Mad Twitching

The Bird Watching Adventures of a Yorkshire Lad

David Houghton

Illustrated by
Naomi Hart

The Pentland Press
Edinburgh – Cambridge – Durham – USA

First published in 2001 by
The Pentland Press Ltd
1 Hutton Close
South Church
Bishop Auckland
Durham

Email: manuscripts@pentlandpress.co.uk
Web: pentlandpress.co.uk

ISBN 1-85821-792-x

Typeset in Adobe Garamond 11 on 13
by Carnegie Publishing
Carnegie House
Chatsworth Road
Lancaster

Web: carnegie@provider.co.uk

Printed and bound by
Antony Rowe Ltd
Bumper's Farm
Chippenham
Wiltshire

Contents

Illustrations

Preface

DEAR READER,
What you are about to read is a series of light-hearted bird watching tales, commencing with my being a rank beginner joining a bird watching club, and progressing through from my early bumbling birding efforts to my meeting and eventually marrying an experienced top birder. From thereon in, the tales tell of some of our adventures together whilst in pursuit of birds in far flung diverse places.

So allow me to take you armchair birding, and for those not familiar with the peculiar esoteric bird watcher's jargon, let me introduce you to it. Before you get too comfortable, to aid your enjoyment of these tales, may I suggest that you pull out your dusty atlas and beg, borrow or steal the relevant field guide for the birds of each region covered. That way you will be able to follow the action and peruse the illustration of any particular bird I mention that happens to take your fancy.

The common names for the birds that I've used throughout these tales, are generally the same names as used in the relevant popular field guides for those regions *at the time of my/our birding trips*. No doubt a few of these names have since changed in later editions of those field guides, but I'm sure that you'll be smart enough to figure out which bird I'm talking about in these circumstances.

I have desisted from using scientific terms and Latin names, to be honest, mainly because I don't know many! Anyway, I don't consider them important to know, unless you have scientific pretensions, or want to impress your next door neighbour. I have included a glossary of Yorkshire Dialect, Swahili and Indonesian words that crop up from time to time for those not familiar with these tongues. You'll find them highlighted in italics, although I've endeavoured to keep the use of these words to a bare minimum for ease of reading.

If these bird watching tales whet your appetite enough to make you go

Mad Twitching

off and bird these localities yourself; or if they revive happy memories of your own bird watching exploits; or even if the odd paragraph brings a smile or two to your face – then my hours spent scribbling them down on paper will have been worthwhile.

Happy armchair birding!
Dave Houghton,
Jakarta, February 2000.

Foreword

Imagine my surprise when I received a letter from David Houghton, a fellow Yorkshireman who had moved to Australia on a ten pound assisted passage, better known by Australians as a 'Ten Pound Pomm' who still, after all those years, considers himself a local lad, proud of his West Yorkshire accent.

The letter was requesting me to write a foreword to a book which he had written about his experience in bird watching.

It did not take me long to discover that David and myself have four things in common. We are both Yorkshiremen, we both smoke a pipe, we love bird watching and also share a passion for the great game of Rugby League Football. This game of course dates back to the eighteen nineties.

The more I read of David's exploits the more envious I became of the thrills he encountered whilst discovering the wonderful birdlife which abounds around the world. I found myself becoming very involved in his descriptions of the surroundings in which he spent his time. From beaches to mountains and forest to bushlands he, along with his wife Kath, shared many hours with these exotic creatures. I must say, Kath sounds a wonderful lady with a great deal of knowledge of the subject, a fact which David is quick to point out.

There is one part in the book which involves them seeing a lion, the description was so graphic it made me feel that I must check behind my chair in order to feel safe.

The dialogue of the book gives one the feeling of being there with David and Kath through their adventures and when they come across a bird they are searching for I feel I wish to reach out and shake hands to congratulate them on their success. There were times during my reading the book, going up and down dirt tracks, climbing over boulders, hanging on to a rope through rushing waters, I felt quite breathless and had to rest a while with a glass red wine and a pipe full of baccie before continuing.

Mad Twitching

Before I finished reading the book I was willing David on to fulfil his ambition of seeing two thousand different species of bird in time for the millennium. A book well worth reading, featuring dedication and the will to succeed the hallmark of a Yorkshireman.

Freddie Trueman OBE

Acknowledgements

THIS PUBLICATION wouldn't have come into being if it wasn't for Pauline Clayton, the former editor of *The Drongo*, the newsletter of the Townsville Region Bird Observers Club. Pauline badgered me into writing a piece about the birds of Papua New Guinea after my work stint there, and from thereon, encouraged and cajoled me into writing more pieces. (Quite a number of those tales appear in this publication too, but in a different form.) It was Pauline and her accomplice Lindsay Fisher who suggested that I should put a few of these tales together and try to get them published in a 'thin volume'. Here it is! Thanks Pauline and Lindsay for your encouragement.

I'm indebted to Naomi Hart for painstakingly producing the beautiful illustrations for this publication, and to the British Museum at Tring for allowing her to wander around freely to peruse their collection of dead birds.

I acknowledge the help of: *The Yorkshire Dictionary* by Arnold Kellet in assisting me in my spelling of dialect words; the *History of Batley* by Malcolm Haigh to get some of my facts straight about my home town; and Brian Cartwright's *The Gallant Youths* for reminding me what a great little outfit is the Batley Rugby League Football Club.

I'm also very grateful to a large number of people in different countries for their hospitality, good companionship, sound advice and for putting up with my clumsy ways and dreadful puns whilst out finding birds. Namely:- In **Australia**: Ian & Pauline Clayton, Keith & Lindsay Fisher, Glen Ingram, Ray Nojeck, Richard Noske, Alan & Chris Oldroyd, Trevor & Annie Quested, Cilla Rose and Townsville Region Bird Observers Club members. In **Papua New Guinea**: Phil Gregory and Ian Schofield. In **Tanzania**: Neil & Liz Baker, Zul & Jenny Bhatia, Stan & Carole Davies, the late Angus & Janey Galbraith, Monica Gorman, Chris Horrill, Trudi van Ingen & Jaring van Rooijen and Alan Tye. In **Uganda**: Greg Roberts.

In **Yorkshire**: Alan & June Blakeley, David & Carol Morrison, David & Janice Reynolds, and Mrs. Kathleen Skelly. In the **United States of America**: Mrs. Elizabeth Sharon and family. In **Indonesia**: Chris & Erin Frost, Paul Jepson, Wayne Klockner, Avi Mahaningtyas and Frank Momberg.

In addition I would like to make a special mention of my daughter Kylie and son Keir, for their love, and accepting the fact that their old man is not around as often as he should be. For if he is not residing in some foreign clime, he is out chasing after silly birds.

It goes without saying that I acknowledge above all others, the encouragement, help and advice, that my best mate and expert birder wife, Kath Shurcliff, has given me whilst compiling these tales. Her limitless patience in getting me onto birds in the bush has made these tales possible. Without her assistance I would have dipped out of seeing many of the species recounted herein.

So to all the people mentioned above, I say a big sincere THANKS.

Glossary

Soiler	A swear word	*Thoil*	Not willing to give
Spadger	Sparrow	*Thowt*	Thought
Starved	Frozen	*Umpteen*	Quite a few
Teem	Pour	*Watter*	Water
Tha	You	*Wahr*	Worse
Thee	You	*Wick*	Alive
Thi	Your	*Wor*	Was
Thissen	Yourself		

Swahili Words

Askari	Security guard	*Ngalawa*	Dug-out canoe with outriggers and sail
Bwana	Mister, master		
Chai	Tea	*Panga*	Machete
Chakula	Food	*Pesa*	Money
Dhow	Wooden sailing vessel	*Pombe*	Local brewed beer
		Rafiki	Friend
Duka	Shop	*Shamba*	Cultivated field
Hamna	There is no	*Simba*	Lion
Hatari	Danger	*Ugali*	Maize porridge
Mgonjwa	Ill, sick	*Wazungu*	White people
Mzee	Old man, village elder		

Indonesian Words

Baru	New	*Losmen*	Cheap hotel
Becak	Bicycle rigshaw	*Mandi*	Bath, bathe
Bule	Foreigner	*Natal*	Christmas
Burung	Bird	*Nasi goreng*	Fried rice
Doker	Decorative pony-drawn cart	*Rumah makan*	Eating house, cafe
		Selamat	Safe
Gunung	Mountain, mount	*Tahun*	Year
Hari	Day		

I

My Introduction to the Esoteric Birding Circle

Townsville, North Queensland, Australia

"HEY DAD!" Kylie shouted out to me one evening whilst she was sprawled out on the living room floor reading the *Townsville Bulletin*, and I was up to my elbows in sudsy water in the kitchen dealing with a huge pile of washing up. "There's a notice in the paper advertising the inaugural meeting of a bird watching club – anyone interested in birds are invited to attend."

"Oh really?" I exclaimed excitedly, for this was the opening I'd been waiting for.

It was February 1992, almost 4 years had elapsed since I'd taken my first tentative steps into bird watching on my 40th birthday, whilst I'd been working at the Ranger Uranium Mine situated in the heart of Kakadu National Park in the Northern Territory of Australia. At that time I'd been going through a sort of mid-life crisis and had been appalled to realize that I'd attained middle age without being able to put a name to most of the common things that surrounded me out in the bush. I'd deduced that this was a pathetic state of affairs, one that I must address. This I did by rushing out and purchasing my first bird field guide and a tree identific-ation book. Since then, my field guide and ancient heavy binoculars had been my constant companions on my regular weekend bicycle jaunts into the bush, for I found that I derived great satisfaction from simply observing birds and got a real buzz when I actually managed to identify a new one that I hadn't seen before. But there were quite a lot of birds that I basically ignored, because I frustratingly couldn't sort out which ones they were in my bird book. These were mainly waders, eagle-type birds, terns and the myriad of small brown things that flew around all over the shop. I'd often wished that I could meet up with a 'proper' bird watcher, who would take me 'under his wing' and give me a few pointers on bird identification, or wished that I could join a bird watching society – but I didn't know of the existence of any such societies. Now here was my big chance to meet at last some 'proper' bird watchers.

I was now residing in Townsville, North Queensland with my daughter Kylie. She was studying at the James Cook University and I was busy fixing up a dilapidated, 80-year old, genuine miner's cottage that I'd bought for some inane reason that I was beginning to regret. The same reason someone brings home from the pound a scruffy looking, flea-ridden mutt, I suspect! I'd been introduced to the city of Townsville when I'd arrived here 3 years earlier, to work on an expansion project at the local Queensland Nickel Refinery. I'd felt at home here from day one, for Townsville, compared to its rival neighbour Cairns, is much less tourist orientated and much more down to earth. It has an interesting mix of inhabitants, the largely working class folk mingling with academics and students from the university and marine institutions, and a large contingent of army personnel from the local barracks. Hence the place has a lot of lively (sometimes too lively!) old fashioned pubs, a thriving folk music club, a rugby league club, a theatre, a couple of cinemas, and a good library – all the things that I derive great pleasure from. Not only did it have all the amenities I enjoyed, it was aesthetically pleasing too, the city being situated right on the coast with the almost 1000-foot tall Castle Hill dominating the skyline. From the top of this giant rock, there are spectacular views over the town centre and harbour below and beyond to Magnetic Island, a smashing place for a weekend retreat, lying peacefully in Cleveland Bay only a 20 minute ferry ride away. These factors, plus the fact that there were numerous good bird watching spots nearby, had influenced me in deciding that this was as 'good a place as any' to settle down in. Unfortunately no sooner had I bought my tumbledown old cottage, and before I actually moved into it, the expansion project at the refinery was 'shelved' and my job came to an abrupt end. Luckily, around this time I was offered a further 18-months work back in Kakadu, and jumped at it. Now I'd just recently arrived back in town jobless, and finally taken up residence in my humble abode, which was falling down around my ears.

Kylie accompanied me to the meeting held in the Thuringowa Library meeting room. She was as curious as I to find out what kind of people would attend. I must say that I felt rather ill at ease at the prospect of meeting a group of bird watchers, for I'd no idea what to expect. Would they all be loony environmentalist types? If so, would they berate me for earning my living in the not-so-environmentally-friendly mines and refineries? Would they all be egg-head scientists / ornithologists who would talk way above my head? Would there be a smattering of my archetypal idea of bird watchers as portrayed in old British motion pictures, i.e., portly, moustachioed retired army colonels with their stout jolly hockey stick wives dressed in tweed country wear and Wellington boots, and possessing 'hooray Henry' accents to match? If so, they would hardly be likely to have anything to do with an unsophisticated Yorkshire lad, would they? I even began to wonder if there would be anyone at all present that was on my own wave-length! I was put at ease somewhat when a swarthy, bearded, pirate looking character, straight out of the pages of *Treasure Island*, gripped my hand tightly at the doorway and introduced himself in a strong Lancashire accent as Ian Clayton. He welcomed us to the meeting and bade us to take a pew, as the meeting would be commencing shortly.

I was pleased to find a couple of chairs vacant at the back of the room, where I could hide and observe the other participants. To my relief they all seemed to be remarkably normal people (It's funny how first impressions can be wrong, isn't it?), a fairly normal cross section of the general public in fact. Except that it was plainly obvious bird watching was an older age group pastime, for there weren't too many people present much younger than I. Kylie stuck out like a sore thumb amongst a pack of little old ladies sat beside us. It became patently obvious too, by the way everyone greeted new arrivals, that most people already knew each other. How could this be so, if this was the inaugural meeting of a new club? It soon became clear when the meeting got underway, chaired by the pirate, that most folk were members of the Townsville branch of the Wildlife Preservation Society of Queensland, and that they wished to form a Townsville Region branch of the Bird Observers Club of Australia. (B.O.C.A.), a Melbourne based organization that I'd never heard of before. A show of hands later in the proceedings confirmed that a lot of people present were already individual members of this club.

There was also, although I didn't know it at the time, quite a number of distinguished bird watchers present. One of them was a rotund, snowy-bearded chap by the name of Peter Britton. (The editor of the acclaimed *Birds of East Africa* – the bible of the East African Natural History Society.)

Mad Twitching

He gave a spiel on how to write up rare bird sightings. Another participant was an interesting looking, self-assured, ginger-haired lass called Kath Shurcliff, whom I was informed was an ardent 'twitcher'. I hoped that she would soon get better from this strange affliction. There was also a clean-cut, neatly attired bloke called Rob Shaw, who later came to prominence when he added the Blue Rock Thrush to the Australian list. This bird he spotted on a nudist beach north of Brisbane – it has never been satisfactorily explained to me what he was actually doing on a nudist beach with a pair of binoculars! I was to meet an entertaining bubbly character over tea and biscuits during the interval, he was affectionately known as Uncle Frank, who apparently was an enthusiastic bird watcher well known for his 'unusual sightings', but to my relief instead of chatting about birds he entertained me with dirty jokes.

On completion of the meeting Ian Clayton took down everyone's particulars and handed out application forms to those not already members of B.O.C.A. I was about to make my unobtrusive escape with Kylie, thankful that no one had questioned my meagre bird watching credentials, when one of the old ladies buttonholed me as we sidled our way towards the door. On being quizzed, I was forced to admit that I'd just returned to Townsville after a long stint working in Kakadu National Park, where I'd spent most of my free time watching birds. I purposely failed to mention that I'd worked at the Ranger Uranium Mine, not wanting to get into an environmental debate, so she assumed no doubt that I was connected with the National Parks and Wildlife Service (N.P.W.S.) in some way. She also assumed wrongly, with my accent, that I was a British bird watcher, by asking how many birds I had on my 'Australian list'. This question completely stumped me! I didn't have any lists, Australian or otherwise. It had never occurred to me, to make a list of all the birds I'd actually seen since I'd started bird watching. Let alone add them all up. She seemed a trifle amused when I told her that I didn't have a clue. Her response made it quite clear to me that bird watchers measure themselves against each other by how long their lists are. Interestingly enough, just like train spotters do!

That same evening I filled out my application form to join B.O.C.A. and got down to the task of ticking off in my bird book all the birds that I had 'knowingly' seen during the past 4 years. I had a grand total of 172 species. I guessed that I'd better keep quiet about it! A week later I received a letter from B.O.C.A. welcoming me to the club. They had enclosed a swathe of literature for me to peruse, including a bird list for the Townsville region. There were, to my amazement, 336 birds listed on it! Flippin' *heck*! Too right I'd keep mum about the paltry number of birds that I'd seen!

Only three weeks after the inaugural meeting, I was informed by the new Townsville Region branch of B.O.C.A. (TOWNBOC) that they were holding a slide show on 'breeding birds', to be followed by a short bird walk and a barbecue – please bring your own food and refreshments, etc. This was my big chance to actually 'get to know' other bird watchers and increase my scant knowledge of birds. So I needed no prompting in setting off on my bike down to the Heritage Cottage in the Queensland N.P.W.S. Regional Centre at Pallarenda, where the event was to be held. This centre, by the way, abuts the Townsville Town Common Environmental Park – one of the top bird watching spots in Queensland. The hall was packed with folk when I arrived, far more than at the inaugural meeting. A chap built like a rugby league prop forward, by the name of John Young, gave a very illuminating and informative slide show, showing rare eagle-type birds, owls and others photographed at their nests. He went on to explain some of the difficulties in obtaining these shots, such as bush bashing over difficult terrain to locate the nests, then shinning way up to the top of gigantic trees to build hides. This well-built fellow certainly was an agile, macho character, more monkey than man – I only hoped that no one would call upon me to help them photograph nesting birds.

After tea and biscuits, Uncle Frank led us on a short bird walk at the back of the cottage. It became apparent that on these walks the keen bird watchers keep up with the leader to spot the birds, whilst the rest lag behind to chat amongst themselves, only regrouping to take an interest in affairs when anything unusual was spotted. I also became aware that bird watchers used different names for the same bird, or a shortened version of the name, and some of them even used the Latin name! On this walk I heard the **Torresian Imperial Pigeon** simply referred to as a 'TIP', others called it the Pied Imperial Pigeon or Torres Strait Pigeon, whilst those wanting to impress called it a *Ducula*. It was interesting but most perplexing! I quietly inquired about this use of different names, and was told that it all depended on the period that a person started bird watching, for they tended to stick with the common English name in current use at that time. And, keen bird watchers often shortened these names down to save them the trouble of repeating long-winded names. These common names apparently keep changing to suit the whims of learned men in national ornithological societies, but the Latin names generally remained the same. It was interesting too to hear birds' names pronounced differently from the way I'd been pronouncing them, not having heard anyone else actually 'say' the names before. I must admit that I found it extremely difficult to pronounce 'Gerygone' as 'jer-**ig**-ony with the same rhythm as 'polygamy', after I'd been pronouncing it with two hard 'G's' for years. We didn't see too many birds on Frank's little walk, but I thoroughly enjoyed it and did a fair amount of chatting myself to some really nice people, although at times they used jargon that I was unfamiliar with. But I let it go, not wanting to show my ignorance. For I thought that I'd asked enough silly questions for one day! Although I did confess to all and sundry that I was a 'rank beginner,' (as if it wasn't plainly obvious). For I figured that by doing so they would be more inclined to help me and wouldn't embarrass me again by asking how many birds I had on my 'Australian list'.

We later adjourned to a picnic area nearby for a barbecue where I was joined by my old mucker Alan Oldroyd. Alan is a bit of a 'card'. He and I go back a long way, from our Batley Cycling Club days in Yorkshire, when we'd trained together, boozed together, sung together at folk clubs and chased lasses together in the local dance halls. We had been a right pair of 'likely lads', *leet-gi'en as posser-'eeads*. He had lived in Australia longer than I had, but it was a coincidence (because we both moved around a fair bit), that this was the first time we had actually resided in the same town at the same time. He had been a joiner and undertaker when I knew him from 'back home', but somehow he had wangled his way into the N.P.W.S. and bluffed his way into becoming a manager of sorts. We had resumed our friendship after all those years by going out on regular Friday night pub crawls, it was just like old times! Needless to say we both had a ball at the barbecue, supping my carton of red wine dry, behaving in a completely outrageous fashion whilst making merry with my new fellow bird watchers. We were the last to leave and rounded off the evening by giving the stayers renditions of 'Ilkla' Moor *baht* 'at', the Yorkshireman's anthem, and various bawdy songs from our extensive repertoire.

The following morning, nursing a hangover, I thought to myself, "Oh no, I've gone and blown my big chance! No one will want to have anything to do with me again in the bird club – we were definitely too 'over the top' last night." To compound matters, it had completely escaped me how to pronounce 'gerygone' properly! On picking my clothes up off the floor I found in one of the pockets a notice announcing a 'Learn Your Waders' event, which was to be held on the coming Monday morning at 5.30 a.m., together with a map showing where to meet. "Funny!" I thought, "I can't recall anyone giving me this last night."

I sheepishly showed up to learn my waders at Bushland Beach, just north of Townsville. There was only Kath Shurcliff there, the ginger-haired lass that I'd been informed suffered from a terrible affliction. She asked with a grin, how I'd 'pulled up' the morning after the barbecue, and graciously left it at that. No one else showed up. It was just the pupil and the teacher who walked the short distance over the dunes onto the quiet undisturbed stretch of beach, where I had time to confess that waders gave me no end of trouble in sorting out. As she set up her telescope she patiently explained to me that the first thing that I should do is to learn to place the birds in their respective 'family' groups, family groupings being based on the overall size and shape of a bird, the bill size and shape, the leg length, and general behavioural features. She gave me a leaflet showing in silhouette form all the different families of waders, and wanted me to place into one of these families the birds that she would show me in the scope, before we proceeded to sort them out any further. I could tell that she had got onto something rather unusual for me to look at when she did an initial pan over the beach with her scope, for she got rather excited and her voice became noticeably shriller. She moved aside pointing at the eye-piece for me to take a sqizz. I found myself looking at a large, strange, long-legged, long-necked bird having a huge yellow eye, an extremely stout black-tipped yellow bill and a white wing-bar. It was the first time that I'd ever viewed a bird through a telescope – it was absolutely terrific. I'd never seen a bird so clearly before, you could almost see what the gawky looking creature had for yesterday's breakfast! I had no trouble in pointing to its silhouette on Kath's leaflet that proclaimed it a member of the stone-curlew (thick-knee) family, before pointing to one of the two

Beach Thick-knee

illustrations in the field guide showing the two stone-curlews that occur in Australia. It was the one with the extremely stout bill, the **Beach Stone-curlew (Beach Thick-knee)** that I'd never seen before. Kath told me, as we watched it canter down the beach away from us, that this bird was fairly rare, and one didn't get the chance to observe it very often, for besides being shy, they were active mainly at night, unlike the other commoner Bush Stone-curlew that roamed around gardens and barbecue areas in Townsville and Magnetic Island in large noisy flocks. Embarrassingly there wasn't much else around on that particular beach for some reason, only a couple of **Silver Gulls** and a small flock of **Bar-tailed Godwits**. Kath soon ran out of things to say about them, and mentioned that the tide was wrong for other waders. So after a long silence she asked me if I'd ever seen a **Garganey Teal**. When I shook my head, she said that she would 'get me one'.

We took off down to Blakey's Crossing, this being a wetland area of freshwater swamps and grassland adjacent to the Townsville Town Common and the R.A.A.F. air strip. In next to no time I was viewing this lovely duck through the telescope, a duck that was a very uncommon visitor to Australia she informed me. This particular one had been hanging around in this area for a couple of weeks. "Now you owe me a drink for getting you two 'lifers'!" she teased. I didn't understand what she was talking about. But on going through the many birds in this spot she got me a further three 'lifers' as she termed them, they being the **White-eyed Duck**, the **Sharp-tailed Sandpiper** ('sharpies' she called them) and the **Marsh Sandpiper**. I was impressed by the way she was able to put a name to a bird, just by its call alone, or after only having a quick glance at it, and I told her so. She said that she knew their 'jizz'. Whatever that was! I offered to buy her a coffee for being so patient and helpful in showing me all the birds and in the process getting me five new ones, but she declined saying that she had to dash off to work. Wow, what a lass! Would I ever get as good as her if I spent hours in the field?

On subsequent well-attended TOWNBOC bird watching trips, which I never missed, I learned a lot of the etiquette involved in observing birds in a group. It was obviously a 'no-no' to walk in front of anyone whilst they were observing a bird, or to talk or fidget whilst someone tried to encourage a bird to show itself out of a tangle of undergrowth by making a squeaking sound. It was also imperative that no one should disturb a bird into taking off until everyone in the group had actually seen the flippin' thing, which the bird often did without any prompting. They also discouraged me from pointing excitedly to a bird that I'd spotted by waving my arm about in the air in the vague direction of it, and shouting, " There's one over yonder!" Instead they told me to describe a definite landmark and give verbal instructions as to the bird's whereabouts from it. To make this easy I was informed to imagine the foliage of a tree to be a clockface. So that I should say for example – "See the huge scruffy looking tree about 60 yards away, well there is a bird in the small bush immediately to the left of it, at about 10 o'clock." I enjoyed my outings with the TOWNBOC crowd immensely. I found them to be a really great fun-loving bunch of people who went out of their way to help me. Indeed they helped me sort out quite a few of the waders, eagle-type birds (which they termed 'raptors'), terns and little brown things, in the process adding more birds to my new Australian list. The outings invariably finished up with a social picnic or we'd all go back to someone's place for a barbecue, where I usually behaved myself if Alan wasn't present. After a while I even got so that I could understand what they were talking about. I became familiar with their esoteric bird watching jargon. I learned a whole new vocabulary of words and phrases of which I'll attempt to explain to those not already in the know.

Bird watchers in the club referred to themselves as **Birders** or **Birdos**, that implies they were actively involved in locating and observing birds primarily as a hobby or pastime, that they call **Birding**, as opposed to **Ornithologists** who are scientists with letters behind their names, who earn a living by studying birds and writing scientific papers about them. To complicate matters some ornithologists are birders too, and some top experienced birders write scientific papers. This practice often gets up the nose of some ornithologists who think that these birders are trespassing on their exclusive professional domain and so try to discredit the papers and the amateur authors. On the other hand a lot of ornithologists are indebted to the large band of birders who happily collect data in the field for them on a voluntary basis.

I learned that all the species of birds in the world can be divided roughly in half into two groups – the **Passerines** and the **Non-Passerines**. The passerines being the smaller, singing, perching birds, all have four toes, always arranged with three toes forward and one back for gripping onto their perches. The non-passerines have very different and varied feet, they include ducks, parrots and swifts. The non-passerines are usually placed in the front of field guides and lists, the passerines, being the later evolved species, at the back.

Scientists have divided the world up into seven different faunal regions. Most bird species are restricted to one particular region but it is handy when referring to birds that transcend these regional boundaries, such as migrant waders, to know where they have come from. Hence I heard the term **Palearctic** used often, which is the name given to the large faunal region comprising of Europe, North Africa, the Middle East, the old USSR and China, where a lot of these migrant waders breed in the northern summer. Other regions which I only heard referred to occasionally were: **Nearctic** – North America; **Ethiopian** – most of the African continent; **Neotropical** – South America; **Oriental** – India and South East Asia; **Australasia** – Australia, New Zealand and New Guinea and **Oceanic** – small islands in the Pacific and Indian Oceans. Birds that are only to be found in one region are said to be an **Endemic** of that region. A bird can also be an endemic of a particular country, or small province of a country, or even a particular mountain range if it is only to be found there.

Birds that spend most of the time living in trees are said to be **Arboreal**, those spending most of their time on the ground are **Terrestrial**, whilst the ones living out at sea are termed **Pelagic**. Ones that eat fruit are said to be **Frugivores** and the ones that eat seeds are for some reason called **Seedeaters**.

If you want to attract a bird into showing itself from out of thick foliage, this can often be achieved by **squeaking** the bird out by noisily kissing the back of your hand, or between your index and middle finger. Alternatively, you can purse your lips and make a **pishing** sound. A few birders use a more sophisticated method – they employ the aid of a tape recorder. They either tape the call of the bird and play the bird's own call back to it, or play a pre-recorded call of a species that they suspect, or hope, it to be. The bird that may come out to take a look, to ascertain what the devil's going on, is more than likely to be one of those hard to identify little brown things or 'Little Brown Jobs' referred to by birders as **L.B.J.s**. Experienced birders may identify a bird that flies by quickly overhead, so that one only gets a fleeting glimpse of it, by its **Jizz**. This term I understand is a corruption of the anagram 'GISS', standing for 'general impression size and shape', a method used by airmen in W.W.II to quickly determine whether another aircraft in the vicinity was friend or foe. Each species of bird, like a make of aircraft, has its own Jizz that obviously can only be recognized after hours of observation in the field. It is something that one cannot glean from a book. Sometimes a birder puts a name to a bird, but on being quizzed by their companions, has to admit that they didn't see much of it, let alone any distinguishing features of it, but they instinctively knew what it was by its jizz. They are often proved correct.

If a bird you happen to observe and identify properly was a new species for you, that you had never seen before in your life, it is termed a **lifer**, and you have gained a new **tick** on your **life list**. Some birders have all kinds of lists, from their garden lists, town lists, local area lists, state/county lists, country lists, faunal region lists right up to a world list, necessitating birders with a lot of lists to have lists of their lists! Some 'ticks' are worth more than other 'ticks'. For example if you visit a region that you haven't been to before, odds on you will see a lot of new birds that will be 'ticks' for you. But some of these birds will be so common in that region you will be falling all over them in your hotel grounds, whilst others may take days of bush bashing through leech infested tropical jungles to locate. Obviously you will rate these latter ones as '**Good ticks**', and if a bird you spent days trying to find in the tropical jungle was a little drab nondescript brown thing, although it was a 'good tick', it wouldn't be quite as good a 'tick' as if it had been a large beautifully plumaged bird like a Resplendent Quetzal say. That would be classed as a '**Mega tick**'. Furthermore, if you had been trying to locate a particular bird for a number of years, say for instance the rare secretive Brown Mesite in Madagascar, and you had spent a small fortune on a number of trips to Madagascar specifically to see this bird, but always failing to find it this would be called your **Bogey Bird**. When eventually you were lucky enough to see it, you would be over the moon with joy, so that could be classed as a '**Mind Blowing Tick**' or any other expletive you wished to call it! If you discovered a new species that hadn't been recorded before in your country, like Rob Shaw did, that would fall into this category of 'tick' too.

The affliction that Kath Shurcliff suffered from, called **twitching**, I discovered to be indeed a terrible affliction, but not necessarily a life threatening one. A **twitcher** is a birder who is obsessively concerned with going farther and farther afield to see and thus 'tick' lots of new birds for themselves, thereby amassing a long list of birds on their country/world list. Bill Oddie is perhaps the most famous twitcher, and may well be the one responsible for coining the jargon relating to the pastime of twitching. Twitchers are very competitive birders, and like other sportsmen, particularly cricketers, get great satisfaction upon reaching milestones – centuries for country lists and thousands for world lists. The really top twitchers in Australia are the ones who have seen over 700 species, whilst in the U.K. (where there are far fewer species) top twitchers are the ones who have amassed a list of 420 species or more. Nothing, and I mean absolutely nothing, will stand in the way of a dedicated twitcher in their quest to see and 'tick' new birds off on their lists. They will endure hell and high water, risk getting the sack from their employment, and divorce from their spouses to go chasing after a reported sighting of a new or rare bird in their country. Some twitchers even subscribe to 'Birding Hotlines' where the news of any unusual bird sighted will automatically be paged to them. Hence they can 'shoot through' at the drop of a hat to travel hundreds of miles to **twitch** it. In England where there are twitchers in abundance, it is not uncommon that hundreds of twitchers show up at the same time to see a poor unfortunate rare bird, which they sometimes hound to near death.

Obviously not all of them get to see it; those that don't manage to get a butchers at it are said to have **dipped out**. If a couple of bird club mates for instance went to 'twitch' a particular bird together, one saw the bird and the other 'dipped out', the one who failed to spot it could say that they got **gripped off** by their mate. But if they get to see the bird the following day, they can say that they **gripped one back**. Most twitchers rely on their network of birding 'friends' to inform them of any unusual bird sightings. It is not quite cricket if one of these 'friends' spots a rare bird and neglects to tell anyone in their circle. They can be accused of **supressing** their sighting. Naturally that person will not be informed of any future sightings! It is a real 'no no' for anyone to see and identify a bird wrongly, say for instance they saw what they believed to be a fairly rare (in Australia) Wandering Tattler, and announced this sighting to all and sundry. When every man and his dog showed up to see the thing only to discover that it was a fairly common, very similar looking Grey-tailed Tattler. That person's sighting would be said to be **stringy**, and that person would earn the reputation of being a **stringer**, their sightings would never be taken seriously ever again, and they would become a source of ridicule.

Mad Twitching

Twitchers not only enjoy competing against each other by the length of their bird lists, but also by seeing who can observe more species in a day, month or year, and often take part in **twitchathons**. These are events organized by birding organizations to raise funds, where teams of birders compete against each other to see the greatest number of species in a set time, usually 24 hrs. I think that the world record was set in Peru in 1982 when a team of two people spotted an amazing 331 birds in a day.

Not all bird watchers are twitchers of course, some being content to observe and attract birds into their gardens. But I'm sure these folk too, whether they admit it or not, get quite a buzz from observing a new species not seen before in their gardens.

I'd been watching birds for four years on my own, but in a matter of months since joining TOWNBOC my bird watching skills, although still rather elementary, I felt had progressed in leaps and bounds. Joining the TOWNBOC mob had no doubt been one of the best moves that I'd ever made. They held meetings once a month where a guest speaker would give an illustrated talk on a particular birding topic, they organized regular birding trips to different locations, including weekend campouts, and even started to put out their own club magazine called *The Drongo*. (Later on when they became firmly established, this enthusiastic band of birders to their credit got involved with bird survey work and local conservation issues too.) I felt privileged to have been introduced to a great bunch of friendly interesting characters, and accepted as a novice into their esoteric birding circle.

2

Earning a Crust

Tabubil, Western Province, Papua New Guinea

AFTER SPENDING HEAPS OF MONEY fixing up my old cottage in Townsville, I decided it was about time that I put my feelers out amongst the employment agencies to get a short-term contract job. I was delighted when I got offered a two-month contract in Papua New Guinea, to work on a new lime kiln project at the Ok Tedi Copper Mine. I had no objection at all to visiting exotic places I wouldn't otherwise get to see, at someone else's expense, and at the same time earning a few bob. The only drawback was that they wanted me to fly out almost immediately, and that didn't give me enough time to procure a 'Birds of New Guinea' field guide which were not readily available in the Townsville bookshops!

I arrived field-guide-less, but otherwise intact, in the small mining township of Tabubil in early May 1992. Tabubil is the operational head-quarters of the giant Ok Tedi Copper Mine, situated in the Star Mountains in the Western Province, only 18 km from the Irian Jaya border. There must have been quite a lot of work going on at the mine at that time, because the single men's accommodation block adjacent to the mess, where I would normally have been billeted, was fully occupied. Consequently I was housed in a small self-contained 'donga' at the bottom of the mine manager's large garden (formerly his gardener's cottage). I was rather pleased with this arrangement, knowing from past experience that it meant that I wouldn't be roped into any drinking/card schools. It meant that I wouldn't have to queue up to use the bog or to take a shower at the peak user time before breakfast. It meant that I wouldn't be disturbed by loud drunken parties raging on into the wee hours, or by some lost, lonely pea-brained soul watching M.T.V. at full volume outside my door. This donga was situated in quite a lovely, secluded setting, amongst trees and shrubbery, where I could sit under the verandah in privacy and look out onto the mist shrouded rugged mountains. At the bottom of 'my' garden, only 40 paces away, ran the fast flowing Ok Tedi River in a spectacular deep ravine.

Mad Twitching

When I first saw it, I vowed that I'd better not sleep walk, for if I went over the high cliff it would be curtains for sure! I was rather surprised when the project manager actually apologised for having to house me there. It took all my powers of self-control to contain my joy and stop myself grinning from ear to ear before mumbling, "Oh, that's O.K., it will do!" I found it even more agreeable when I discovered that some good fairy, whom I never did get to see, would come and clean the room, make the bed, leave me a fresh towel and replenish the stock of tea bags each day, whilst I was out at work. I was spoilt. I liked it! The only drawback being that it was a 20-minute walk away from the mess, a small price to pay for my privacy, wouldn't you say? The mess food too was to my liking, even though I soon discovered that pork seemed to be on the menu quite frequently. I later learned that the local chaps simply love it. When they have a celebration in their villages, they traditionally roast a few pigs and gorge themselves for days on end. I heard some legendary tales of these folk in the course of such festivities, making themselves deliberately vomit by sticking their fingers down their throats, so that they could make room to carry on feasting! After witnessing the huge pile of pork these blokes devoured in the mess at one sitting, I had no reason to disbelieve these stories at all. They must have thought that their prayers had been answered, by working for a company that provided a feast for them every other night! It was interesting to see that different tribal groups sat together on the same long tables, the expats too! A case of 'birds of a feather flock together' no doubt.

I was working with a small multi-national team of agreeable engineers and draughtsmen in an office in Tabubil. (I kid you not, there was an Englishman, Irishman and a Scotsman, together with a Dutchman, Zimbabwean, Albanian and an Australian, not forgetting the Yorkshireman!) My part of the job was to do all the piping work, which meant that I would spend quite a bit of the time at the mine-site itself designing my new pipes and pumps to fit into the spaghetti network of existing pipework. A task that most draughtsmen find rather daunting, like novice bird watchers find in sorting out waders, but I specialise in piping and find it a rather agreeable and satisfying job, even dare I say – a quite simple job, but I never let on!

Tabubil is 630m above sea level and is connected to the mine-site by a twisting, steep, gravel road running up the Ok Tedi River valley. The mine-site being at 2053m above sea level, is shrouded in thick cloud most of the time. The annual rainfall being over 10m, deems it necessary to wear wet weather gear most of the time too, or at the very least every afternoon. I was quite awe-struck when I first clapped eyes on the ore refining plant up at the mine-site, (pun intended) when the mist cleared for a few minutes that is. The sheer logistics and ingenuity involved in building this entire engineering masterpiece, in such rugged, remote terrain was mind boggling. The plant snaked down the narrow valley, at all different angles and levels, using the gradient to minimize the need for slurry pumps. I found it to be quite a remarkable engineering feat, a tribute to the engineers who designed it. It's a pity that the tailings dam collapsed during construction, and a political decision was taken to commission the plant without one. Now all the tailings go directly into the river! A shame really!

All in all I found this place to be, despite the rain – what shall I say, well yes – rather agreeable! What else! During my first week I'd even seen a few birds. My favourite part of the day was at the first light of dawn, when I'd contentedly sit out under my little verandah with a cup of tea, watching the drifting clouds on the mountain as it changed to differing hues with the approaching day. Each morning a pair of **Sacred Kingfishers** would show up and hunt lizards in the grass from an exposed branch directly in front of me. I spotted a lovely dark brown sunbird, and three or four very large grey-coloured noisy crows on a few mornings, but I'd no idea what they were without a field guide. I did recognise the **Sulphur-crested Cockatoos** though, that flew in small noisy parties across the ravine each morning. Yes, it was a smashing peaceful half hour I spent each day, before having to break the spell and set off to work. In the town itself there were a few **Willy Wagtails**, numerous swallows to be seen gracefully swooping all over the place, and quite a number of woodswallows resting on the overhead wires. They looked like Welcome Swallows and White-breasted Woodswallows respectively to me, they being species I was now familiar with in Australia. There was also a different small swift that I'd watched up at the mine-site, it having a lovely blue glossy back. There again, I'd no idea what it was. I somehow had to remember them all until I could get my hands on a field guide. I'd been informed that the Tabubil branch of the Australian Country Women's Association ran a craft/gift shop in town and a small library. Maybe they would have one there? But with the long hours I worked I had to wait until late Saturday afternoon to catch them open. When I did get to the library, I was out of luck; they didn't have a copy. It was a library made up of paperback novels that people had read and discarded. Nevertheless I had now a source of literature to while away my evenings and lull me to sleep, besides the pitter patter of the rain on the tin roof, and the sound of frogs copulating in the drainpipes.

I didn't take much persuading to put my 'glad rags' on and go down to the golf club bar on my first Saturday night in town. The place was quite lively, and it got livelier and livelier as the night wore on. I think the whole expat community was present, and somehow, fortunately for me, I got introduced to an Englishman called Phil Gregory, a teacher at the International School. He was introduced to me as a 'twitcher'. When I mentioned that I was a 'rank beginner', my ignorance of birds only being surpassed by my enthusiasm, and that I was a member of the Townsville Region branch of the Bird Observers Club, we arranged to go out at 7.00 a.m. the following morning. I can't remember much of the night after that, but my work mates say I had a good night, and that they enjoyed my rendition of 'The Rose of Tralee'! My party piece! I'd remarked that I'd let them off lightly, because I could have sung them 'Ilkla Moor *Baht 'at*' – all the way through!

Sunday morning loomed, I was up but not exactly raring to go, when Phil came around to pick me up! I felt like death warmed up, so I made us a cup of strong coffee, as he went off to check out the ravine. He called me over to look at a **Tawny-breasted Honeyeater** he had got onto in a tree below. Why hadn't I spotted it during the previous week? (I don't wish to hear your answers.) We set off in his vehicle out of town and into the bush on narrow boulder strewn tracks. The strong coffee was working and I was slowly beginning to start feeling almost human again. I was enthralled to see local blokes walking along these tracks carrying nothing but bows and arrows, in most cases with their women following close at their heels, some burdened with babies slung at their breast by a cloth, and all carrying huge, heavy laden string bags, called billums, on their backs, the handles of these bags passing across their foreheads so that their heads took a lot of the weight. "Goodness me, in Western societies it is the men who have to struggle with heavy suitcases. Where have we gone wrong?" I asked Phil. We chatted for a while, where it became clear that Phil was a passionately keen birder indeed. He was a fair dinkum 'proper' bird watcher, it wasn't just a pleasant pastime for him, birding was his whole way of life. It transpired that he even led birding trips for well-known tour operators in this area. I was beginning to feel uncomfortable, like a real raw prawn! I needn't have worried unduly, for when we reached the Ok Mani Road and started watching birds, I found that he had endless patience for a novice such as I, even though I must have asked some pretty silly questions.

The Ok Mani road ran up a little valley, on either side were very tall trees. With most of the birds being at the very top, I could understand why Phil lugged about and preferred to use his telescope. He managed to scope most of the birds for me to have a look at, so I had excellent views of a lot of the species we came across. We had three species of parrot-type birds, the **Dusky Lory, Rainbow Lorikeet** and a female **Eclectus Parrot**; three species of raptors, the **Crested Hawk, Long-tailed Buzzard** and **Brahminy Kite**; together with **Grey-headed** and **Golden Cuckoo-shrikes, Yellow-faced Myna, Black** and **Hooded Butcherbirds, Brown Cuckoo-Dove, Ornate Fruit-Dove, Moustached Tree-swift** and **Mountain Peltops**, without naming all the other birds we saw that are fairly common in Australia. Some quite lovely birds indeed, my favourites being the **Golden Cuckoo-shrike** for its striking yellow/orange plumage and the **Moustached Tree-swift** with its prominent long white eyebrow and long white 'tash', giving it a rather unusual appearance. Phil also recognised the call of a bird of paradise and a **Yellow-billed Kingfisher**, but they never showed themselves. Wow, I'd had an excellent morning's birding and managed to pick Phil's brain no end; he even let me peruse his field guide. I only hoped that I hadn't got in his way too much! I gleaned from him that the swallows and woodswallows I had seen in town were in fact the **Pacific Swallows** (Welcome Swallow being an extremely rare vagrant) and the **P.N.G. Great Woodswallow** (slightly bigger and darker than the White-breasted Wood-swallow). That the crow and sunbird I'd seen in 'my' garden were the **Grey Crow** and **Black Sunbird**, the swift, up at the mine-site being in all probabilities the **Glossy Swiftlet**. That meant I'd seen 18 new birds so far. I was quite pleased, and eternally grateful to Phil. Would he invite this hungover Yorkshireman with a deadpan sense of humour birding again?

I enjoyed my pork in the mess that evening, whilst reflecting on the good birds I had seen that day. On strolling back to my lovely retreat I heard a strange honking / whooshing noise coming from the Ok Tedi River ravine. "Flippin' *heck*!" I exclaimed, "What the bloomin' *hummer's* that?" I ran over, and peered into the ravine and saw two of the strangest creatures that I'd ever clapped eyes on. They were two huge black birds with white tails, flying with slow wing beats (hence the whooshing noise) across the ravine, honking as they went. Their enormous pale bills and golden yellow heads and necks being caught in the fading sunlight was a joy to behold. They were of course the wonderful **Blyth's Hornbill** (two males), the only hornbill that occurs in P.N.G., and the first I had ever seen. What a grand sight to round off a smashing day.

I spent the following Sunday wandering around town, with my binoculars dangling around my neck. Like most mining towns that I had lived in, there wasn't much to it! The town centre consisted of a large open area, used as the local produce market. Around this square stood the large Woolworth's supermarket, a bank, a travel agents, the Australian C.W.A. gift shop/library, a hardware shop, a post office and that was about it. What more do you want? Further afield there was an expensive hotel (appropriately named 'Cloudlands'), the golf club, a rugby league club, a hospital, schools and churches of every denomination that you can think of. The mine staff lived in houses of differing sizes and quality, depending on the occupants' status at the mine. These bougainvillea-clad houses were situated higher up the valley, north of the town square, in lovely tree lined avenues. South of the town square is where the mess, single men's and single ladies' accommodation blocks were located. (The small ladies' block being known colloquially as the 'fur farm'.) Further down were warehouses and contractor's workshops, with the local indigenous folk, who were not employed by the mine, living lower down the valley still, in what can only be described as a shanty town. They had been drawn to the area because of all the facilities that were on offer here, besides all the goodies that were available in Woolies.

I scoured the forest edges looking for new birds, but on 'not knowingly seeing any', only youths hunting them with catapults, I retired to go up to watch the local rugby league match. I had my best sighting of the day on my way to the ground when my eyes alighted on a young woman walking towards me, wearing a simple cloth that showed off her slender figure. Her sheer elegance captivated me. Her gait could have graced the catwalks of Paris. She passed by me, giving me a shy 'Mona Lisa' smile. Her tribal tattoo markings on her cheeks and forehead only enhanced her beauty, in other settings maybe they wouldn't have been accepted as being *de rigueur*. I stopped in my tracks and swivelled around to watch her rear view. She turned around too and gave a little giggle, before carrying on. Wow, she was absolutely drop-dead gorgeous! I was madly in love! (When I mentioned this to the lads later, I got bombarded with a lot of politically incorrect and sexist remarks, but none the less they were bloody funny!) I ambled on up to the ground, consoling myself with the thought that we probably wouldn't have anything in common. Probably she would even be a Manchester United supporter! That wouldn't do at all! The game was in progress when I arrived at the football field, *by gum* it was a cracking match. The vocal locals were there to egg on their team in force. It was quite a colourful, entertaining spectacle all round. I bumped into Phil on my way home, and yes, he did invite me to go birding with him again the following weekend!

This time we birded a narrow stony maintenance track that ran beside a pipeline heading steeply up a forested hillside. Phil called it the 'pipeline track'. On our way there he had got quite excited about seeing an **Intermediate Egret** flying over the valley, apparently he didn't see too many of them here. We also saw a lovely **Pied Chat** by the roadside, my first new bird for a few weeks! I had in fact quite a few new birds that morning, a further six to be precise. They were in order of appearance, **Scrub White-eared Meliphaga, Little Red Lorikeet, Red Myzomela, Torrent Lark, Western Black-capped Lory** and **Boyer's Cuckoo-shrike**, the stunning vivid red **Red Myzomela** taking the cake for being the prettiest of the day. I also learned that *meliphaga* and *myzomela* were posh Latin names for genera of honeyeaters, some of which occur in Australia too. (Some of which I'd actually seen, but was ignorant of their fancy Latin name!) I filed this useful information away, and practised how to pronounce them properly. I couldn't wait to have a bit of fun by showing off my new found knowledge and impressing my fellow bird club members back in Townsville!

That evening in the mess having my pile of pork, I was sat next to an engineer called Ian Schofield who spoke with an accent remarkably similar to my own. No wonder – he came from Batley … my home town too! You could have knocked me over with a feather. What a remarkable coincidence, two Batley lads meeting in the middle of the jungle, in P.N.G.! When he learned that I'd spent my day birding, it transpired that he enjoyed bird watching too. He had taken it up whilst living in Africa for a number of years. He told me about a sacred mountain lake that was close by, called Lake Wangbin. This lake reportedly contained ancestral spirits and a few 'ducks'. He asked if I'd like to check out these 'ducks' to see what they were. Up to now he told me, he couldn't get anybody else interested in going with him, and it was only about 4 km away. How could I refuse? So we got permission from the village elders to go up there the following Sunday. Apparently there used to be a village by the lake up until the mine opened, whence it re-located closer to Woolies so the path up there was now little used, and we were advised to hire a guide. The idea I had in my head was to stroll up there in the early morning, find out what kind of ducks inhabited the lake, returning in time for the Sunday lunchtime session at the golf club bar with the other lads. It turned out quite differently.

We left the bitumen in Tabubil, guide-less, at daybreak, and headed up the mountain path. It went up and up and up. It was a treacherous track. It was like climbing up the stairwell of a kilometer high skyscraper building, except that every second step was on moss-covered rock as slippery as ice, and every third step we sank ankle deep in stinking mud, each step being just too high to reach comfortably, necessitating us to pull ourselves up on tree roots and saplings. We forded many fast flowing mountain streams, and we were never able to glimpse the sky, the vegetation being too high and too dense. We arrived at the lake 4½ hours later, absolutely shattered and covered in leeches! I burned them off with a cigarette, just like I'd seen Jack Hawkins do in a jungle picture! We had only seen one bird on our ascent, it being a lovely little pied job, having a black back and breast, and a white belly. We had seen it sitting contentedly on a branch close to the ground, and I'd made a mental note of it. I would have to find out what it was later in Phil's field guide. We collapsed by the lake and ate our meagre rations, before spotting the 'ducks'. They were actually **Eurasian Coots**. On not spotting anything else before the clouds rolled in and it starting to rain heavily, making it impossible to see anything at all, we set off back. If I thought that climbing up the mountain had been quite difficult, going back down in the pouring rain was another story. It was HORRIFIC! Every step had to be carefully placed, and on the steepest sections I found that the safest way to descend was on my backside. I was relieved to see the house roofs of Tabubil appear just before dusk. It had taken us 10 hours to traverse 8 km! I had no energy left at all, or as I remarked to

Ian, in Batley talk, " '*Ee* Ian lad, I *dooan't* know *abaht thee*, but I'm *jiggered.*" We 'staggered' through town, wet through to the skin, covered in mud and with our legs running with blood from the leeches. Ian said, with typical Yorkshire understatement, "Quite tough in parts, wasn't it?" My reply waxed on the lyrical, but I'm afraid is not printable here! I collapsed on my verandah chair, too knackered to even untie my bootlaces, let alone walk down to the mess for more pork. I reflected wryly that in Batley, I'd often seen **Eurasian Coots** on Taylor's Mill dam on my way to school! I had nightmares for weeks after that 'stroll', replacing my sweet dreams of the drop-dead gorgeous, Manchester United supporting, dusky maiden I had fallen in love with the other day!

The following week there was held a 'Sing-Sing' called Hamamas Wik, where visiting dance troupes from different regions came to the town for a big week long competition. Out of curiosity on the first night I went along to watch. They were held on the covered floodlit netball courts and well attended by the locals, but not as many expats as I'd expected. One troupe after another danced, each with their own drummers beating out trance inducing rhythms on the kundu drums. I was enthralled by the near naked dancers' movements as they no doubt played out some ancient story, which I could only guess at. The men were adorned by only penis sheaths made from gourds, (some comically having a twirl, like a pig's tail at the tip), and headdresses made from plumes of birds of paradise and cassowary feathers. The women were bare breasted and wore grass skirts, and had crowns of pretty flowers on their heads. This was not a dancing exhibition for tourists, this was the real thing. They were dancing for the honour and pride of their respective villages. Rather like at a brass band contest in Yorkshire! I could make out that birds figured prominently in their stories as they mimicked strutting cassowaries and birds of paradise in their courtship displays. I appreciated it immensely and went along to most of the performances. I couldn't get any of the other lads interested funnily enough. If I'd mentioned the bare breasted bit, I'd have got trampled in the stampede!

When I had occasion to meet Phil again and flick through his field guide to look for the 'pied job' Ian and I had seen, I had no hesitation in proclaiming it a Mountain Robin. Unfortunately Phil gently advised me that they had never been seen around these parts, and that they inhabited mountain tops far higher than we had been at. I looked for other species that it could have been, and got totally confused trying to remember what I had actually seen. I came up with nothing, most frustrating indeed. It did teach me a valuable lesson though, that is – the importance of taking comprehensive field notes *at the time of sighting*. I never did find out what that lovely little dicky bird was! Never mind, Phil said that he would try and get me a bird of paradise on my last weekend in town, as up to now I'd only heard them, and seen their plumes adorning dancers' headdresses. Yes, my two months were almost up already, and I had nearly completed my task at the mine.

We took off looking for one up the Ok Menga Road, having to leave the vehicle and cross over a stream onto a small track into the forest. There were birds everywhere. I'd a right job trying to keep up with Phil as he pointed out one bird after the other. He got really excited about seeing a small flock of black starlings with yellow eyes. They were the – yes you've guessed – the **Yellow-eyed Starling**, a species having a very restricted range, and I don't think he had seen them here on his own patch before. No wonder that he couldn't contain himself! He taped their call to send off to the museum in Port Moresby. In this location we saw **Torrent Flycatcher, Stout-billed Cuckoo-shrike, Black Fantail, Northern Fantail, Spot-winged Monarch, Pygmy Honeyeater** (the smallest bird in P.N.G.), **Orange-breasted Fig-Parrot, Papuan Mountain Pigeon, Papuan Black Myzomela, Spotted Honeyeater, White-shouldered Fairy-wren** and a beautiful **Beautiful Fruit-Dove**, plus others that I had seen previously. I was very pleased to have seen all the lovely birds that I had that morning, but nevertheless a little disappointed that I'd 'dipped out' of seeing a bird of paradise yet again. We were slowly wending our way back to the vehicle, when lo and behold, you will never believe it, because I couldn't, a large chestnut coloured bird with a long plumed pale tail flew across the track in front of us, and perched in a tree posing for me. It was the **Greater Bird of Paradise**. I'd heard so much about these much admired birds that have quite extraordinary courtship displays, and now I'd actually seen my first one. I was *chuffed*, and eternally grateful to Phil. What a fantastic bird to end my P.N.G. work trip on. I was quite happy with my tally of 54 species, 39 of them being 'lifers', considering that I'd only managed to get out birding a few times, because of my work commitments.

When I arrived back home in Townsville, I asked Kylie if she had got anything in for our tea. She answered casually, "Yes dad, I've got some

Greater Bird of Paradise

nice PORK CHOPS in the fridge." Poor lass couldn't understand why I fell about in hysterics!

A few weeks later at the Townsville Region Bird Observers Club monthly meeting, Kath Shurcliff was asking me about my P.N.G. trip, and wanted to know how many species of birds I'd seen. She completely deflated me when I told her, by saying "Oh is that all!" I was lost for words, and only managed to stammer, "Well I didn't go on a birding trip, I was up there EARNING A CRUST." That confounded woman ! I thought, "Just you wait, I'll get you!"

3

Twit-a-Wooing a 'Proper' Birder

Townsville, Darwin, and Cairns, Northern Australia

IT WAS SUNDAY AFTERNOON 9th August 1992. I was in the packed Townsville Art Gallery for the launch of Jo Wieneke's book *Where to find birds in North East Queensland*. My mate Alan Oldroyd and I were strategically positioned next to a table loaded with 'finger food' and cartons of wine, which we were freely guzzling down. We had only been there for a short while chatting to other TOWNBOC members that were among the throng of renowned birders present, but we were already at the giggling stage and having ourselves a ball. Some local lady dignitary, wearing an outrageous silly hat, that looked like an oversized flat cap borrowed from an actor in the musical *Oliver*, was giving a speech. I started to sing quietly for the benefit of folk in the immediate vicinity, the old music hall song 'Where did you get that hat, where did you get that hat?' to be met with a few glares that implied, "Behave yourself!" That is all except Kath Shurcliff, who happened to be stood in front of us, for she turned around, flashed me a smile and chuckled. So I whispered theatrically into her ear, "She looks like one of Ken Dodd's 'Diddy Men' in it!" Alan nudged me in the ribs, assuming that I was trying to chat her up, and said in his Yorkshire way, "You don't stand a chance with yon lass, old lad, she's far too good for *thee!*"

I didn't know Kath all that well really, considering that I'd been on numerous TOWNBOC outings where she'd been present. All I really knew of her was that she was one of the 'top birders' in the club, worked in some sort of managerial position for the Great Barrier Reef Marine Park Authority and that she was a bit of a women's libber. This last bit of info I'd played upon no end, for I'd never let a chance slip by to make sexist remarks when she was within earshot. She always rose to take the bait and never failed to respond in a suitable forthright manner, much to my amusement. It came natural for me, hailing from the Broad Acres of Yorkshire, to address all members of the fair sex as 'love'. When I'd addressed Kath in this fashion on a club outing a few weeks previously, it hadn't escaped me that she had responded by addressing me back as 'darling'! Had it been a Freudian slip? On that same outing she had stunned me by saying that she would be starting a new job in Cairns shortly, and consequently would be leaving Townsville. I must confess that my heart had sunk at hearing this news for I enjoyed pulling her leg, and I would sorely miss her presence on club outings, not to mention her expert guidance on identifying birds. She invited me to her 'leaving do' to be held in a local restaurant after Jo's book launch, so Alan and I were getting well primed to party on there later.

Kath's leaving party was attended by a dozen or so stalwarts of the bird club. It was quite a jolly boisterous affair. We washed down our Thai cuisine with copious amounts of wine, which embalmed me with a pleasant feeling of bonhomie towards my new birding companions. Consequently I issued a general invitation to carry on partying at my place when they kicked us out of the restaurant, for I had a stash of posh wine that had fallen off the back of a lorry, and with which I needed help in disposing of. Kath and Alan were the only ones to take up my offer, nevertheless the three of us made a heroic attempt at demolishing my wine stock.

During the evening I mentioned to Kath that I had worked on the expansion project at the local Queensland Nickel Refinery a few years ago. I must explain that this project came about because the nickel ore that was mined nearby at Greenvale, and railed from there to the refinery, was almost exhausted, so the company had proposed to bring in ore by ship from overseas and modify the refinery to handle the new ore. This entailed the ore carriers having to negotiate the Great Barrier Reef before anchoring up in the bay, where the ore would have to be transferred onto barges, then from the barges onto a long conveyor that was proposed to be built way out into the bay. The Great Barrier Reef Marine Park Authority for obvious reasons weren't thrilled with this idea one bit, and said as much in an environmental impact study. Hence the project, which I'd worked on for 12 months, was abruptly shelved and I had lost my job.

Kath seemed to find this very amusing for she howled with laughter and spluttered, "I bet you didn't know that I was in charge of assessing the environmental impact study!" Well I'll be blown! So she was the faceless

bureaucrat responsible for throwing me out of work! We both laughed till
our sides were sore. Later on, when the right moment arose, I told her that
I was leaving town too, but only for a short while, for I had just landed
a contract to work for B.H.P. in Darwin on their oil rigs in the Timor
Sea. Did I detect even in my *druffen* state that she was a teeny weeny bit
sad to hear that I would be leaving to work in the Northern Territory,
which is miles away from Cairns, her future workplace? I hoped so, for I
thought she was a grand lass, despite her having scorned the paltry number
of birds that I'd seen in Papua New Guinea. I would miss her!

I had the mother of all hangovers the following day, but brightened up
a bit when I discovered a scrap of crumpled paper on the messy, empty
bottle strewn table that I was half heartedly cleaning up. It had Kath's
name, phone number and a scribbled message, in appalling 'doctor's'
handwriting that I had great difficulty in deciphering, saying simply that
I should ring her before we both left town. This I sheepishly did a day
later, asking if I'd any reason to apologise for anything I may have done
on the Sunday, but she said to my relief that there was no need to. So we
went out that evening to a local Indian restaurant and had a very relaxed
pleasant evening. To my surprise she accepted my invitation to a port and
coffee at my place to round our farewell evening off. Well what can I say?
Except that we rounded the evening off very well indeed and that we got
to know each other a lot better! So well in fact that we got to know each
other even more the following evening, my last in Townsville before my
trip to Darwin.

A week later, after a three day, long tiring drive to Darwin where I'd
settled myself into a small cheap room in the Larrakeyah Lodge, a backpacker style hostel in the heart of town, I was on the oil rig *Skua Venture*
in the Timor Sea. B.H.P. operated three such rigs in close proximity to
each other, but they were not the standard oil rigs that you would imagine
them to be, for this was a fairly small scale operation compared to the
North Sea oil fields. Two of these rigs were in fact converted old oil tankers,
the third being a purpose built barge that looked like an oil tanker, the
correct term for these vessels being Floating Production and Storage
Facilities, or something like that. These were each anchored around a huge
pipe, called a 'riser' which brought the crude oil at high pressure from wells
on the sea bed onto the fo'c's'le of the vessel, where it was refined in a
plant built on the main deck before being stored in the cargo holds. It

took about two weeks to fill these holds whence it would be sold and transferred to an ocean going oil tanker that would anchor up astern. The transfer of oil was achieved by pumping it through a long, large diameter 'floating hose' that was hooked up to both vessels. When not in use it was left floating on the water, forming a huge circle, for the free end or discharge end was securely lashed to the 'rig'. You may wonder why I'm telling you all this? Well there's a quite simple explanation – the floating hose was used as a roosting spot by hundreds of pelagic birds!

I was quite astonished when I first clapped eyes on all the bird activity around the floating hose. The Chief Engineer had just given me a Cook's tour of the stinking hot, sauna like engine and pump rooms, showing me the jobs that he wished me to tackle. Then he led me out onto the oven hot poop deck where I'd to adjust my eyes after emerging from the dark bowels of the vessel to be confronted with such an unexpected terrific sight on the shimmering sea. There were many dark-backed tern-like birds sat side by side on top of the hose, with lots more gracefully flying around the immediate vicinity and skimming the surface of the sea. I'd no idea which terns they were at that stage but managed to get half an hour before tea to take a look at them properly when I fetched my binoculars and field guide up from my cabin. I still had great difficulty in deciding whether or not they were the fairly similar Bridled or Sooty Terns until observing the juvenile birds. For these juveniles weren't dark all over like Sooty Tern juveniles were supposed to be, but they had white undersides like the adult birds, so that was a good enough reason for me to tick them as **Bridled Terns**. Those sorted out I scanned the hose with my binoculars and spotted to my delight a small group of different tern-like brown birds with snowy crowns. I found that these were Noddies, but which ones? Now these posed a greater problem in identification than the dark-backed terns had been, for the illustrations of Common, White-capped and Lesser Noddies in my field guide looked identical to each other. I figured out that they were probably **Common Noddies** on their distributional range only, but made a mental note to ask someone sometime if I was correct in my assumption. I knew that a 'proper' bird watcher wouldn't identify a bird on such a premise, for it was remotely possible that vagrants of the other two similar species could show up here in the Timor Sea.

On not finding any further different species on the hose I was about to go down to the galley for tea when I spotted a few swallow-type birds flying around. I watched one land on a pipe on the main deck, so hurried off to get a closer look. It was a **Tree Martin** with a mucky white rump and tiny patch of red on its forehead, there were perhaps a dozen of them hawking insects around the vessel. I watched them contentedly for a while until I spied a bird perched alone on the ship's rail. I moved closer, it was some type of brown little seabird, having a hooked bill with a strange looking tube nostril. Some kind of petrel or prion I guessed after thumbing quickly through the field guide illustrations, afraid that it may fly away at any moment, before I'd had the chance to identify it. But it didn't take off, so I edged stealthily closer and closer to get a better look at it. The dopey thing just sat there nervously watching me, occasionally shuffling its black feet on the rail. I guessed that it must be knackered and didn't have the energy to fly away from me. I eventually finished up beside it only an arm's length away from the poor thing, but even at such close range I failed to observe any distinctive features on it. It was brown all over with a black bill and black webbed feet. What was it? I deduced that it could have been any of about four storm petrels illustrated in my guide, until the bird summoned up enough energy to fly off in an arc and re-land on the rail about six yards away, where I got the opportunity to see that it had no white on its rump and that it had a forked tail when it had spread it to alight. I left the poor exhausted creature to rest. I reckoned it was a **Matsudaira's Storm Petrel**, a rare vagrant in Australian waters. It was probably on its migration from Volcano Island south of Japan into the Indian Ocean.

By gum, I didn't half enjoy my tea in the galley! The three near retiring-age ex-merchant navy cooks had whipped us up rainbow trout and oysters – with all the trimmings. It was grub fit for a king. I'd never had a better meal anywhere before, even in a swank fancy-priced restaurant. I told them so too, just to get on the right side of them, knowing from past experience that cooks can live up to their reputation and get a little cranky at times, taking it out on their patrons. I relaxed in the evening, like I did on many a future evening by watching a titillating blue movie, and availing myself of the bottomless supply of soft drinks, potato chips and chocolate bars provided gratis for us. Then I took a stroll on deck in the humid tropical air before turning in, to watch the noisy wheeling terns in the vessel's lights, discovering that at night there were perhaps twice as many birds present than during the day. *By heck*, this was the life for me! I only regretted that

I hadn't gone into the Merchant Navy when I'd left school. My job incidentally was based in the Darwin office, but the nature of my work meant that I would have to spend a lot of time on each rig at some time or other. I wasn't complaining, on the contrary, I was as happy as a sandboy on the rigs. Everything was to my liking and I even got the chance to observe pelagic birds at someone else's expense, most of them being 'lifers' for me.

To get to the rigs B.H.P. had their own Fokker Friendship aeroplane in which they flew their personnel from Darwin to a titchy island, called Troughton Island, located just off the coast of northern Western Australia, which was barely big enough to fit the short runway on. This island in days of yore was home to a weather station that got blown away by a cyclone, but now was the place where we 'de-planed' and boarded helicopters to take us the short distance out to the rigs. It was a flat windswept desolate place covered in grass, that was *wick* with dozens of tiny **Brown Quail**, scurrying hither and thither like rabbits all over the shop. On my first return trip from *Skua Venture* it was here that I spotted my first **Australian Pratincole**, a bird that flies like a swift and hops around on the floor like a pipit, and had time whilst waiting for the flight back to Darwin to write my first ever letter to Kath, telling her about the birds I'd seen. Would she bother to reply? Would she say, "Dave who?"

The following week B.H.P. informed me that I had to undergo a Helicopter Underwater Escape Training course if I wished to remain employed by them. The mere mention of this dreaded course filled me with fear, because I'd heard that they put you through quite a rigorous ordeal. They were not wrong for they tried to drown me in quite a number of ingenious ways! My fellow course participants and I, all attired in boiler suits and plimsolls had to jump with trembling knees from a great height into a swimming pool, inflate our life vests and scramble into a flimsy life raft – a feat much more difficult than it sounds, believe me. Just as we all got cosily settled inside to take a breather, we were instructed to jump out of it one by one to be winched out of the water in a harness, simulating a rescue by helicopter. That was the easy part of the course!

We had learnt in the classroom before getting wet that when a chopper ditches in a controlled manner into the sea, which had happened not so long ago, that flotation bags located near the skids should automatically inflate and keep the thing afloat on a calm sea. However if a chopper ditches in a not so controlled manner, or the sea is choppy, the chopper being top heavy will turn upside down and sink, taking approximately 8 seconds for the deadly whirring rotor blades to come to a complete stop under the water. Now we were going to sit in a helicopter simulator and practise how to escape under water! Bloody Nora! Our first attempt they'd made easy for us, or so they said, for they were not going to fit any windows in the mock-up chopper cabin. I paired off with another pale looking chap and we climbed nervously into the simulator at the side of the pool, each of us taking a window seat and fastening ourselves in with the seat belt, all as instructed. Before I had the chance to call out, "I want my mum!" the thing was magically lifted into the air and plonked unceremoniously into the pool, where it proceeded to sink and turn upside down simulta-neously, leaving us poor souls inside strapped upside down in our seats. I managed to take a last life-saving gulp of air before being engulfed and disorientated in a torrent of bubbles. Then as instructed beforehand, I counted off 8 agonizingly long seconds, released my seat belt as in a trance and floated out of the window to surface with much spluttering and coughing, my lungs at bursting point. *By gow*, I never realized that I was capable of holding my breath for that length of time!

Our second attempt was much tougher because they fitted windows in the simulator, and like proper helicopter windows they were 'emergency' ones, designed to be punched out when the need arose. Would I be lucky enough to take a vital last gulp of air before being submerged like I had on the first run? Would my seat belt spring open without any fuss after my count of 8? Would the window be easy to punch out with my elbow, or would it require Herculean strength to do so? These were all questions running through my head before being dunked again. I survived. Our final run we had to sit in the middle seat of the simulator, and wait for the person sat by the window to jettison it and escape, before following them out. This time I asked myself did I really want to work on the oil rigs? Surely there must be an easier way of earning a living? "Splosh" we went once more, and wouldn't you just believe it – the blithering idiot who I was to follow out couldn't undo his seat belt! I was already up to the count of 13 and floating around like a spaceman inside the cabin looking for an alternative exit, and could see the frogman coming to rescue us, before the useless so and so finally pulled his frigging finger out and escaped enabling me to do likewise. I miraculously survived this ordeal to tell the tale and was given a certificate that gave me the dubious privilege of allowing me to continue to earn my living on the rigs.

That same evening, suffering from slight shock, I found a letter awaiting me at my lodgings from Kath. It was more than I'd hoped for in my wildest dreams – not only did she remember who I was, but also said that she enjoyed our times together and that she missed me. Wow! So I dashed another letter off to her, a much more intimate one than my first. I wondered how she would respond to it?

A few weeks later I was out on another rig the *Jabiru Venture*, where luckily for me a large flock of storm petrels were present fluttering about, skipping and bouncing daintily on the sea's surface with their legs a-dangling. These ones had a distinctive white rump that I'd no reservations in identifying as the **Wilson's Storm Petrels**. Their antics were an absolute delight to watch. I also discovered a few more species of birds to be present on the floating hose here, besides the many **Bridled Terns** and a few **Common Noddies** (which had been present on *Skua Venture* remember?) There were six strange looking large brown birds with white bellies, yellow pointed bills and yellow webbed feet, that I had no problem in sorting out as **Brown Boobies**. Nor did I have problems with two little **Ruddy Turnstones** that stood out amongst the throng as they busily pecked at the weed growing on the hose – but hang on a minute, there were a few darker looking terns on the hose too. Some of them were juveniles that were dark all over with lovely white scallop marks on their back and wings. These I deduced were the other dark-backed terns, the **Sooty Terns**. It was easy to distinguish these two species of dark-backed terns from each other when you could observe them side by side. I was engrossed in watching all the birds, instead of getting on with my work, when a chap came up behind me and asked what I was doing. He'd caught me swinging the lead. This quietly spoken moustachioed fellow I'd seen before in the Darwin office. He was some kind of production boss, so I thought that he was going to play *hummer* with me for *laiking* about. As I was about to bluff it out by explaining to him the intricacies of the job on deck I was supposed to be undertaking, whilst *siding* my binoculars away into my tool bag, he simply smiled knowingly and asked if I was a birder. When I stammered, "Sort of!" he strode away laughing, saying over his shoulder that we must have a chat sometime.

It transpired that he was an experienced birder by the name of Ray

Wilson's Storm Petrel

Nojeck. He helped me out no end in sorting out all the species present on the rigs, explaining in depth the finer points of differentiating between the different Noddies and in doing so confirmed my sighting of the **Common Noddies**. He didn't seem surprised when I mentioned that I'd seen what I believed was a **Matsudaira's Storm Petrel** a few weeks earlier, saying that he'd observed them on a number of occasions. What I found really interesting was his tale of picking up a distressed Nicobar Pigeon one time from off the main deck. He took it down to his cabin to look after it for a few days before releasing it in a much better condition. Knowing that these particular distinctive looking pigeons had never before been recorded in Australia, he'd sent off photographs that he had taken of it to the curator of the Western Australian museum in Perth, only to receive a short reply saying that the rig we were on was not considered to be in Australian waters, so the species could not be added to the Australian list. This fact had never occurred to me, even though I knew we were closer to Timor than to Australia. For I'd seen maps of the oil fields showing a thick line running through the area carving up which fields belonged to Australia and which belonged to Indonesia. I was also aware that birds observed on Christmas Island, which was located many miles further away from Australia than we were, could ironically be legitimately added to the Australian list. There was something terribly wrong surely? We were only a short chopper ride away from the Australian coast. There was no doubt whatsoever in my mind that we were in Australian waters. It was Ray who put me on to some great birding spots in and around Darwin, and even told me 'his spot' for the Gouldian Finch. A bird that I would have dearly loved to see but had dipped out of seeing so far in my two long stints working in Kakadu National Park.

There was a fax from Kath waiting for me when I arrived back at my lodgings in Darwin from *Jabiru Venture*. I was elated to read that she would be spending a week in Darwin to attend a conference – would I be free for dinner on the night of the 2nd October? You bet!

I had a spare weekend before Kath arrived, so I spent it camping in the Yinberrie Hills, just north of Katherine, looking for the elusive Gouldian Finch in Ray's spot. I saw quite a few lovely birds that I hadn't seen before, such as the **Yellow-tinted Honeyeater**, **Banded Honeyeater**, **Black-chinned Honeyeater**, **Varied Sittella**, and **Grey-crowned Babbler**, my most memorable sightings being when I got onto a beautiful turquoise bellied, black crowned, long-tailed small parrot sat on top of a termite mound – the **Hooded Parrot**. Then a large quail walked into my campsite at dusk and actually walked over my bloomin' foot as I was sat quietly having a cup of tea. I kid you not. This *gaumless* creature I deduced was a **Chestnut-backed Button-quail**. Although I tramped for two days all over the dry sparsely wooded hillsides in the overpowering heat, and along many a dried up creek bed where just small pools of stagnant water remained, until my feet were sore, I never did clap eyes on any flippin' Gouldian Finches. Funnily enough I observed quite a few small flocks of other finches, such as **Long-tailed Finches**, **Masked Finches** and **Double-barred Finches**, but where were the Gouldians? When I reported this to Ray, he couldn't believe it, for he told me that all the times he had been down there he had seen them on every occasion! You can imagine what a hopeless jerk this made me feel!

Kath arrived in town; it was lovely to see her again. We had a very memorable romantic interlude. We condensed 9½ weeks into one! We even had time between wining, dining and so forth, to visit the Northern Territory Wildlife Park on the Saturday after her conference concluded. It was here, whilst strolling contentedly around hand in hand with her, that I first realized that we were behaving like a couple. Were we now 'an item'? Consequently on her return to far away Cairns our letter writing became more intense and we even started ringing each other up on a regular basis for lovey-dovey chats. This often annoyed Kath's flatmate Nikki, as I sometimes rang in the wee small hours of the morning on my way home from the aptly named Pickled Parrot Bar on a Friday night!

The months leading up to Christmas I spent almost every Sunday at Buffalo Creek checking out the waders with a brand new telescope that I had treated myself to. It was grand being able to ride my bike to this beach area at the mouth of the said named creek along a cycle path that hugged the coast almost all the way from the centre of town. I felt like a 'proper' bird watcher out on the beach with my swank new scope. I got so that I could recognize a lot of the common waders' 'jizz' after a while and felt quite comfortable with them. In fact I began to really enjoy watching them, for unlike forest birds that flittered by and quickly disappeared, the waders stayed put for hours in more or less the same place, where you had a chance to observe them properly. My most memorable sighting was when I was flabbergasted to see the beach chock-a-block with **Burdekin Ducks**

Gouldian Finch

(White-headed Shelducks). There were simply hundreds of them vying for space with the regular Northern Hemisphere winter visitors:- **Great Knots, Grey Plovers, Whimbrels, Eastern Curlews, Bar-tailed Godwits, Curlew Sandpipers, Large Sandpipers, Red-necked Stints** and the resident **Red-capped Dotterals.** In this idyllic fishing/birding spot one could observe **Gull-billed Terns, Crested Terns, Lesser-crested Terns, Little Terns** and even **Caspian Terns** on occasions – species that I was now becoming familiar with too and being able to recognize at a distance. A little walk into the mangroves near the car park was a good place to get onto **Yellow White-eye, Mangrove Warbler, Red-headed Honeyeater** and **Green-backed Warbler,** with the occasional **White-breasted Sea-Eagle** and **Brahminy Kite** flying over the area to keep an eye on things.

I always checked out Holmes Jungle at least once a week (if I wasn't out on the rigs), sometimes calling in for an hour after work. This spot is a small patch of protected monsoonal rainforest, just about the only notable patch left in Darwin. It is surrounded by grassland, with a swampy area between it and the town dump – a favourite spot for duck (Magpie Geese) shooters, so this area with its different habitat types was definitely worth checking out on a regular basis. In the rainforest I often saw **Orange-footed Scrubfowl, Yellow Oriole, Figbird, White-bellied Cuckoo-shrike, Emerald Dove, Bar-shouldered Dove, Torresian Imperial Pigeon, Rose-crowned Fruit Dove,** and even got onto a **Little Kingfisher** one evening perched on a branch overhanging the creek that meandered through this delightful forest. (Ray was sceptical about this latter sighting, for he went looking for it himself, but failed to find it!) The picnic area on the edge of the rainforest was a great place to sit quietly and observe things that came through the shade trees, such as: **White-throated Honeyeater, Bar-breasted Honeyeater, Dusky Honeyeater, Lemon-breasted Flycatcher, Restless Flycatcher, Varied Triller, White-winged Triller, Northern Fantail, Forest Kingfisher** and not forgetting the **Rufous-banded Honeyeater.** This latter species is very common around Darwin suburbs, there being no House Sparrows to take over its role – as yet! In the grassy areas there were **Golden-headed Cisticola** and small active flocks of **Chestnut-breasted Mannikin, Crimson Finch, Double-barred Finch, Long-tailed Finch** and on one memorable evening I saw my very first **Star Finch** here, all on its own. But I never did get to see a Yellow-rumped Mannikin that were reputed to mix with the very similar, common Chestnut-breasted, although I spent hours and hours until

I went boss-eyed, checking out all the flocks of these that I came across. The swampy area was the haunt of **Magpie Geese** where one evening when I was creeping through the long grass to sneak up on them I flushed out a little quail. I saw clearly its red patch on its lower neck as it flew away from me, the distinguishing feature of the **Red-backed Button-quail**.

Occasionally I checked out the Darwin sewage ponds on my way home from Buffalo Creek. These smelly ponds I'd first visited with Ray, who had a key to let himself through the gate, as had most local birders. He informed me that this particular collection of man-made lagoons is where many a rare vagrant to Australian shores had been spotted in the past. I never saw any, but there certainly was an abundance of birds languishing here in peace, that I enjoyed observing at close range, such as **Australian Pelican, Magpie Goose, Burdekin Duck, Pacific Black Duck, Wandering Whistle-Duck, Australian Grey Teal, Hardhead, Pied Heron, Pied Stilt, Sacred Ibis, Little Pied Cormorant, Little Black Cormorant, Australasian Grebe, Eurasian Coot**, and on one occasion even a few nomadic **Pink-eared Duck**. The mangroves surrounding the sewage ponds were great too, for it was here I spotted my first **White-breasted Whistler**, a species that is rather uncommon and sought after by birders, or so Kath informed me in one of our chats over the phone.

Beside the Darwin birding 'hot spots' of Buffalo Creek, Holmes Jungle and the sewage ponds, I kept adding new species to my list in unusual locations all over the place. Like the time I was astounded to come across a flock of perhaps 300 or so whimbrel-type waders wandering around in a field where vegetables were grown. These I figured out were **Little Curlews**, but why on earth were they not on the beach with the other waders? Similarly I also spotted a few wader-type birds behaving strangely by running about with their heads held high in a mowed field housing an array of radio masts. These I reckoned after a lot of deliberation were **Oriental Plovers**, here again, what were they doing in a field? I'd never come across waders in fields before! Naturally I had a lot to discuss with Kath over these sightings.

Kath was entering my thoughts more and more, especially after she posed the question in one of her letters, "What are you doing in Darwin, the birding is so much better in North Queensland?" I read, rightly or wrongly, into this innocent remark that she wished me to return to Townsville. I actually tackled her about this question in one of my letters, by asking if she was trying to encourage me to return so that we could at least see each other occasionally! She had replied by simply saying, "Be encouraged!"

As Christmas drew nearer my initial short-term contract with B.H.P. had been extended twice and looked to becoming a permanent never ending one. I was quite happy with that for I enjoyed the work, and Darwin in general, but my ex-wife Karen, had informed me that she was kicking our son Keir out of the family home in Brisbane because she could no longer handle the big (6'–3" tall) *gaumless* lump. She proposed that he should come to live in Darwin with me, but that was impractical, with me living as I was in a backpackers hostel so I suggested that she should send him up to Townsville to live with his sister Kylie, who was looking after my house there in my absence. I planned to return there to spend Christmas with Kylie and hopefully catch up with Kath again too. I thought that if Keir was there, I would be able to give him a kick up the backside and frighten him into getting a job, before escaping up here again after Christmas to avoid all the traumas for I knew that Kylie and Keir both fought like cat and dog together. Kylie predictably wasn't too keen on this idea at all, and insisted that if Keir came to stay, I should return permanently too, for she couldn't handle him on her own either. I didn't really appreciate the problem. I knew that he was a big bone-idle, good-for-nothing pain in the bum, but he wasn't that bad! He was just a lad being a lad! I was quite proud of him in fact. The outcome of a lot of further family discussions is that we decided that we would all spend Christmas together (my ex-wife too) in my home in Townsville and sort it out from there. This posed a further problem for me, because Kath had said in one of our lovey-dovey chats, "May I bid for some of your time over Xmas?" This I dearly wished to grant, but I was losing control of events, and it was beginning to look pretty hopeless that I'd even get the chance to see her.

Kath's 'be encouraged' remark and Keir's arrival into the equation made me start to think that maybe I should pack in my lucrative contract in Darwin at Christmas time and return to face an uncertain future in Townsville. But how could I tell Kath that I wouldn't be able to see her over Christmas because I would be spending it with my family? I plucked up the courage to tell her straight out and was astounded when she replied, "Well, aren't I invited to your place too?" I never thought that she would even entertain spending Christmas with me *and* 'the kids', let alone my ex-wife too. She took the whole situation calmly in her stride and didn't seem phased at all at the prospect of spending Christmas with us lot, even though I warned her what it would be like. She just mentioned that we must find time to do a bit of birding and catch up with friends in TOWNBOC. Wow! I couldn't believe how events were quickly unfolding!

My mate Alan flew up to Darwin to spend the last week there with me before we drove back down to Townsville together. What a mad week that was – we painted the town red, and every other hue, but I can't go into details on the grounds that it may incriminate us both! I don't think I've ever laughed as much since my Great Auntie Minnie got her tits caught in t' mangle!

Our first night on the road we stopped in the Yinberrie Hills, my third visit to this spot and my last chance for a while to look for the maddeningly elusive Gouldian Finch. Unfortunately we arrived in a tremendous electrical storm and were forced to spend the night sitting in the front seats of the vehicle telling dreadful jokes to each other, for it was impossible to sleep in such cramped conditions. We didn't see any Gouldian Finches, for it was still *silin'* it down with rain the following morning, but we did spot a 'lifer', the **White-plumed Honeyeater**, when we stopped on our southward trek down the Stuart Highway at Renner Springs to fill up with diesel. We observed many gigantic **Wedge-tailed Eagles** feasting on kangaroo road kills, groups of **Spinifex Pigeons** in the road verges, **Fork-tailed Swifts** flying high overhead, and the odd **Australian Bustard** and comical looking ungainly **Emus** strutting about in the paddocks, when we headed eastward on our long tiring drive towards Mount Isa on the never ending Barkly Highway. We didn't make it to 'The Isa' that day, for we crashed into our swags by the roadside completely exhausted at about midnight near Camooweal on the Northern Territory – Queensland border where the lullingly smooth, wide, straight tarmac road that we had traversed changed abruptly into a bumpy, narrow, winding cart track at the border. Change your clocks not ½ hour forward but ½ a century backwards! The heavens opened up again at about 3.00a.m., when we were forced to retreat back into the dry interior of the vehicle once more. Unable to sleep we plodded on to the barren, slag-heap landscaped mining town of Mt. Isa for breakfast, where a road sign informing us to "Keep Mt. Isa Beautiful" brought a smile to our tired faces. We were relieved to finally arrive stiff and zombie-like back in Townsville at 11.00pm that evening. It's a bloody long 2500 km drive I can tell you!

I rushed around like a madman in Townsville, frantically getting the house and garden in order and doing last minute preparations for a house-full of folk to descend on us over Christmas (Kylie had invited two of her friends from Brisbane to join us too) before taking a few days off to go up to Cairns to pick up Kath. I met her on the beach at the aptly named northern suburb of Yorkeys Knob. She looked absolutely ravishing with her green smiling eyes and red hair billowing across her face in the strong wind. We fell into each others arms, the prelude to a blissful few days spent in a secluded beachfront chalet lost in each other … and to the world. There was no way that I would be going back to Darwin in the New Year!

We arrived at my home in Townsville on Christmas Eve, it was heaving with noisy family members and friends – just like a home should be at Christmas. Keir greeted me with a 'give me five my man' handshake, dressed in long baggy shorts and tee shirt, with a baseball cap worn back to front. Bloody Nora! I was appalled. Karen hadn't told me that he was going through a rap music phase. Yanks have a lot to answer for, ain't they?

Kath surprised me with how serene and relaxed she was amongst my family throng, and I was relieved that everyone accepted her presence there. Christmas morning when the rest of the household hadn't even stirred from their slumber we took off down to the Kissing Point rockpool on the Townsville foreshore for a dip, before spending a relaxing hour down at Blakey's Crossing checking out the waterbirds in the swamp. *By heck*, we had come a long way in our relationship since she had first brought me to this spot to show me a Garganey Teal on the TOWNBOC 'learn your waders' morning way back in March. We were most definitely an item now. She got me a **Tawny Grassbird** for my Christmas pressie down at Blakey's, besides presenting me with a framed painting of my bogey bird, the Scarlet Pimpernel Gouldian Finch during our family pressie opening ceremony on our return home when everyone took it as a cue to get stuck into the Christmas Cheer, although it was still only mid morning. I had won a Santa Claus hat, so wore it to get our traditional Yorkshire roast turkey dinner underway whilst listening to the strains of Bing Crosby crooning Christmas Carols. That is after threatening Keir with an untimely death if he didn't turn off his dreadful New Kids On The Block rap album that he had been assaulting my eardrums with. I was deliriously happy. By the time dinner was on the table, everyone was very merry indeed. Karen managed to say her little maudlin 'goodwill to all men' speech twice over dinner, and had to be restrained by Kylie from delivering it a third time! Yes, it was a real Mad Hatters Christmas dinner party, the food a-blood-and-guts, no-holds-barred, get-stuck-in affair, but most memorable. Alan with his wife Chris and daughter Karen came around later to join us all for our traditional ham and pickle supper, with Christmas cake and cheese for 'afters', followed by a sing song, which continued well into the night.

Our Christmas celebrations carried on in this sort of fashion, with folk coming and going and doing their own thing. Kath and I found time to do a bit of bird watching and catch up with our friends in TOWNBOC none of whom seemed really surprised that we were 'stepping out' together! On one of our daily mucking about dips in the Kissing Point rockpool, Kath gazed into my eyes and said shyly, "I think I'm falling in love with you!" I was taken aback a bit, but managed to compose myself before replying, "I'm glad you feel that way, for I'm a bit soft on *thee* lass an' all!" Two days later the two of us had snook out to the fancy Yongala Lodge restaurant to celebrate Kath's birthday. The air was filled with romance as we sipped our pre-dinner champagne. I slipped onto my bended knee, feeling like a real twit, and with quivering voice asked her to marry me. "YES" came her reply.

Three months later at the appointed hour, I was waiting nervously with my best man Alan for the bride's party to arrive. We stood beside the pool at The Point Resort, built high on a promontory overlooking the sea at Mission Beach. Kath took my breath away when she made her entrance on the arm of the jovial, bushy bearded Glen Ingram, who was to give her away. Flanked by the elegant bridesmaids, all of them barefoot, she looked so radiantly beautiful that my heart skipped a beat. During our exchange of vows a **White-breasted Sea-Eagle** flew over this wonderful tropical setting to make it absolutely perfect. A twit had wooed and finally married not only a wonderful lady, but also a renowned 'proper' birder.

4

Letter-winged Kite Expedition

Southwest 'Outback' Queensland, Australia

MY NEW BRIDE AND I set off out of Cairns on the Kennedy Highway, early on Good Friday, Easter 1993. Our intentions were to see a Letter-winged Kite at all costs! This particular bird is the only raptor occurring in Australia that Kath has not yet seen, despite her having been on two previous unsuccessful expeditions searching for them. This time she had done her homework via the 'birding grapevine' and been informed, by a reliable source, of two possible locations where they might be found, one site being south-west of Mt. Isa, near Lake Nash, the other being north-west of Windorah, near Davenport Downs, a known breeding site.

The nomadic Letter-winged Kite is a small grey and white hawk, having black shoulders. It looks almost identical to the far more widespread and common Black-shouldered Kite, only being distinguishable by having a black line like a letter 'W' on its underwing. Hence its name. It feeds nocturnally, mostly on plague rats (*Rattus vilissimus*). After rain or flood in the 'Channel Country' when conditions are right for the grasses to grow and seed, and thus rats to breed in plague proportions, the Letter-winged Kite is also to be found in large numbers. When the land dries out again and rat numbers decrease, the kites disperse in search of prey and can show up anywhere in Australia. With the Georgina and Diamantina Rivers being in flood only a few months back, we decided that the time was right to go searching for them.

We reached Hughenden, a small town on the Flinders Highway between Townsville and Mt. Isa, with 620 km on the clock. Over a welcome break in a small café, we were faced with the dilemma of deciding which of the two locations we should go for. Could we manage to check *both* locations in the five days we had at our disposal, before having to be back in Cairns? After some short deliberations and considering our prospects for other good 'ticks', we plumped for Davenport Downs. So we headed south-west down the Kennedy Development Road towards Winton, saying goodbye to the

letter-winged Kite

bitumen for the next five days. We came upon Winton, a pleasant little outback town, with a further 215 km on the clock. Winton is the centre of a vast sheep and cattle grazing area, its claim to fame being that it is here where Qantas Airlines commenced operations in 1920, and where 'Waltzing Matilda' was written nearby in 1895 too! There were still a few hours of daylight left, so being anxious to get as far as possible in our first day, we wearily pressed on south towards Windorah, finally calling it a day, 100 km or so further on when we reached Lark Quarry just before dusk. Lark Quarry is the place where fossilized dinosaur footprints were found. These 100 million year old prints are now protected under a large roof against the affects of the harsh outback elements, with interpretive signs placed near these 'trackways', telling the imaginative story of how a mob of small dinosaurs stampeded when a large carnosaur stalked them! We had time to have a look at them before making camp close by.

At first light the next morning I surveyed the dry desolate 'moonscape' from our swag. "What a dry barren land," I remarked to Kath. "This must be hell! Yesterday we left a tropical paradise. Why have you brought me to this godforsaken place?"

I was to find out half an hour later when we checked out some 'mulga' beside the Winton to Jundah road. (Mulga being the name given to describe habitat comprised of mainly small acacia bushes that thrive in dry desert conditions.) For we found ourselves amongst a large multi-species feeding flock. There were unbelievably four types of woodswallows present: **Black-faced**, **White-browed**, **Masked** and **Little Woodswallows**; and four types of thornbills:- **Yellow-rumped**, **Chestnut-rumped**, **Brown** (white-bellied form) and **Slate-backed Thornbills**. I was amazed at all the activity, and could not keep pace with Kath. No sooner had I got one species in my sights, then she had spotted another for me to take a look at. There were **Hall's Babblers** and **Apostlebirds** noisily feeding in the understorey, **Hooded Robin**, **Red-capped Robin**, **Singing Honeyeater**, **Grey-headed Honeyeater**, **Spiny-cheeked Honeyeater**, **Crested Bellbird**, **Grey Shrike-thrush**, **Variegated Fairy-wren**, **Spinifex** and **Crested Pigeons**, plus all the usual ones like **Willy Wagtails** etc., that seem to be present wherever you go. It was all too much for me to take in at once, but quite a marvellous frustrating experience. I had just got 11 'lifers' in less than 40 minutes! I exclaimed, "What are all these lovely birds doing out here? Nothing in its right mind would live here through choice surely!"

Mad Twitching

We continued on our journey south, the vegetation alternating between mulga and open grass plains. We stopped occasionally to identify raptors overhead, seeing **Australian Kestrel, Brown Falcon, Black Falcon, Australian Hobby** and the gigantic **Wedge-tailed Eagle**. And we started checking out stands of eucalyptus along watercourses, looking for the Letter-winged Kites roosting during the day – but no luck. We carried on in this manner, bypassing Jundah, until reaching Windorah, a one-horse town in the middle of nowhere and the start of the 'Channel Country', where we took a break at the local store cum café cum petrol bowser. The 'Channel Country' is so named because of the extensive network of channels carved into the landscape by the tributaries of the Diamantina, Thomson and Barcoo Rivers, which drain south into Lake Eyre in South Australia. These rivers are normally dry, but when the rains come they flood their banks and spill into the 'channels'. It is then that this area comes alive overnight, turns green, and rare plants blossom, only to revert back to desert just as quickly. We set off west out of Windorah heading towards Bedourie. After driving a further 110 km we came upon a left fork that takes you onto Birdsville, where we stopped a little further on and made camp at dusk near Mornay Station beside a 'turkey's nest' borehole. What an oasis for birds! Parrots abound, there were large flocks of noisy **Red-tailed Black Cockatoos, Little Corellas, Gallahs,** and **Budgerigars**, together with **Emus, Brolgas, Pacific Herons, Wood Ducks, Black Ducks, Crested Pigeons, Masked Plovers, Australian Ravens, Black-faced Woodswallows** and hundreds of little pretty **Zebra Finches.**

Easter Sunday we continued in a north-westerly direction along the 'main road' to Bedourie for perhaps 50 km, where we turned right up a station track heading towards Davenport Downs. We headed north for a further 100 km or so up this track until at lunchtime we finally reached our Letter-winged Kite location, a stand of coolabah trees along Davenport Creek. It was hard to believe that we had taken 2½ days to drive 1,600 km just to get HERE! The middle of nowhere! This was beyond the 'Black Stump' alright, this was beyond the pale! Kath was anxious to get going on foot to check out the trees along the creek-bed straight away, but I knew that if we did this we wouldn't get our lunch and a cuppa for hours. So I doggedly insisted that we boil the billy first, or else! This we did and we were kept amused by an inquisitive **Jacky Winter**, who helped calm the mounting tension, as we ate lunch 'under the shade of a coolabah tree'.

We were both twitching with anticipation as we finally set off in the blazing midday sun along the creek-bed, looking for sleeping kites. Two hours later, wreathed in sweat, we had come up with – nothing. Kath was sullen. I kept quiet. I thought to myself that at a time like this, she wouldn't appreciate any of my facetious comments. We made camp, slung a few 'tinnies' under a damp cloth to cool for later and took a refreshing bush shower using the tepid muddy creek water, before settling down to await darkness, so that we could go spotlighting. I guessed that Kath was thinking it looked pretty hopeless ... there being no fresh signs of rats, only abandoned holes. I was amusing myself by playing with the telescope, whilst Kath sulked. She insisted that she was not sulking but was considering possible alternative sites. Unfortunately time would not allow us to get to the Lake Nash spot now, even if we had enough fuel to get to Boulia (which was debatable if it was necessary to engage 4wd all the way), as I'd just emptied my last jerrycan of diesel into the tank. I interrupted Kath in her deliberations to come over and take a look at the lovely **Black-faced Woodswallow** that I'd got in the scope, thinking that it would cheer her up a bit. She sauntered over unenthusiastically, and upon glancing through the scope, shrieked, "Eureka!" I wondered what on earth was happening. "What do you see next to the woodswallow?" she cried excitedly. "Some sort of black and yellow honeyeater," I said, taking a look, "with a red bill. Rather like a White-cheeked." It was in fact, a **Painted Honeyeater**, a nomadic bird that had eluded Kath for donkey's years, until this very moment. A 'lifer' for her, her first one in Australia for quite some time (Kath's Australian list being in excess of 650 species). No wonder she was hopping about delirious with glee!

There were in fact two adult male **Painted Honeyeaters**. They were feeding among the acacias in the creek-bed. Although there were flowering and fruiting mistletoes around, the birds never touched them. They were gleaning among the acacia leaves (or phyllodes of the shrubs as Kath put it). We watched them for about 5 minutes, before they flew into the top of an acacia perhaps 3 m high, and just sat there, about half a metre apart, completely silent. They stayed there, doing nothing, until darkness fell. Just like us!

So in a better frame of mind, we set off spotlighting for the kites. We tripped and trailed for hours along the creek-beds and floodplains, under a clear star-bejewelled sky. But we never set eyes on any sign of rats or kites. I think we'd left our expedition a bit too long after the recent floods, as the kites must have already dispersed! We reluctantly packed it in and retired to our swag for what was left of the night. Well you win some and lose some don't you? Or as I said more aptly to Kath, "You look as though you've just lost a bob and found a tanner!"

Over breakfast on our fourth morning, Easter Monday, which we shared with millions of flies, we were visited by the **Jacky Winter** again, this time with his Channel Country mates, the **Singing Honeyeater, White-plumed Honeyeater, Weebill, Variegated Fairy-wren, Mistletoebird, Red-browed Pardalote, Yellow-throated Miner, Grey Fantail, Rufous Whistler, Red-capped Robin** and **Crested Pigeons**. The **Painted Honeyeaters** had departed by first light so we realised how fortunate we were to have seen them for the brief time that they had passed through, never having emitted a single sound.

We decided that time had run out for us to return home the long way, via Lake Nash, to check out the other location. We had gambled all our chances at this one spot, and it had not paid off, well – not for the Letter-winged Kites at any rate. So off we went retracing our tracks, still checking out stands of trees in a last ditch effort at trying to see a kite. On passing over an area of gibber, Kath excitedly called me to a stop. She had spotted a number of wader-type birds on the ground, I don't know how because they blended in so well with their surroundings, and it took me an eternity to get onto them even with Kath's assistance. They were the lovely little, nomadic **Inland Dotterels**, having a narrow black Y-shaped band on their breast and resplendent with black vertical stripe through their eye. A good tick indeed. It amazed me how they manage to thrive in this arid stony habitat. There was a large group of perhaps 15 of them, but we had to leave them and press on. That day we planned to drive all the way to Opalton, not too far from Lark Quarry, where we had camped on our first night, an area that Kath assured me was good for spinifex specialities such as Striated Grasswren, Spinifexbird, and Rufous Emu-wren, species that I hadn't encountered before. We only made one stop from there on, back at Windorah to refuel the vehicle and ourselves, where I discovered that we had collected a **Crimson Chat** on the radiator grill. Kath wouldn't allow me to tick a dead one, and it refused to respond to my mouth to mouth resuscitation, but a live one obligingly flew across the road when we got going again. This time thankfully I didn't collect it. As night and our destination approached, the vehicle started playing up. It felt like a fuel starvation problem, probably too many miles and not enough rest like us. I tried to coax it on by bashing the fuel filter with a dirty great big wrench, but it finally stopped altogether and refused to budge an inch further. We were now stranded on a little-used track between Maynesville and the 'main' Winton to Windorah road. There was little else to do, as now it was dark, except to push it off the track, have dinner with the stars and a bottle of red wine to celebrate the day's adventure and birds.

The next morning I awoke to find the vehicle resting at a crazy angle, one of the tyres was flat. I realised then that it was going to be 'one of those days'! I changed it whilst Kath got breakfast cracking. I then discovered that I had every type of spare imaginable, except a new fuel filter! There was only one thing to do – that was to try and clean the old one out, whereupon I found it to be clogged up with bits of rust from the bottom of my ancient jerrycans. I re-assembled it all, filling the filter back up with fuel, but it wouldn't fire. I figured that I must have an air lock somewhere and almost flattened the battery trying to pull it through by turning the engine over. In my ignorance of diesel engines at that time, I didn't know that the vehicle manufacturers in their wisdom had provided a priming pump specifically for the job in hand! It was beyond my level of expertise and I was getting rather frustrated with it, so we set off to find some technical assistance. A 15 km hot hike through the mulga yielded some good birds. We found that the **Hall's Babblers** were locally common, and we had excellent views of more **Little Woodswallows**, a **Chestnut-breasted Quail-thrush** and **Slate-backed Thornbills**, to name just a few. Eventually, wreathed in sweat, we arrived at Elvo Station on the main Winton to Windorah road. It was rather embarrassing to have to explain to the station owner that we were in a 'spot of bother'. He was a rather obliging, friendly sort of chap, who promptly gave us a lift back to our vehicle and had it running again in 5 minutes flat, after showing me where the priming pump was! I felt such a *chump* and would have expected a dressing down from a lesser man, on the perils of travelling in the outback without having rudimentary mechanical skills, but he didn't, he humbled me by being a perfect gentleman. I have nothing but respect for these self-reliant Australians who are perfectly at home and at one with the harsh outback conditions. I didn't wish to offend him by offering him money, but he was delighted when I presented him with our last bottle of posh red wine with our many thanks. He was obviously a man of taste too!

Mad Twitching

By now it was almost midday, and having nearly 1,000 km to cover to get back home to Cairns that very day, we decided that time had run out for us to go looking for the spinifex specialities at Opalton. We had no option but to head for home post haste. We were obviously rather disappointed in not achieving our objective of seeing a Letter-winged Kite, but Kath did get one 'lifer' and I got 21, bringing my Australian list up to 336 species. We also had our fair share of fun, saw some quite unique country, which was by now growing on me, and I'd had a well overdue mechanical lesson. Sooner or later, to use the words of General MacArthur, 'I shall return' – for yet another try for the elusive Letter-winged Kite.

5

A Bored Househusband in Tanga

Tanga, Tanzania, East Africa

"WOULD YOU LIKE to live in Africa for three years, Dave?" Kath excitedly shouted down the phone. She was ringing from Nairobi, where she'd gone to attend an interview with the I.U.C.N. (The World Conservation Union) for the job as the Chief Technical Advisor for a new project they were setting up in Tanga, Tanzania. Before I'd chance to say anything, she gabbled on at 20 to the dozen about how she had been successful in her interview and they were offering her the job. She wanted my blessing before accepting it. "Yes!" I replied, with adrenaline surging through my veins. For Africa was a dark mysterious continent that I'd dreamt of living in ever since I was a boy, intrigued by the tales of Livingstone and Stanley, which I'd heard at Sunday school. Kath had made my boyhood dream come true!

We arrived in Dar-es-Salaam in July 1994. There was disappointingly no one to greet us at the airport, so we had to make our own way up to Tanga with our mountain of luggage, Tanga being about a 5 hour drive north of Dar-es-Salaam and not too far from the Kenyan border. When we eventually arrived there, we surprisingly discovered Tanga to be quite a pleasant sleepy seaport town, despite it having a population of over 100,000 souls, with its streets thronged with bicycles and colourfully dressed pedestrians. It is hemmed in by enormous sisal plantations to a beautiful coconut fringed, turquoise bay, with the nearby purple coloured Usambara Mountains lending a picturesque backdrop to this idyllic setting. The town centre consists of crumbling, rotting, colonial buildings, badly in need of maintenance, and the poor state of the pot-holed roads are quite frankly beyond belief to anyone first arriving from a developed country. So one gets the overall impression that the place has seen much better days, but decay has its own special charms don't you think?

Mad Twitching

Kath was straight away engaged in setting up the new project (the Tanga Coastal Zone Conservation and Development Programme) from scratch, in conjunction with the regional government. The regional government had previously agreed with the I.U.C.N. to make available suitable office space for this new project, and a government house for us to live in. Neither was forthcoming, just a lot of quite ingenious excuses, so Kath had to hunt around for an office and I a house for us to rent. This was by no means an easy chore as there were no estate agents, nor a local paper. It was all apparently achieved by word of mouth, and we didn't know a soul. We ended up living in the Panori Hotel for three whole months until we finally found a place to rent. This was no real hardship, as we learned that we had chosen at random on our arrival here, the friendliest, cleanest, little hotel in town, serving what Kath described as, 'the best food in the whole of East Africa'. In the meantime our container from Australia arrived by ship, with my old faithful 4wd vehicle packed to the brim with our camping gear inside. What an incredible frustrating struggle that was to get it out of the port without actually having to bribe anyone. I had after all got all the relevant documentation and could see no reason why I should have to cross anyone's palm with fistfuls of U.S.$, in fact I was determined not to. It just took a long time, a lot of patience, a lot of acting dumb and sheer dogged persistence, in the face of the customs officials' expertise in extracting *chai*-money (as they called a consideration) from their customers. After that harrowing experience, in which I learned a lot of their ploys, I vowed that I would never set foot inside the port ever again. (The port complex was actually the only place in Tanga I observed **House Sparrows**. I wonder how long it will be before they colonise the town?)

Our arrival here in July was quite good timing as far as I was concerned. It meant that when I wasn't otherwise engaged in taking Kiswahili lessons, house hunting, or spending hours at the port trying to get my vehicle out, etc. I could get acquainted with the local non-migratory birds before being swamped by the Eurasian migrants arriving a few months later. There were plenty of interesting new birds for me to observe within the town itself, along the foreshore and around the hotel. (We regularly saw the huge **Verreaux's Eagle-Owl** in the evening near the hotel.) But when Kath and I finally moved into a charming, whitewashed, colonial bungalow, that was perched on top of the ancient coral cliffs overlooking the Indian Ocean, in a quiet fishing village only 10km south of Tanga, called Mwambani, we found it to be a bird (especially wader) watcher's paradise. We also found that this house needed a lot of work done to it to make it habitable, as it had been empty for over a year, and that the electricity supply in Mwambani was rather erratic to say the least. It would go off without warning at all hours of the day or night, sometimes for 10 minutes and sometimes for days on end. The I.U.C.N. hadn't made matters easy in this regard, for in their wisdom they supplied us with an electric cooker and an electric fridge!

We joined the Wildlife Conservation Society of Tanzania and were informed that they were compiling records on a map grid system basis to enable them to publish a Tanzanian bird atlas. Neil and Liz Baker were in charge of this endeavour. They sent us reams of atlas cards for us to record our sightings on a monthly basis. We had to tick off the bird species seen, estimate the number, and note if we suspected them of breeding. They told us that there were no other birders resident in our Tanga map square, so we were it! I remarked to Kath, "They don't know us from a bar of soap! How on earth do they know we are competent enough birders to compile their records accurately?" Kath shrugged her shoulders, obviously having no such fears. This responsibility of compiling bird atlas records gave me an added impetus to get to grips with the local birds quickly, and I might add, kept me relatively sane, as I would creep out and escape from our new household staff for an hour or so to go bird watching most days, as they did their utmost to drive me crazy!

I must explain that before we moved into our new home I'd told Kath that I most certainly didn't want any servants, because I was quite capable of running the place on my own whilst she was out at work. To be honest I didn't fancy the idea of having strangers wandering around the house invading my privacy, which I value highly. But Kath was insistent that it was expected of *wazungu* to have household staff, not only that, she said it was 'our duty' to employ local people. She kept reiterating the adage, "What's the point of working for an aid project if you can't help the people around you!" To keep the peace I relented and we actually finished up with five staff members can you believe? For when we moved our camping gear into the house we discovered that the previous tenant's cook with his large extended family were living in the servants' quarters at the bottom of the two acre garden. This well built elderly fellow, called *Mzee* Musa, had been squatting there for over a year without any income since the previous tenant departed. He was consequently bare footed and dressed in rags and it would have been a heartless person indeed who could have evicted him. We set him on as our house-boy (as they refer to their house keepers here, a term I could never bring myself to use!) and found that he was quite an amiable character, if not a bit of a rogue. To my relief I found he even spoke a bit of English, which was to prove a godsend in dealing with day to day matters. We also set his mate on, a Mr. Hassan, as our *shamba*-boy (gardener); this perpetually grinning character with a hacking smoker's cough needed a job badly to support his two wives, and burgeoning family. Kath's regional government counterpart, Solomon, meanwhile had stressed upon her that we also needed an *askari* to guard the place during the hours of darkness. *Mzee* Musa insisted that we needed *two* on each night, as there had been a spate of armed robberies in the area recently. So we employed three *askaris* so that they could each work five nights on and take two nights off. That was our full compliment of staff, not deeming it necessary to employ a cook just for the two of us.

I found it ironic that all my working life I'd been a committed trade unionist and here I was reluctantly being thrust into the role of being an employer. It wasn't easy to come to terms with, nor the fact that I didn't have the place to myself. I couldn't even scratch my backside in my own house! In our naivete, Kath and I decided that we would pay our staff well above what other people paid theirs. And we only had them work five days a week instead of the usual six or even seven that all other household staff seemed to work. I initially bought them all that they asked for, raincoats and Wellington boots for all of them, plus torches, whistles, bows and arrows and Maasai spears for the *askaris*. In addition they enjoyed a limitless supply of tea and sugar, the latter running to a staggering 2kg a week! We thought this would keep them all happy and content. We were wrong. Instead they thought I in particular was a soft touch and took every advantage of me, making quite extraordinary demands! Within a few weeks I found myself running around looking after them, surely it should have been the other way around? They turned me into a blubbering wreck and my life a complete misery until I eventually learned to say, "NO."

One *askari* asked me if I would make his dinner for him each night, because sometimes his wife hadn't got it ready for him before he left for work! I told him that if he liked I would especially bake him a cake each day. He thanked me profusely, obviously my sarcasm completely went over his head! After a while things settled down a bit and we got into a routine, they even started calling me *bwana*. (I rather liked this term, for it is the term that Tarzan was referred to in the old pictures!) What with the mammoth task of fixing up the rusted plumbing and arranging to have sticks of furniture made for us, you will understand that it took us months to settle into our new home before we could even begin to really appreciate the wonderful setting and the abundance of birdlife.

A few weeks after we moved into our new abode, and long before we'd sorted ourselves out properly, Kath received correspondence from Don Turner in Nairobi. He was compiling a new field guide on the birds of Kenya and Northern Tanzania and wanted to know the status of **Kurrichane Thrushes** in our Tanga area. He said that there were several old records from the 1930s, when they had been seen in the hospital grounds and in the cemetery, but no records since. Tanga was the most northerly extent of their range apparently. When Kath told me this I blurted out that I'd seen a thrush in the garden of a house across the road from the Panori Hotel whilst we had been staying there. (The Panori Hotel being not too far away from the hospital.) I had meant to check it up in the field guide, but what with checking up other new birds too, it had completely slipped my mind. Silly me, and now for the life of me I couldn't describe it adequately to Kath's satisfaction, other than to say that it had had a bright orange bill and I thought that it had been an Olive Thrush that I had seen before in Kenya. (I now know that Olive Thrushes don't occur in Tanga.) So we spent one weekend traipsing around the grounds of the hospital and cemetery looking for one, but to no avail. Funnily enough the weekend after when we were taking a walk in the *shambas* / coconut plantation near our new home we came across a pair of thrushes on the ground. "These could be the Kurrichanes!" Kath excitedly shouted. Now we had to be certain on this one, or it could have proved rather embarrassing, so I rushed home to fetch the scope. After a great deal of deliberation we agreed that they were indeed **Kurrichane Thrushes**. Glad to be of service, Don! We later discovered that they were actually quite common in Mwambani, and we even saw a pair nesting in a coconut palm in December. Neil Baker however was rather sceptical as he said that they didn't nest in such palms, and would come down to our place sometime to take a look for himself.

Wader watching was a delight, and involved no effort on our part. We simply had to set up the scope on our verandah to enable us to survey the reef flat below our cliff. It reminded me very much of watching waders on the Cairns esplanade in Australia. Not only because we were sat comfortably and had excellent close-up views when the tide came in, but because we observed a lot of the same species that frequent the Cairns foreshore too. Such as **Green-backed (Striated) Heron, Great White Egret, Bar-tailed Godwit, Common Greenshank, Whimbrel, Common Sandpiper, Curlew Sandpiper, Terek Sandpiper, Ruddy Turnstone, Greater Sandplover, Lesser (Mongolian) Sandplover, Grey Plover, Gull-billed, Little, Lesser Crested and Crested Terns**. In addition we also had on a regular basis **Eurasian Curlew, Ringed Plover, Little Stint, Grey Heron, Black-headed Heron, Woolly-necked Stork, Sacred Ibis** (a recent split from the Australian one), and the wonderful African specialties such as **Crab Plover, White-fronted Sandplover, Black Heron, Yellow-billed Stork, Open-billed Stork, Dimorphic Egret,** (a 50/50 mix of white and dark phase) **Long-tailed Cormorant** and **Sooty Gull**. On occasions too we saw the odd **Greater Flamingo, African Spoonbill, Oystercatcher, Ruff** and **Common Tern**. Kath and I would go into raptures watching the **Black Herons** fish. They have the unusual habit of bending forward and folding their wings up over their heads in a quick motion to shade the sun's glare from the water's surface. They hold this pose for a few seconds, flick their wings back down, step forward and repeat the whole process over again. They are locally called umbrella birds because of this canopying feeding style. We have seen up to 40 birds feeding together in this manner in the same rock pool, and then moving off en masse to fish the next. My favourite shore bird is the **Crab Plover**, their 'jizz' rather resembles that of a Thick-knee (Stone-curlew), but they are endowed with a striking black and white plumage like an Avocet, and have a powerful stout black bill for dealing with crabs, their main diet. These plovers we found to be quite numerous on our stretch of beach throughout the year, they being most abundant between September to April, when we could usually count 30 to 40 of them. Unlike the Black Herons, they don't feed collectively, they space themselves out individually along the foreshore, but they do roost together in tight flocks on sandy beaches. This I discovered one evening at dusk that coincided with a high tide, when I was walking the dog on the cliff tops overlooking a small sandy cove, nearby our residence. I was surprised to startle a large roosting flock into taking off and flying in tight formation low over the sea. They circled around and around and went this way and that, but

Crab Plover

wouldn't return to their roosting spot until I'd cleared off. I estimated that there were about 250 of them. They used that small sandy cove to roost for a few weeks, but I was never able to sneak up on them to take a photograph, they were far too skittish for that. They apparently breed around the Arabian Gulf and are unique in the fact that they are the only wader in the world to nest colonially in burrows underground. Even during their breeding season between May to August we usually could count upwards of 10 over-wintering on our patch. These we deduced were mainly 1st or 2nd year juveniles.

Waders were not the only interesting things to watch from our verandah either, there was plenty of other activity. A large contingent of village ladies would swarm into the shallows most days to catch miniscule shrimps in mosquito nets. These they used to flavour their *ugali*, a stiff maize meal porridge, the stodgy starchy staple diet of Tanzanians, who simply love huge helpings of the stuff. Youths would scour the tidal flat for crabs and dive out of dug-out canoes collecting lobsters, whilst the men folk went out fishing on the reefs in their small handcrafted outrigger canoes called *ngalawas*, these being rigged with a small triangular sail. Old men checked their fish traps and repaired and finely adjusted them daily. Consequently we were never short of fresh seafood; I actually got a bit tired of eating lobster three times a week! Kath never did! On a regular basis I would hear the muffled explosion of 'bombs' going off in the water, or in other words hear people dynamite fishing. This is an extremely destructive and illegal practice of course. Our village had a simple flag system of letting these fishermen know if it was all clear to use dynamite. They hoisted up a red flag if any officials or police were present in the village or a white one to signify it was all clear. One morning whilst watching waders through the scope, I spied an old chap with one arm missing at the elbow, standing up in his dug-out canoe. He was scattering what must have been bait onto the water. This completed to his satisfaction, he sat down and lit up a fag. A few minutes later I watched him light a stick of dynamite from his fag, and hold it for what seemed to me to be an awful long time before tossing it into the water. Then came the expected muffled explosion, with the accompanying eruption of water, and he calmly slipped into the water with a small net and started scooping up dead and stunned fish. What I didn't expect is that numerous **Gull-billed Terns**, a few **Crested Terns** and **Sooty Gulls** and two **African Fish-Eagles** were quickly at the scene trying to noisily steal his fish. They obviously recognised the sound of the bomb going off! I found it rather amusing watching him waving his stump around in the air trying to fend off the birds, whilst frantically scooping up fish with his good arm. It wasn't funny though the day I heard a tremendously loud bang, it must have been dynamite going off out of the water. I rushed out onto the cliff top but couldn't see where it had gone off, it was out of my field of vision. I later learned that a young newly wed lad from the village had tragically blown himself up. He had lost both hands and was blinded for life. This illegal, lucrative and highly organised practice is one of the big issues that Kath's project had to address. They used photographs of this poor soul taken at the hospital to try and dissuade other lads from ending up like him.

A typical day usually began with the song of the **White-browed Robin Chat** before first light. My field guide describes it as a 'series of sustained flute-like whistles of great beauty', but I'm afraid at that time of day it was sometimes hard to appreciate, especially after a heavy night. At day break it was joined by the many **Common Bulbuls**, they seemed to chant 'rugby league, rugby league' to me. That was my cue to get out of bed, enjoy my first cup of tea and fag in peace whilst watching the sun climb quickly above the horizon, before I served breakfast on the verandah to my Dearly Beloved. We would watch **Striped Swallows** swirling around our cliff top, see the **Pied Kingfishers** hovering stationary over the sea before plunging in to take small fish, and observe large numbers of **Cattle Egrets** flying low over the water in 'V' formation from their roost in the mangroves. (Contrary to some field guides that say they are not to be found in marine environments!) Our resident **Brown-hooded Kingfisher** surveyed our lawn for tasty morsels whilst perched in his usual spot, and a pair of **African Pied Wagtails** would be wandering and fluttering around on the lawn. The **Little Purple-banded, Collared, Amethyst** and **Scarlet-chested Sunbirds** (on rare occasions the odd **Mouse-coloured Sunbird**) flitted around in our hedgerow along with the **Speckled Mousebirds**. The **Red-fronted Tinkerbird** and **Black-backed Puffbacks** put in regular appearances in our flamboyant (poinciana) tree. (So did the **Lesser Honeyguide** to check out the bees nesting in our eaves before we reluctantly had to have them removed, because they kept attacking Mr. Hassan as he slashed the grass.) We could always hear the tranquil call of the **Red-eyed Dove** (saying, I-am-the-Red-eyed-Dove, I-am-the-Red-eyed-Dove!) and **Emerald-spotted**

Wood Dove, and they sometimes nervously came in to our bird bath for a quick drink. If we were lucky on occasions the lovely rather shy **Peter's Twinspot**, the odd **Yellowbill** and **Grey-Headed Bush-shrike** or a small party of noisy active **Green Wood Hoopoes** would pay us a visit. We often saw **African Fish-Eagle, Palm-nut Vulture, Peregrine Falcon** or **Lizard Buzzard** hurrying by. Periodically we had passing through, and often staying around for a month or two, the migratory **Eurasian Marsh Harrier, European Golden Oriole, Red-backed Shrike, European Rock Thrush, Olivaceous Warbler, Blue-cheeked Bee-eater, Madagascar Bee-eater,** and the largest, most beautifully coloured bee-eater that I have ever been privileged to see, the **Northern Carmine Bee-eater**! What a stunning bird, what a grand sight, with its carmine red plumage set ablaze in the sun, contrasting with the pastel blues of its forehead, throat and vent, gracefully making aerial forays for insects right along side our verandah. An unforgettable sight! Pure magic! A great start to the day.

One morning I was mucking about doing some task or other on our cliff top with Mr Hassan, the wind was whipping up and the sky was as black as night over the bay, a storm front was heading our way. A large stationary object caught my eye, as it hung motionlessly in the air just above us. I recognised it instantly as a frigatebird. Luckily Kath hadn't as yet set off for work, so I bellowed, "Frigatebird!" at the top of my voice to make myself heard over the noise of the wind billowing the trees. She dashed out with her binoculars at the ready and had plenty of time to pronounce it a **Lesser Frigatebird**, as it hung there for ages before being carried off by the wind. On checking up in *Birds Of East Africa* by Britton we found that in Tanzania there had only been one definite sighting recorded in Dar-es-Salaam in 1974, and a few probable sightings in 1973 and 1975. Here we had another sighting in Tanga! I was really pleased that Kath had been home to see it, or else she would have grilled me for hours over its description, to determine whether it was the Lesser or Greater Frigatebird. It spared me that ordeal at least!

Kath would have to dash off to the office, whilst I usually set off for a walk on the maze of footpaths winding through the coastal scrub and scattered *shambas*, leaving *Mzee* to get on with the chores. In these *shambas* the village folk grew maize, cassava, bananas, paw paw, cashews and oranges in amongst the many coconut palms, mango trees, kapok trees and the strangely beautiful baobab trees, these baobab trees, being the favourite

Northern Carmine Bee-eater

Naomi 2000

haunt of the **Lizard Buzzards**. I often saw **Black-winged** and **Zanzibar Red Bishops**, **Winding** and **Rattling Cisticolas**, **White-browed Coucals**, **Little Bee-eaters** and **Spotted Flycatchers**, perched high on small shrubs in these cultivated fields. Small flocks of **Bronze Mannikins, Rufous-backed Mannikins, Red-billed Firefinches, Red-cheeked Cordon Bleus** and **Yellow-rumped Seedeaters**, plus enormous flocks of **Red-billed Queleas** would take off out of the long grass when I disturbed them. The **African Golden Oriole, Collared Palm Thrush (Morning Thrush)**, **African Drongo, Southern Black Flycatcher, Brown-breasted Barbet, Broad-billed Roller, Green Pigeon, Violet-backed** and **Black-breasted Starlings** preferred the taller, leafier trees. The gregarious **Village Weavers (Black-headed)** with the odd **Masked Weaver** mixed in with them, made a terrible din near their wonderful colony of woven nests hanging precariously from their chosen borassus palm. The **Spectacled Weaver** was much more reserved than its relatives and preferred to nest on its own. The colourful **Fisher's Lovebirds** would invariably try to compete with these weavers to see who could make the most din, whilst a faint tap tap tap noise would betray the presence of a **Mombasa Woodpecker** digging for insects in the trunks of the coconut palms. Walking through the coastal scrub I often saw **Black-headed Oriole, Arrow-marked Babblers, Zanzibar Sombre Greenbul, White-browed Scrub Robin, Grey-backed Camaroptera, Tawny-flanked Prinia, Pale flycatcher, Black-headed Batis, Black-headed Tchagra, Didric Cuckoo, Pin-tailed Whydah** and **Grosbeak Weaver**. In a large area of grassland fringing the tidal flats there was usually to be seen **Yellow-throated Longclaw** and **Richards Pipit,** and on one occasion after a long dry spell in February we saw a lone **Northern Wheatear** and a lone **Capped Wheatear**. In the mangrove vegetation on the sand dunes I would never fail, whatever time of year, to flush out a pair of **Mozambique (Gabon) Nightjars**, nor fail to observe the slender **Palm Swifts** as they wheeled high above.

I never tired of my walks through the *shambas*/coastal scrub or along the beach. There was always something new to see or observe at different times of the year, and I was constantly adding new species to our list. I would return from these walks at peace with the world and ready to tackle the numerous trivial household problems I knew that *Mzee* and Mr Hassan would have in store for me. These out of the way, I usually spent the rest of the day either sorting out staff problems and keeping track of all their advances and loans; keeping up correspondence with family and friends;

doing odd jobs around the house; repairing my old vehicle which was well past its used by date; boiling up fresh lobsters and crabs and preparing tea; or running around town shopping and banking. Apart from my little walks I found that I rarely had a spare moment left for myself! Kath would arrive home from work each day and I'd excitedly tell her of my day's birds. If I'd spotted a new one for our list, spotted a bird nesting or feeding a fledgling or I'd had trouble sorting one out that day, we would nip out before dusk and try and find it again. On the other hand if she had passed anything interesting on the track home, which she often did, we would go back to have a look.

In the evening very rarely did we miss out on hearing our resident pair of **African Wood Owls** calling whilst having our tea. Kath could never resist replying to its loud 'HWOOOO' call, which would frighten the life out of the *askaris* and the dog. Not having a T.V. I spent most evenings reading old novels, as often as not by the glow of a paraffin lamp, for I'd discovered the Tanga Library, which was a godsend. This library was built by the British before independence in 1961 and was stocked with a good selection of books donated from British libraries. (They were all stamped – Cancelled – Bognor Regis Public Library Service, or some such thing!) Their collection had not been expanded since independence as far as I could see, except for a few books on communist dogma donated by communist block countries trying to woo Nyerere. The books themselves were generally in a dreadful moth eaten filthy condition. But this didn't deter me at all as I discovered a lot of quite compelling pre-1960s reading. On the weekend we entertained frequently at home, having Kath's fellow technical advisors from her project and visiting consultants as regular guests. Among these were Monica Gorman, a really smashing outgoing Irish lass, Trudi van Ingen a lovely Dutch lady with her househusband Jaring, and Chris Horrill a likely, darts-playing, Geordy lad. They were a fun loving bunch. Needless to say we had many a good bash, always with mountains of lobster and crab on the menu, and copious amounts of wine on hand.

We had joined the Tanga Yacht Club, the only place in town where the small expat community hung out. They had quite a lively social scene going with regular fancy dress parties, dinner dances and suchlike, and it was pleasant to hang out there and sip gin and tonics in the convivial atmosphere overlooking the harbour. But I had been annoyed a little when a few of the hoi polloi types, leftovers from the British era, upon being first introduced had immediately asked me what I did for a living. (It is taboo in working class Yorkshire to ask such a question, for it reminds folk about 'work' when they are trying to distance themselves from it!) On learning that I was a 'HOUSEHUSBAND' they had guffawed and sniggered and rudely quizzed me about what on earth I did all day at home. (No one ever asks housewives this, do they?) I'd nonchalantly replied, "Nothing!" Flabbergasted, they'd eventually got around to saying that surely I must get BORED doing nothing. "No way!" I'd retorted. These initial encounters led to me, when having a tête-à-tête with Kath, jokingly referring to myself as – 'THE BORED HOUSEHUSBAND IN TANGA!' It was our little private joke.

We often went down to Kingfisher Lodge in the fishing village of Kigombe, near Pangani. Pangani incidentally, being an old slave trading port on the mouth of the Pangani River, where they used to ship slaves captured in the interior over to the slave market in Zanzibar. This delightful lodge, only a 45-minute drive from our place, was run by Janey and Angus Galbraith in the palatial old sisal plantation manager's residence on the beach-front. It catered for a small number of guests who generally were interested in staying there to go out deep sea fishing. (Angus's passion). But they had more than a passing interest in birds and we became firm friends with them, as well as being regular guests. (Janey's mother, known by her nickname of Kimbo, is in fact a well-known East African birding identity). Often we would go out on their Sunday morning trips in a local *dhow*, snorkelling on the reefs, to return for the traditional East African Sunday curry lunch served on the lawn. Other times we would go out birding with them, and seeing that Kigombe just sneaked into our Tanga bird atlas square, it meant that we could add the species seen onto our Tanga list. Angus would lure us down there by his tale of seeing a **Bat Hawk** each night on dusk. We spent many a happy evening with them sipping gin and tonics on the lodge verandah on dusk, waiting for the flippin' Bat Hawk to show up, but we never did get to see it! He would always swear that he'd seen it the previous evening, to be met by our peals of laughter, or send us a message that it had shown up the following night!

The short drive down to Kingfisher Lodge was quite interesting. We would encounter **Ring-neck Doves** and occasionally the lovely little **Namaqua Doves** on the road, and see numerous **Lilac-breasted Rollers,** a few **Striped Kingfishers** and at the right time of year big mobs of **Eurasian**

A Bored Househusband in Tanga

(**Barn**) **Swallows** on the telegraph wires. During June, the wet season, small depressions in the *shambas* would fill up with water, making little ponds for a few months, before drying out again. These were always worth checking out as we often saw **Red-billed Teal**, nesting **Little Grebes** and the beautiful little **Malachite Kingfisher** taking advantage of them. The road meandered through sisal plantations where **White-throated Bee-eater** where to be found, and **Common Button-quail** scampered about between the weed choked rows of sisal. It was also a good place to observe **Wahlberg's Eagle, Bateleur, Black-chested Snake-Eagle** and **Harrier Hawk** flying high overhead. The road headed inland before descending, (and deteriorating) into a swampy marshy area. This we never failed to check out for we regularly observed **Black Crake, Squacco Heron, African Reed Warbler** and **Lesser Swamp Warbler** in the reeds, and on one memorable occasion during June saw a pair of **Senegal Plovers** and a lone **Spur-winged Plover** in this location. What a thrill that was to add these unexpected visitors to our Tanga list.

The lodge had a resident **Red-necked Falcon**. The first time I observed it was through the scope from the upstairs bedroom verandah of the lodge. I was on eye-level with it as it sat in a nearby tree, its red crown and nape lit by the golden dawn glow, with its finely barred belly ruffling up in the gentle sea breeze. Then I jumped back into bed for a 'morning glory' before enjoying a leisurely full English breakfast! Just the sort of stuff memories are made of! Janey said that she felt sorry for the **Wire-tailed Swallows** nesting under the eaves, as the falcon would pick off all the fledglings as they took their first tentative flight out of the nest. She informed us on our first visit to the lodge that there were some salt pans nearby, sited behind the mangroves, where a lot of shore birds gathered on high tide. She wasn't wrong for we counted over 5,000 birds! That's quite a lot by anyone's standards. These being mixed flocks of mainly **Grey Plovers, Greater Sandplovers, Curlew Sandpipers, Whimbrels,** and **Common Greenshanks**, and to our delight a few **Pink-backed Pelicans** and **Yellow-billed Storks**. She also took us to the local sisal factory to check out the dam system. Here we saw **Wood** and **Marsh Sandpipers, Pied Stilt, Blacksmith Plover** and **Ruffs**, these birds obviously unperturbed by the less than pristine state of the water, as the factory emptied their effluent into it. Janey had also discovered a large freshwater lagoon at the back of the village. Here we set up the scope on the top of the vehicle to peek over the fringing vegetation, but were disappointed that there weren't too many birds on it. We did see an **African Darter**, a couple of **African Jacanas**, **Hamerkops**, 40 **Open-billed Storks** in a lakeside tree, and to our surprise a pair of **African Pygmy Geese**. Kath informed me that I had now seen all the world's species of pygmy geese. (The two species in Australia being the only other ones.) These birding spots that Janey put us onto we would check out on a regular basis, but we never did set eyes on the darter or pygmy geese ever again.

We got a message from them one time that there was a huge flock of **Crab Plovers** on a sand bar at the mouth of the little river just south of their lodge. They thought that we might be interested in going down to take a gander. What a wonderful sight greeted us when we did just that. We estimated that there were 750 of them! We saw **Water Thick-knee** and **White-winged Black Terns** too as a bonus. When Neil Baker heard of this sighting he paid us a visit. He said that since the world population of Crab Plovers was estimated to be around 43,000, the numbers around Kigombe were quite significant, over the 1% required to make it a Ramsar site. This is what he intended to do. He was also sceptical of our sighting of the **Kurrichane Thrushes,** as I mentioned earlier, so we found one in the *shambas* around our house for him to take a look at for himself. He confirmed that our identification had been correct!

I'll certainly never forget the time Angus said that if we came down to the lodge for the weekend he would guarantee us seeing the **Bat Hawk**, because it had shown up every evening without fail for weeks! Kath, Janey and a sweet English lass, Naomi Hart, took me around all the birding spots in the afternoon, and I wondered why they were dragging their feet in getting back to the lodge for a 'sundowner' before dinner. Then they wouldn't let me park in the car park by the lodge when we did get back on dusk. They insisted that I should drive down to the beach, only a few minutes walk away, for they said that was where the Bat Hawk was to be seen. (This beach, by the way, was the only place in our Tanga map square that we ever observed **Sanderlings**.) I found Angus and his staff had set up a bar there and he plied me with a welcome gin and tonic. He said, "This is where we are going to have our barbecue dinner this evening." I thought to myself, "Oh, how super." Meanwhile Kath had strolled onto the beach and beckoned me down. When I followed her, I got the shock of my life, for 20 or so people, all our friends from Tanga, jumped out from behind the dunes, shouting, "Surprise! Surprise! Happy Birthday!"

Bloody Nora, you could have knocked me over with a feather! They had completely hoodwinked me! Monica, bless her, had even made me a smashing cake!

Kath and I were devastated not long after, to hear that Angus, who we had seen only a few days previously, and who had complained that he was feeling a bit out of sorts, fell unconscious and passed away with malaria! A bloody tragedy! Poor Janey went back to Nairobi with their toddler to live with her mother, and the lodge closed.

We had in our Tanga map square one small area of coastal rainforest. I should say 'titchy' really because there was no more than maybe two dozen rainforest trees left. These were in a limestone gorge just north of Tanga at a place known as Amboni Caves. To someone coming from Yorkshire, abounding in spectacular cave systems, these caves were not up to much. That said, it was still worth going down with a guide, mainly for the fact that the guide lit the way with a lighted palm frond twisted up into a taper, and told outrageous tales of dogs going missing in them, only to be found later, mucky miles away on Mount Kilimanjaro! All the stalagmites and stalactites had long since been souvenired and the place was covered in graffiti, but the titchy forest was great. It surprisingly held a small population of Colobus Monkeys and quite a few birds that we rarely saw anywhere else in our Tanga map square. So we checked it out on a regular basis. We'd take the path beyond the cave that ran alongside a beck that had illegal *shambas* on the opposite bank. (I say illegal because it was supposed to be a nature reserve.) We often saw the wonderful **Giant Kingfisher** plying this beck, with **Common Waxbills** and **African Golden Weavers** playing around in the beck-side vegetation. We always tried to turn the latter species into the very similar Golden Palm Weavers, the main difference being the colour of the eyes. It had irked us a bit that some visiting birder had cheekily recorded Palm Weavers in *our* Tanga map square, but despite searching high and low for them in different locations, and deliberating over eye colour, we in all honesty only ever did see the Golden Weavers! This gorge was an excellent spot for swifts and swallows, there always being quite a few species flying around to sort out. **Black Roughwing Swallows** flew low, making us duck for cover at times; **White-rumped Swifts** would be high in the sky, together with a few comical, ungainly, tailless **Boehm's Spinetails** (the swift family's equivalent of the ungainly Puffin!); and **Mosque Swallows** could often be seen perched on top of the crags. Further along the path the gorge narrowed. In the low scrub we'd find **Yellow-bellied Greenbuls** and in the rainforest trees themselves quite an array of birds which often included: **African Paradise Flycatcher, Black Cuckoo-shrike, Tropical Boubou, African Scimitarbill, Trumpeter** and **Crowned Hornbills** and one of my favourite birds the rather lovely **Narina's Trogon**. This latter bird is a favourite of mine, not just because of its striking plumage of bright green head and back and crimson belly; nor the fact that it was named after a prostitute, but for its habit of bobbing its dark blue tail up and down when it called.

At the end of our stay in Tanga, after compiling the monthly atlas cards religiously, I could clearly see patterns emerging of what species passed through our area and when. Not only the European migrants but the inter-African migrants too. Of course it was easy to see at a glance which birds were our all year round residents. We finished up with a 'garden list' of over 160 species, (this included the beach and surrounding *shambas*!) and our Tanga map square list was to us a respectable 240. I say 'to us' because this Tanga tally was considered by Neil Baker, with whom we had become good friends, to be abysmal. The cheeky so and so often told us that we should pull our fingers out! We could only counter that our Tanga map square consisted of two thirds sea and the rest sisal plantations, which was almost true! Besides our excellent birding, things had gone extremely well for Kath in her project too. She often received glowing praise from the most unlikely quarters regarding the remarkable results that her project team had achieved. We enjoyed our life in Tanga; it was both exciting and rewarding, but not without its trials and tribulations. I remember well the time when Kath went off with Monica for a week to a conference in Uganda …

I knew that when Kath went off anywhere our household staff, knowing that I was a soft touch, always gave me a hard time, so on the first Monday morning of Kath's absence it didn't surprise me to find them lined up waiting to see me. I was only peeved that I hadn't managed to sneak off birding before they all showed up. Yes, as I'd expected they all wanted advances on their wages, or further loans for a variety of different reasons. I had to sit through all their quite ingenious heart rending sob stories, all of which were deserving of Oscars. I couldn't quite understand why they were all apparently flat broke, *hamna pesa, hamna chakula*, when I'd only just paid them their wages a few days earlier. Knowing they were trying it on as usual, but at the same time thinking of Kath's maxim of, 'What's the point of working for an Aid project if you can't help the people around you!' I caved in to agreeing to give them most of their demands, not wanting to have them sulking for weeks on end. The only thing was, I didn't have any money in the house to give them, which meant that I had to make a special trip into town to go to the bank. This really peeved me off. For besides the ride into town being a rather bone jarring experience, and for the fact that it never took less than an hour in the bank to perform a simple withdrawal transaction, I had intended to stay at home all week to get on with drawing some maps up for Kath's project. These, I'd faithfully promised her, I'd have completed on her return. To cap it all, when I got back from the bank all tired, dusty and sweaty, Mr Hadjee, a chap that I regularly bought fish from, was waiting to see me. He sadly told me that his brother had just died, and he needed a loan of 20,000Tsh. (US$40) to transport the body back to their village of origin for burial. I conveyed my sympathy, but told him that seeing as I had five of my own staff and their extended families to look after already, I simply couldn't help him. I added that if I did, I would have all the inhabitants of Mwambani seeking my assistance too. He started to cry. I gave him the money. *Mzee* told me as he disappeared down the drive that Mr Hadjee was very happy, and had rejoiced that God had sent me to Tanga to help him! I never slept that night for thinking about what a soft *chump* I was!

Tuesday morning I was determined to go out for a little bird walk then make a start on drawing up Kath's maps. Unfortunately *Mzee* showed up earlier than usual to tell me that the night before, Biro, 'my dog,' had chased and injured the next door neighbour's goat. He went on to say that he thought Biro was *mgonjwa* because he was frothing at the mouth, and said that he thought that it could be RABIES! Naturally he was concerned about Biro attacking his children and rightly suggested that he should be put down! Bloody Nora! Biro had come with the house. When we moved in *Mzee* had informed me that the mangy, scrawny mutt, with huge red sores on its back, running around the yard uncontrollably was mine! I'd never seen such a pathetic looking dog before and thought then that it should be put down. Instead I'd got some pills from the vet and nursed it back to health over a long period of time. Hence I was the only person that it would let stroke, and it enjoyed coming out with me on my little walks. I'd grown quite fond of the silly thing, and what's more I'd felt safe on my walks along the beach with it, as there were quite a few desperate *panga* wielding thieves about. These characters were petrified of dogs and would keep their distance, but I had over the past few days noticed Biro behaving strangely, and it had chased and worried a couple of chickens, which I'd had to recompense the irate owners for. Furthermore it hadn't shown up for its grub that morning which was highly unusual. I found it wandering around the yard listlessly. It wouldn't let me near it and it was indeed foaming at the mouth. I was unable to corner it into the shed, so I told *Mzee* that I wanted everyone to give it a wide berth, whilst I went into town to get some pills from the vet to put it to sleep. The vet was out, and wouldn't be back until later in the afternoon, and the receptionist couldn't find the pills I wanted. I had no option but to hang around town for 3 or 4 hours awaiting his return. This I did at the Tanga Library, where would you believe the librarian, who I normally passed the time of day with, asked me, seeing that I was his *rafiki*, if I could loan him 50,000Tsh (US$100) to buy a bicycle. I laughed it off as a huge joke! The vet had been and gone when I returned to his surgery. He had left me a note to say that he had no pills left, and asked if I knew anyone with a gun! Back at home I didn't know what to do! It was clearly obvious that Biro had to go, he was a danger to everyone. Then I had the brainwave of sending *Mzee* into the village offering anyone 10,000Tsh if they would kill him for me. I thought that this could be done with a little dignity, in the same way that they slaughtered goats, by slitting their throats whilst facing Mecca. I had no takers until one of my *askaris* showed up for work in the evening. Without much ado he calmly picked up a hoe that was lying around and whacked poor old Biro a mighty blow over the head with it. Biro dropped dead. I had never witnessed anything so brutal in all my life! That night I couldn't sleep for thinking about poor Biro, and pictured him frolicking about in the shallows, putting all the waders up in the air on one of our many beach walks. Would he come back to haunt me for having him put down in this brutal fashion?

2.00a.m. Wednesday morning when I'd eventually nodded off to sleep I was awoken by Mr Mwachalika, the only *askari* that I really trusted, as he tapped on my bedroom window calling, "*Bwana*! *Bwana*!" I groaned, so he carried on. "Hassani is fast asleep! He won't wake up!" I knew exactly what this meant. Hassani was a young *askari* that kept giving me no end of trouble. I'd even had to bail him out of the police lock-up on one occasion, and he was forever asking me for extra money, as I later learned, to support his drinking habit. I'd always regarded him as a sneaky, sneering individual who treated me with what is described as 'dumb insolence' in the army. The other *askaris* didn't like him either and often told tales about him to me behind his back. But what really concerned me was his habit of coming to work drunk on *pombe* and sleeping it off all night, for whichever other *askari* was working with him on a particular night had to cover for him, when they couldn't wake him up to do his turn at patrolling around the yard. I'd insisted that there was always to be one *askari* awake doing patrols whilst the other rested, for if any intruders were encountered they could summon the resting *askari* to give assistance by blowing their whistle. After a few complaints about him I'd got *Mzee*, who I regarded as my head man, to tell him to pull his socks up, or else he would be out on his ear. He behaved himself for a while until slipping back into his former ways. After more complaints I wrote him a letter in my best Kiswahili telling him more or less the same thing, that if he came to work drunk and was unable to perform his duties, he would receive his marching orders. The sneering prat only jeered at my poor Swahili grammar, but he got the message all right. A few months later after more complaints, I decided that I'd had enough of him, and instructed the other *askaris* that if it happened again they were to wake me up, at whatever time of night it was, so I could catch him in the act. So that night was the night! I sneaked around the corner of the shed to find him snoring away in a drunken stupor on a chair. He had his Maasai spear leant up against the wall beside him, so I thought it prudent that I should move it out of his way in case he woke up with a start and stuck me with it. It took me three attempts to wake him up and when I finally succeeded I'll never forget the look of utter surprise and bewilderment on his beer sodden face. I told him that if he wanted to sleep all night he could do it at home from now on because he was sacked! Luckily he accepted this without any fuss, only asking if he could stay the rest of the night because he considered it too dangerous to go home in the dark! I returned to bed and realized that I was shaking. I'd never sacked anyone before. It had been a most unpleasant but necessary task.

Needless to say he was still hanging around when I surfaced in the morning. He wanted his job back. When I didn't relent he belligerently demanded a month's salary. I pointed out to him that he owed me a lot more than a month's salary with all his outstanding loans, and added that I wanted him to leave behind all my property that he had in his possession – torch, whistle, bow and arrows, spear, raincoat, etc. He fled on his bike with the lot, and I thought, "Good bloody riddance." That unfortunately wasn't the end of it, for mid morning, just as I was about to get started on drawing Kath's maps, one of her project vehicles pulled into the yard. It was Kath's office manager to tell me that he had been visited by an official from the Labour Office, to say that I'd unfairly dismissed an employee, and that I owed him wages. I told him the full story, about Hassani's behaviour, and that he'd had a verbal and written warning over a long period of time, and that I'd actually caught him in the act. Furthermore that Hassani actually owed me money and property. Kath's work colleague kindly agreed to handle the dispute for me, having dealt with the Labour Office before. He requested that I should write a report about it and make a full list of all wages, overtime payments, bonuses, housing allowances, and travel allowances that I'd paid him, and a list of outstanding loans and property. This I did. It took me the rest of the day to complete it. (Later the Labour Office ruled in my favour, and added that Hassani had been a fool to lose his well-paid position! They even got me back all my property, but I never did see the money that he owed me!) What a right carry on! I was weary of it all!

Thursday morning 3.30 a.m., I was awoken this time by *Mzee* tapping on my bedroom window. I thought, "What the Dickens now!" He cried in a falsetto voice, through the louvers, "*Bwana, Bwana.* My daughter is having two babies. One has come out, but one is stuck. I think she need go to hospital." I mouthed, "Oh my Giddy Aunt!" or words to that effect and sprang out of bed. I pulled my vehicle up outside the servants' quarters in the back yard, where a knot of people were gathered in the dark. *Mzee* and his wife came out of the house grim faced, with a lady carrying a new born baby swaddled in cloth, to be followed by his sobbing daughter being half dragged and half carried by 4 or 5 village midwives. They all piled into my vehicle dragging his daughter in on top of them. Now I've mentioned before that it was a bone jarring ride into town, which entailed weaving around huge craters in the road in low gear, there only being one reasonably good bit where you could actually get up into third gear for a short distance. Well here I was with a quandary. Should I go fast and get to the hospital quickly but give her a horribly bumpy ride, maybe inducing the birth in my vehicle? Or should I go slow and risk her and the baby's life by not getting to the hospital in time? I took the middle course, but every time I went over a bump she cried out in pain. Luckily I got her to the hospital in time, where smartly dressed nurses manhandled her inside. *Mzee* and I hung around for an hour until a doctor came out to say she hadn't given birth to the other baby yet, but we should go home and come back at 10.00 a.m. This we did and on our return were greeted with the news that she had given birth and mother and child (children) were all doing fine but for some reason I had to transfer them all to a different hospital. I finished up paying the bill, being the only person with any money, and took the patient with all her entourage to another hospital. Here again I was told to return later at 6.00 p.m. I did and they discharged her, I having to foot the bill once more. I was utterly exhausted. I'd been up since 3.30 a.m. and had made three bone jarring trips into town that day taxi-ing folk about.

Friday morning I had bags under my eyes after the torrid week I'd endured. I didn't feel inclined to start work on Kath's maps. In fact I was waiting for some other calamity to occur. I felt that I'd been let off lightly when all that happened was that the bank teller, that I normally dealt with, came down to see me. He handed me a letter with my name neatly written on it. It informed me that he was getting married, and requested politely in old fashioned 'your humble obedient servant' type language, seeing that I was his *rafiki*, that I should contribute 50,000Tsh (US$100) towards the cost of his wedding!

Kath returned home on the Saturday. She inquired, using reference to our little joke of me being a 'bored househusband', by saying, "I hope that you weren't too bored on your own whilst I've been away?" I snapped back, roaring, "BORED! BLOODY BORED! FAT CHANCE OF THAT! IF YOU MUST KNOW I'VE KILLED THE DOG! SACKED AN ASKARI! DELIVERED TWINS! AND NOT EVEN HAD A CHANCE TO START ON YOUR #@*# MAPS!"

6

The Man-eaters of Mkomazi

Mkomazi Game Reserve, Tanzania, East Africa

ALMOST A YEAR had elapsed since Kath and I had arrived in Tanga. Not only had my lifelist just reached the momentous milestone of 1000 species with my sighting of a **Golden-winged Pytilia** in Mikumi National Park, but in that time we'd taken every opportunity that presented itself to take off and bird the recognized locations within easy reach of us, there being one notable exception – the Mkomazi Game Reserve – that we had inadvertently overlooked. If you pull out a map of Tanzania you will find that this reserve lies between Mount Kilimanjaro and the coast, bounded to the south by the Pare and Usambara mountain ranges and to the north by the Kenyan border. (It actually abuts onto the Tsavo West National Park in Kenya.) You will notice on the map that it is an area (about 3600 sq. km.) strangely devoid of any sort of geographical feature – no mountains, no rivers to speak of, no human settlements, and no roads – just a big blank empty space. No wonder Kath and I had overlooked it! In fact if it had not been for Monica Gorman, who went into raptures about the place after she'd spent a long weekend camping there, it would have taken us a great deal longer before we eventually cottoned on to its existence. She told us that the area was basically a dry savanna grassland plain that was broken by many beautiful steep sided wooded hills, and that there was an abundance of game to view, besides heaps of birds. There was only one thing to do after Monica's enthusiastic appraisal of the place, that is, go and take a look for ourselves. We were keen to do just that, for up until then we hadn't got around to birding any dry savanna grassland habitat at all, so we thought that with a bit of luck we ought to get a few new birds.

Thus one Friday afternoon in mid July 1995 we were in the small dry dusty town of Same (pronounced Sarmay), that lies sleepily on the main road from Dar-es-Salaam to Arusha. I was relaxed and in a happy-go-lucky mood after our rather pleasant 250 km drive from Tanga. The road itself, which we had travelled along a number of times before, was a smooth tarmaced, well-constructed affair by African standards and relatively traffic free. Only occasionally had I been forced to pay attention to my driving when we'd encountered speeding, maniacally driven, dilapidated though gaudily painted, jam packed buses that had seemed to try their damnedest for some reason to run us off the road with their lights a-flashing and air horns a-blaring. This disconcerting behaviour by the doped up bus drivers hadn't in any way distracted us from the fact that this highway passed through some of the most breath-taking scenery in the whole of East Africa. The highway lay to the north of and followed loosely the course of the Pangani River, the river's lush green ribbon of riparian woodland being easy to pick out as it starkly contrasted against the vast endless expanse of the parched looking Maasai Steppe beyond. And the road closely skirted the southern steep slopes of the majestic Usambara and Pare Mountains, which I'd felt that at times I could almost reach out and touch. We'd had fun too on coming across many small villages, just clusters of straw thatched mud huts really, where the cheerful ragged-arsed inhabitants had suicidally run out onto the road in front of us to sell us their wares. We could have purchased any number of items, from sacks of charcoal to eggs, live flapping chickens, bottles of dark looking honey, cobs of corn, bunches of bananas, mangoes and even boxes of tinned food, stamped, 'A gift from the people of the E.U.'. But we'd only arrived in Same with a bunch of over ripe bananas and a large, flimsy, hastily woven basket filled to the brim with rock hard mangoes, such was our skill at dealing with these entertaining rascals.

Whistling a happy tune we turned off the main highway in Same, and climbed up through the little town on the bumpy *duka* lined main street, soon leaving the straggly town behind as the muck road gently climbed up between a gap in the Pare Mountains, coming out onto a fertile plateau where the townsfolk grew their produce and grazed their scrawny cattle. Hereabouts we came across a sign in the middle of a fork in the road announcing the Mkomazi Game Reserve, but it gave no indication of which fork we should take to get there. Predictably we chose the wrong one. Half an hour later realizing that in theory we should have already come across the entrance gate (Monica had informed us that it was only 11 km from the main highway) we retraced our steps and tried the other way. We were relieved, after travelling only a few kilometres, to come across a stone portalled, securely padlocked gateway across the road, which brought us to an abrupt halt. There was a small stone built office attached to the fancy gateway structure and it was set in the shade of a large attractive stand of acacia trees. We could see that there was a conglomeration of bougainvillea clad buildings through the trees not far away, but there was no sign of life anywhere. We presumed we were at the Zange Gate Reserve H.Q.

We stiffly slid out of the vehicle with a view to rousing someone, someone who possessed a key hopefully, but got distracted on seeing a few birds flitting about in the acacias. In what seemed like no time at all, but must have been in reality about 45 minutes, we kicked off our Mkomazi bird list with : **Southern Black Flycatcher, Northern Brubru, White-bellied Tit,** the colourful **Red-and-Yellow Barbet,** the smaller and duller **d'Arnaud's Barbet, Black-headed Oriole, Black Cuckoo-shrike, Red-fronted Tinkerbird, Black-necked Weaver,** (its lovely black eye-line and black throat patch among other things distinguishing it from Reichenow's Weaver), and a rather unexpected **Shelley's Greenbul** that was foraging about acrobatically on a tangle of vines. We were broken off our birding activities when a grinning bare footed chap wearing a threadbare green uniform appeared from out of nowhere, like the genie out of Aladdin's lamp. He informed us in slow careful Swahili, (guessing correctly that ours wasn't up to much), that we were indeed at the Zange gate of the Mkomazi Game Reserve, and what's more that he was entrusted with a key to it. He proudly held the key aloft like a prized trophy for us to see. On inquiring what our intentions were, and on satisfying himself that we were not big game hunters, just harmless eccentric bird watchers, he said that we must pay our daily entrance fees and camping fees first before we could proceed. He did this whilst pointing to a list of charges pasted onto the wall. These we didn't mind paying, for this being a Game Reserve the fees were very modest, compared to the alarming prices that the National Parks now charge. (Here it only cost an astronomical amount to enter if you wished to hunt, an amount far beyond the reach of our pockets, and hunting was strictly controlled – top government officials and their cronies excluded of course!) Furthermore it didn't have a big list of rules and regulations one has to adhere to in a National Park, as we were informed that we could camp anywhere that took our fancy. Formalities out of the way he unlocked the gate and let us through with a cheery warning. *"Hatari, Simba"* or in other words beware of the lions. I just grinned back at him, knowing that people somehow took a great deal of delight in scaring the living daylights out of you needlessly. In the past whilst on my lone bike rides, I'd had folk warn me about bears in America, tigers in Sumatra, crocodiles and deadly snakes in Australia, and I was, by the grace of God, still in one piece. A few measly lions would be no problem, or would they?

We drove about 5 whole yards before Kath bade me to stop. She had spotted one of those little tailless crombec warbler things. When I glimpsed it, without much ado I pronounced it to be the fairly common Red-faced Crombec. Kath with a grin told me not to be too hasty in my judgement, for she pointed out that this one had predominant facial stripes. Well blow me down, so it did! That made it the dry country **Northern Crombec**, my first 'lifer' in Mkomazi. Before I'd chance to get going again a **Green-winged Pytilia**, a **Grey-headed Bush-shrike** and a small party of busy **Speckled Mousebirds** showed up too. This spot by the gate was certainly an excellent birding location, and we should have stayed there a great deal longer, but alas, the day was getting on and I was anxious to find the camping spot overlooking Dindera Dam that Monica had raved about.

So we pressed on through fairly open country until coming across a large patch of recently burned out grassland, with a few small singed bushes scattered here and there, where Kath pulled me to a halt once more. This time her eagle eyes had fastened onto two of the most wonderfully coloured, the most splendid drop-dead gorgeous starlings that I've ever been privileged to clap eyes on, as they fossicked about on the blackened ground and proceeded to fly about from one little bush to another. They had an iridescent green/blue head, an iridescent blue/purple back, a patch of mauve on their upper breast, a startling bright yellow belly, an extremely long slender copper coloured tail and white beady eyes. They were **Golden-breasted Starlings** a definite mega-tick for yours truly. I was captivated by their sheer resplendence, and was reluctant to take my eyes off them when Kath shouted out that she had got onto two plover-like birds hiding in a corner of the burnt out grass patch. This pair we found from the field guide to be **Temminck's Coursers**. The guide mentioned that these were the commonest and most widespread courser in East Africa, but they were nevertheless yet another 'lifer' for me. I was more than rather pleased; I was as *chuffed* as buggery.

The track passed through an area of acacia woodland, and climbed up through a low gap in the hills. At the crest I was brought to a halt once more, but not by Kath this time, but by what had come into view from

Golden-breasted Starling

behind the hill on our left. I was speechless – I *wor reight capped*! For there, before our very eyes lay the stunning sight of the highest peak in the whole of Africa – the snow-capped Mount Kilimanjaro. A sight that visitors to Tanzania rarely get, for more often than not it is enveloped in thick cloud, but we were lucky that day for it stood there in all its glory, just like a picture postcard. Wow! It was unbelievable. No wonder the Royal Geographical Society in London didn't believe it when first informed that an almost 20,000 feet high snow-capped mountain, lying just 3 degrees south of the equator actually existed. They were convinced that the inform-ant must have been stark raving bonkers. But, take it from me, it does really exist. Honest! We feasted our eyes on this marvel and surveyed the expanse of dry savanna plain below us to our right, which was totally enclosed by distant wooded hills. I perfectly understood now why Monica had raved about this reserve. I must confess that up until then I'd had my suspicions that her perspective of the place had been clouded by her romantic attachment to the person she had been here with, rather than with the place itself!

The track descended onto the edge of the plain and hugged the bottom of a lightly wooded hillside. We spotted from the vehicle quite a number of different species of birds, such as: **Yellow-necked Spurfowl, Little Bee-eater, White-bellied Go-away-bird, Northern White-crowned Shrike, Lilac-breasted Roller, Red-billed Hornbill, Von der Decken's Hornbill, Red-billed Buffalo-Weaver, Red-headed Weaver**, and both **Hildebrandt's** and **Superb Starlings**. We were enjoying pointing out these particular birds to one another, when a cluster of white washed buildings on the hillside came into view overlooking a small airfield on the plain. The track took us quite close to the buildings so we decided to call in to get firm directions to Dindera Dam. The place looked deserted when we pulled up outside an open sided dining area, which had commanding views over the plain, but an elderly white aproned chap, who we presumed to be a cook, came out to greet us. He was quite an obliging fellow who explained that we had stumbled on the Friends of Conservation Ibaya Research Station, which had been taken over by the Royal Geo-graphical Society as their H.Q. whilst they were undertaking some kind of research here. On inquiring where the dam was, he showed us a map of the reserve that was pinned to a board on the wall. Before we had a chance to orientate it, he laughingly pointed to a small rounded hill not too far away, telling us that Dindera Dam was located just at the back of it.

We drove through a thicket, driving a **Crested Francolin** before us along the track before it darted to safety in the thick scrub. The track climbed a gentle slope around the hill that had just been pointed out to us where another large savanna plain opened up in front of us. "This looks like the place," I needlessly exclaimed to Kath, as I pointed to big mobs of animals congregated around a waterhole at the foot of the hill about ½ a mile away. A side track took off in that direction, so I followed it. At the base of the hill this deeply rutted track branched into two, one going crazily straight up the steep hillside, the other zig zagging its way up. I gunned the vehicle up the lesser of the two evils and we came out onto a narrow ridge close to the summit, where I was surprised to find a knee high, circular stone walled structure perhaps 8 ft in diameter. I guessed that it was a game viewing platform, or maybe it was intended to be a shooting box? This looked like the camping spot all right, for there was a pile of ashes with old rusty tins poking out enclosed by blackened stones near the entrance to the stone structure. Whatever this structure was supposed to be, I thought that it would make an excellent level space for us to set up our picnic table and chairs and our telescope. This area certainly measured up to Monica's glowing description of it, for we had an uninterrupted view over the surrounding countryside and were directly overlooking the small dam, only 200 or 300 yards away down a steep rocky slope, where now, on closer inspection we could see that the big mobs of animals that had congregated to drink, were in reality a large herd of zebra and quite a number of giraffes. I was intrigued by the way the giraffes splayed their front legs apart to enable them to bend their necks far enough down to drink. An old silly joke came into my head, so I tried it on Kath: "Why do giraffes have long necks?" When I got no response from her, I informed her, "So their feet will touch the ground!" Kath often doesn't appreciate my juvenile jokes, and this one was no exception. We quickly pitched our small hiking tent on the grassy ridge, so that we could take the opportunity to pan the area with the scope before the sun disappeared behind an adjacent hill.

We spotted quite a number of different bird species pottering about in the mud around the dam, namely: **Woolly-necked Stork, Yellow-billed Stork, Sacred Ibis, Great White Egret, Egyptian Goose, Red-billed Teal,**

Blacksmith Plover and **Hammerkop**. These were species that we had come to expect to be at such a dam, so we didn't get too excited about them. But I must confess that I did get rather excited at spotting three lovely dry country species around our campsite before the sun finally disappeared altogether. For all three of 'em were 'lifers' for me. First of all a pair of parrots screechily flew into a nearby bush. They were fairly drab looking predominantly grey and green things, but one of them had an orange belly (the male), which gave it away instantly as the aptly named **African Orange-bellied Parrot**. Then we heard a loud metallic clicking call emanating from a clump of bushes. We took off to investigate and got onto a grey bush-warbler type bird, which was constantly moving its tail up and down, a dead give away trait of the **Grey Wren-Warbler**. Last and least was when we heard what sounded like a child playing with a squeaky toy amongst the rocks below the stone walled structure. It was one of those dreaded non-descript cisticolas that was scampering around like a mouse on the rocks. This one was plain backed and had a reddish crown. I happily let Kath sort it out as the head banging **Rock-loving Cisticola**. I have put the identification of cisticolas in the too-hard basket, for there are *umpteen* species of them in East Africa and they all looked very much alike. Nonetheless I was happy to tick a new one that had brought my day's tally of 'lifers' up to six. When it got too dark to see anything we reluctantly gave our birding up to prepare and devour our tea in the flickering light of our smelly paraffin lamp. Much later, all chores completed, we sat back relaxed and replete, I with my pipe in one hand and a G.&T. in the other, as we watched the stars and listened to the crickets shrilling. We were at peace and at one with the African bush. That is until a loud resonant grunt rent the evening air. It was unmistakably that of a LION. One that was most definitely too close for comfort, perhaps only a matter of 20 or 30 yards away! I came over all queer and threw up.

I knew exactly why I'd reacted in this way, for I'd made the fatal mistake of reading a book by Colonel Patterson called, *Man-eaters of Tsavo* only the week before. An intriguing story, told in a clipped British military manner, about his trials and tribulations with lions whilst he was assigned to build a bridge over the Tsavo River for the Mombasa to Kampala railway in 1898. The lions in that region (only a few miles away from where we were now) had developed a taste for human flesh and preyed at will on his Indian coolie workforce. Indeed they made a meal of 28 of these poor souls in a

12-month period. These cunning lions evaded all types of ingenious ways that Colonel Patterson devised to repel, lure, trap and kill them and in the process they inevitably, in the eyes of his workforce, took on supernatural powers. Understandably the Indian coolies, not knowing when it would be their turn to be stalked and devoured by these beasts, in the end deserted the construction camp, only to return after the lions were eventually shot. So you can well imagine that a lion's grunt at close quarters was the last thing I wanted to hear just after reading this true and chilling tale.

This was not our first encounter with lions by any means, for naturally we'd come across them before on our visits to various national parks in both Kenya and Tanzania, where we'd watched them during the day, when they'd been peacefully lolling about in family groups under shade trees, or sat contentedly, full stomached, around a kill. Then they appeared to be nothing more than big cuddly soft toys from the safety of our vehicle. Only two months back we'd even camped in our little tent in a deserted camping-ground in the Mikumi National Park and listened to the sounds of lions grunting and growling all bloomin' night. But those sounds had come from a fair distance away, perhaps a mile or more. Although I'd been a trifle disconcerted – I could handle that. (My main worry in Mikumi had been when five bloody great elephants walked uninvited into our campsite just after dusk. Scared stiff we had quietly and slowly vacated our seats by the camp fire, where we had been busy cooking our tea and retreated into the relative safety of our dwarfed vehicle. From there we had watched them, with bated breath, for over an hour in the light of our fire as they munched unconcernedly away on the trees surrounding us, before my prayers were answered and they moved off en masse, leaving us a might concerned that they would return later and our sausages sizzled to cinders.) But this was my first encounter with a lion at close quarters whilst not protected by the confines of a vehicle, in the dark of night, and my first one since reading about man-eaters in Tsavo. When it had grunted, I didn't need to say anything to Kath, for we both instinctively walked rather quickly towards the vehicle, jumped in slamming the doors behind us and winding the windows firmly shut. My mouth tasted of bile, my hands trembled, my heart was doing somersaults and I was wreathed in nervous perspiration from head to toe. I glanced at Kath, who looked to be sitting rather serenely considering the circumstances, and managed to say with a wry grin, "Phew, that was a rather close shave, Batman!"

We sat in the vehicle for maybe an hour staring out into the inky blackness for any signs of movement, and listening intently for grunts of any description, secretly wishing that I'd had the presence of mind to grab the gin bottle from the top of the wall during our scramble to safety. We didn't see anything, but we heard the chilling grunts at regular intervals. They never failed to make me jump out of my skin, although to my immense relief they seemed to be coming from further and further away each time. Kath figured that there was not one lion but two of 'em. "Thanks a lot Kath, that makes me feel tons better!" I sarcastically remarked, obviously in dire need of a stiff drink. Then I suggested that we should throw all of our gear out of the back of our short-wheel based vehicle and bed down there for the night, even though I knew from past experience that this idea wasn't a particularly good one for we would be cramped and uncomfortable, there being no leg room in the back of it whatsoever. Kath pooh poohed this idea and coolly told me that she was going into the tent, now that the lions had moved off. She reasoned that there would be no danger in any case, because lions didn't recognize tents as food. "Pigs bum!" I retorted, "I've just read that the lions in Tsavo pulled many a screaming Indian coolie from out of their tents in the dead of night. Not only that but they then dragged them half dead through thick thorn brush fences that they'd built especially to keep the ruddy things out." Kath ignored my outburst and made for the tent. I meekly followed her like a lamb to the slaughter, twiddling up the wick in the paraffin lamp so that it glowed its dull brightest and left it outside the tent flap before turning in.

As you can well imagine I couldn't sleep. My mind dwelled on all manner of scenarios, and I actually started talking idiotically to myself, like: Was the lion prowling around our campsite because it was attracted to the smell of our cooking? No, I don't think so 'cos we'd had spaghetti hadn't we – unless of course it was a vegetarian, or god forbid a vegan! Could it smell our corned beef? What, through the unopened tin! Don't be silly! Could it smell my sweaty feet? Of course it could, but that would have repelled it surely! What should I do if it came prowling around again? I don't even have a weapon to protect myself. Not even *a stick with an 'orses 'ead 'andle, the finest that Woolworth's could sell*. (So that I could poke it in the ear with it, like poor little Albert Ramsbottom did to Wallace the lion in the zoo at the *famous seaside place called Blackpool, that's noted for fresh air and fun*, all as depicted in the monologue made famous by Stanley Holloway.)

But then he finished up by being swallowed whole by Wallace, *and 'im in his Sunday clothes too*! I do have a small penknife though that I use to clean out my pipe; maybe I could gouge its eyes out with that. Or maybe as a last resort I could throw our rock hard mangoes at the thing!"

I knew that I was getting pretty desperate and tried to tell myself that to get taken by a lion one had to be very very unfortunate indeed. But it did happen didn't it? It had happened in Tsavo which wasn't very far from here, and now and again I'd read in the paper that some wretched villager had come across an untimely gory death by one. I lay awake listening to every grunt and roar which continued well into the night, and listened for any padding of feet or hot pants of breath coming from just the other side of our thin flimsy tent wall. I was petrified. I wished that I were in Batley or anywhere else for that matter, as long as it was miles from here.

Kath shook me awake at first light, (so I must have dozed off eventually) and she crawled out of the tent to put the billy on for our early morning cuppa. I rejoiced in the simple fact that I was still of this world and groggily followed her out. It's amazing how daylight puts a different perspective on things isn't it? I was full of the joys of spring when Kath pointed down towards the dam with a silly grin on her face. For there on the banks of the little dam were two lions, a male and a female. My heart skipped a beat of course on spotting them, but I soon relaxed when I realized that they were engaged in four-paw-play, mating and generally frolicking around with each other having a good time. They weren't remotely interested in us, or for that matter anything else around them. I was quite happy just knowing where they were, that is at a safe distance of 2 or 300 yards from our vantage point, so if they disappeared from out of our sight, even for a second, we would have enough time to jump into the safety of our vehicle.

We breakfasted, closely keeping an eye on the honeymooning couple. They were oblivious to the fact that a big mob of zebra and a dozen or so giraffe were stood off a fair distance from the dam watching them too, patiently waiting for them to hop it so that they could go down to the water's edge to take a drink. We were pleased to see a few additional birds down at the dam. An **African Fish-Eagle** was perched on a fallen log, a **Little Grebe** was swimming around in the middle of it, an **Emerald Spotted Wood Dove** was picking about in the grass, and small flocks of **Yellow-rumped Canaries**, **African Firefinches** and **Red-cheeked Cordon-bleus** showed up spasmodically to take a drink. In the bushes around our camp we had an **African Drongo**, a **Long-tailed Fiscal Shrike**, a pair of **Grey Hornbills**, a **Striped Kingfisher**, and a **Black-shouldered Kite**. All very nice birds to watch whilst partaking of breakfast and discussing our plans for the day ahead. Kath suggested that we should head off in the direction of Mount Kilimanjaro, which was hidden amongst the clouds that day, to check out the dry savanna plain for grassland birds. I agreed, but hastened to add that I wasn't over keen at the thought of camping in this self-same spot again that night, it was far too close to these ruddy lions for me. Kath didn't argue with me, so we broke camp and packed up all our gear. We were taking one last look at the frolicking lions before we headed off, when we heard a very loud resonant grunt coming from somewhere very very close behind us. It was without doubt ANOTHER LION. We both sprinted for the vehicle and dived in. "Bloody Nora!" I exclaimed all of a dither when safely locked inside. "I bet that it's been watching us all along. That does it, I'm definitely not camping here tonight. Not for all the tea in China." My unflappable Dearly Beloved replied to my relief, "Me neither." We looked around in the direction of where the grunt had come from but we frustratingly failed to see it. Where the *hummer* was it?

Happy to be leaving this location we headed off down the hill trying to compose ourselves. I muttered to Kath that I bet that it had been one of Wallace's relatives who had just given us a fright. Kath who hails from the land of the brave and the free, had never heard of the tale of 'Albert and the lion' so I had to laboriously tell her who Wallace was, in the process having to recite to her the few snippets of it that I could remember. Kath couldn't quite believe that a simple monologue such as this would be someone's party piece at a family gathering in the north of England. But I could tell that she was somewhat slightly amused.

At the base of the hill, Kath mentioned that she had just got onto some kind of thrush on the ground under a tangle of thicket by the dam wall, just before the lion had rudely interrupted us. She requested that I drive towards the dam to see if it was still there before we went back to rejoin the main track. I complied, but made it quite clear that I for one wouldn't be getting out of the vehicle again in this neck of the woods. Not on your Nellie! I parked the vehicle up by the edge of the dam, the two lions gave us a cursory glance from the other side, only a matter of 30 yards away, and carried on with their mucking about with each other, leaving us in peace to get onto a heavily spotted thrush that was happily playing around on the ground flicking its wings and cocking its rufous tail. It was a **Spotted Morning Thrush**, my first 'lifer' of the day. We were enjoying watching its antics when a pair of small, predominantly black and white, batis flycatchers came into view as they gleaned insects from the foliage in the thicket. These we deduced were the **Black-headed Batis**. They are very similar looking to the more common Chin-spot Batis, in that the males have a black breast band and the females a chestnut one, but having a darker crown and the female lacking the chin-spot.

Not long after viewing my first 'lifer' of the day, we were along the main track on the edge of the dry savanna plain, heading in the direction of Mt. Kilimanjaro, where I was viewing my second 'lifer' of the day. A large pipit like bird, the **Pangani Longclaw**, its more orange coloured throat and less yellow on its belly differentiating it from the more common Yellow-throated Longclaw. I was rather pleased, 'cos it is a rather striking, colourful bird considering that it is a grassbird. For the next few hours we proceeded through this savanna grassland in fits and starts, hardly covering any distance at all for Kath kept pulling me to a halt every few yards so that she could sort out a few typical, non-descript, drab looking, 'L.B.J.' grassbirds. Quite frankly I lost my concentration after a while, (another way of saying that I got bored!) but I was happy in the knowledge that my missus was obviously getting a great deal of enjoyment in sorting them all out. She enjoys a challenge, I suspect that is why she got lumbered with me! All in all she sorted out the **Red-winged Bush Lark, Fawn-breasted Lark, Flappet Lark, Rattling Cisticola, Zitting Cisticola, Desert Cisticola**, and **Ashy Cisticola**, the latter two species being new birds for me, that I somehow couldn't get too excited about! But I did show some interest when we got onto a large **Kori Bustard**, weighing in at up to 18kg it is the heaviest flying bird in tropical Africa. It was striding slowly through the grass, as was the much smaller but more elegant **Secretary Bird** that we came across too. This is a striking grey plumaged, long-tailed bird, wearing black 'plus fours' on its long legs, has bright red bare skin around the eye and sports long floppy crest feathers at the back of its head. This fascinating bird of prey hunts snakes and rodents by stalking them on the ground, and is so called because its long crest feathers were once used as writing quills. Meanwhile we spied flying over a **Bateleur**, a **Brown Snake-Eagle**, a **Harrier Hawk** and a **White-backed** and a **White-headed Vulture** just to liven up proceedings a little, and give me a respite from the 'L.B.J.s'.

The Man-eaters of Mkomazi

With the sun getting high in the sky we ran out of savanna grassland when the track took off up a hillside. It got quite rocky as we slowly climbed up into an area covered in strange looking stilted thick bushes about 5 feet high. I pulled sharply to a halt after rounding a bend when confronted by a large herd of elephant munching on the bushes. We patiently waited for them to move off the track so that we could proceed, and in the meantime managed to spot another new bird, the **Brown-crowned Tchagra** whilst twiddling our thumbs. But after half an hour, the bloomin' *gurt* big things never budged, so Kath suggested that we should turn around and go back to Dindera Dam to eat our lunch. Was she serious? I gave her an old fashioned look to say that I wasn't very keen on that idea with the lions and all, but not wanting to appear to be too much of a 'scaredy cat', complied.

There wasn't a lion to be seen back at the dam, so we ventured gingerly out of the vehicle to partake of our fermenting banana lunch. But I must confess that I never relaxed, I was forever furtively glancing around into the surrounding bush. We spotted a lovely little grey goshawk with a brilliant white rump, which turned out to be another 'lifer', the **Gabar Goshawk.** This sighting took my mind off lions for a moment or two, but I wasn't really happy until we finally moved off again. Driving back to the main track we startled a large mob of giraffes into loping off in their ungainly long legged lolloping trot with their necks slowly sawing back and forth in the air. Clinging to them were a number of **Red-billed Oxpeckers.** These starling type birds are quite interesting creatures, in that they spend a great deal of their time clambering about on large mammals, where they feed on ticks and other blood sucking insects. They can often be seen comically sticking their head up every orifice that a beast possesses, with the animal's apparent consent. A case of I'll scratch your back if I can have all your parasites.

We called back in at the Ibaya Research Station so that we could peruse the map to figure out a good place to camp that night. I secretly was hoping that the cook we had met the other day would offer us accommodation there, especially if I recounted our night of terror to him and threw myself onto the ground, sobbing at his feet. Unfortunately we didn't come across him again, but was met by a fair-haired lanky chap who introduced himself as Jonathan Kingdon. "THE Jonathan Kingdon, the world renowned author, artist, scientist chappie that I've heard so much about!" I wanted to say in awe. But I kept my mouth firmly shut, and let Kath talk intelligently to him. They covered all types of topics from giraffes (which he was currently studying here) to bush babies in the Usambara Mountains, to birds, to other various conservation projects going on around the country. He only laughed when I managed to blurt out about the lions in a lull in their conversation and he retorted, rather matter of factly, "Yes, there are quite a number of them here on the reserve." On inquiring about a good place to camp, he suggested another small waterhole where game converged to drink, which was someway over the plain in front of the lodge, and pointed out the track we should take to get there. So we bade him farewell and set off, me rather unwillingly, for it was rather like being cast into the lion's den once more.

We observed a large noisy flock of agile **Blue-naped Mousebirds** on exiting the lodge and took off over the airfield into the middle of the large dry savanna grassland plain. What was left of the day Kath spent happily noting the subtle differences in the plumage and vocal variances in the drab grassbirds. I occasionally adding my, 'Yes dears' and 'Is that so dears' at the appropriate time, whilst stifling my yawns. Eventually we came off the plain at the other side and entered a wide sparsely treed valley where we came across a small waterhole by the side of the track that had a few zebra mulling around. We decided to pitch our tent about 200 yards away from the waterhole on a fairly open grassy slope opposite, where we had uninterrupted views of anything that may come our way. We made camp, relaxed with our customary sundowner and had our tea when night fell, not once seeing or hearing any sounds of lions, only the loud high pitched mournful call of a **Pearl-spotted Owlet**. Not wanting to temp fate we didn't leave our campsite to go in search of it. This was bliss; this was more than I'd dared hope for. That night I slept like a baby.

I fell out of the tent at first light to the tranquil call of **Red-eyed Doves**, a sure sign that all was well with the world, and startled a covey of **Shelley's Francolins** into crouching low in the grass trying to hide from me as I put the billy on. Over breakfast we relaxed watching our wonderful world change colour as the sun came into view over the head of the valley and noting that a pair of fat, pied **Spur-winged Geese** and a lonesome **Crowned Plover** were present beside the waterhole. Game was conspicuous by their total absence. That is until we heard a trumpeting noise in the distance, and got onto a lone elephant that was heading surprisingly fast in our direction up the valley with its ears flapping madly and trunk waving wildly in the air. Up until then I had regarded elephants as large lumbering creatures incapable of moving at speed, but this one was fair shifting along. I had always given elephants a lot of room, for I never felt easy in their company, they having a reputation of getting a little cranky with anyone who invades their personal space, and trampling all over them. (They had frightened me to death when they had invaded ours at Mikumi National Park that time, when all we could do was cower quietly in the vehicle until they moved on.) This particular elephant was obviously agitated, so we thought it best if we retired to the relative safety of our vehicle again where at least we could hide from it. We were relieved when it went straight by us a good 80 yards away, not even taking the slightest notice of us as it carried on up the valley with great urgency. It was definitely a distressed elephant on a mission. Why and what we could only surmise. Maybe it was Nellie the elephant going to town and saying goodbye to the circus!

Potential danger out of the way we relaxed once more. I was loath to move out of my comfy canvas camp chair when our attention was drawn to a group of grey and white starlings by their noisy chattering, as they played around on the dusty track. They were the dry country **Fischer's Starlings** my first 'lifer' of the day. I was intently viewing them through the scope when Kath got onto a 'L.B.J.' that flittered by and landed in a bush not far away. She took off after it. I, not wanting to 'dip out', followed her. The thing was hiding in the bush; it was reluctant to let us have a good view of it and eventually broke cover and flew off into another bush with us in hot pursuit. It led us a merry dance as it flew from bush to bush on the sloping hillside until Kath managed to see enough of it to identify it as a **Tiny Cisticola**; yet another dry country 'lifer' for me. Kath was still intently observing it when my eye caught the sight of 30 or 40 zebra on the opposite hillside holding off from going down to the waterhole on the valley floor. They were behaving very skittishly, just like the zebras had been the previous morning when the two lions were frolicking about by Dindera Dam. Knowing that something was amiss, I trained my binoculars down on the waterhole and got the biggest shock of my life. A male LION with its shaggy main was stood up in the grass staring directly at me with great interest! We were eye balling each other at a distance of no more than 150 yards, and the flippin' cisticola had led us a good 200 yards from the safety of our vehicle! Holy smoke!

Mad Twitching

I was struck dumb, paralyzed with fear. After what seemed like an eternity I managed to hiss, " Flower, there's a LION watching us from the waterhole. I think we could be in a spot of bother if we don't hop it quick smart!" jerking my thumb in the direction of our campsite. For some reason we didn't actually run, instinctively knowing that the lion could easily intercept us on our retreat to the vehicle if it so wished. Nevertheless we didn't exactly hang about either as we moved along at a fairly brisk walk, keeping one eye on the lion all the while. It unnervingly never took its eyes off us either; it just moved its head to keep us in its sights like a lazy docile dog would. Out of breath, our hearts pounding and wreathed in sweat we reached safety, where the lion quickly lost interest in us, for it turned away from us and flopped down into the grass leaving its head protruding out of it so that we could easily keep an eye on it. Phew! So we quickly packed up all our gear with one of us keeping an eye on the thing all the time. Luckily it never budged. All ready to roll we were both watching the lion's shaggy head in the grass when to our great surprise ANOTHER LION emerged next to it from out of nowhere, whereupon the first lion got to its feet and they both slowly slinked off together up the sandy track. They were both young male lions that I was rather glad to see the back of. I wasn't the only one glad to see them depart, for seconds after they vamoosed the zebras appeared at the waterhole to slake their thirsts. This was all too much excitement for this particular Batley bred lad, especially after it dawned on me that they may have been bedded down next to us the whole night!

We moved off, retracing our steps back over the plain towards the Ibaya Research Station, frequently stopping for Kath to check out the grassbirds, and once trying to flush out on foot a **Common Button-quail** that had darted out from under our vehicle's wheels.

We reached the main track that ran below the lodge and headed back to bird the acacia woodland that we had to pass through on our return to the Zange Gate, surprisingly only stopping the once to observe at close quarters a pair of **Ostriches** that were grazing near the track. These flightless creatures are the world's largest living bird, and *by gum* they are whoppers. They stand almost 8 feet tall in their stocking feet and they have chunky thighs on 'em like a rugby league prop forward's. I personally wouldn't want to pick a fight with either species. We pulled up in the midst of the acacia woodland in what must have been a recognized camping ground for the game hunters for there were numerous old fireplaces, bits of string dangling from the trees, piles of rubbish and a few temporary grass thatched shelters that were in various stages of collapse. The place needed a good clean up, but nonetheless we could hear quite a few birds chirping away, obviously they didn't worry too much about the mess. Indeed some of them relished in it as straight away we got onto a large flock of noisy, red rumped **White-headed Buffalo Weavers** foraging around in it. Then a titchy **Cardinal Woodpecker**, an **African Hoopoe** and a **Lesser Honeyguide** showed up too in the space of 20 minutes or so. This was a good birding spot so we decided to stay and have our lunch here in the shade of the trees where our roaming eyes, (mine naturally still looking out for any signs of lions) picked out a rather cute tiny grey and white **Pygmy Falcon** perched quietly on a branch. (I've since learned that this falcon often uses an unoccupied nest of the White-headed Buffalo Weaver for breeding purposes, and that its range is almost identical to that species.) On throwing away the remains of our weeping, soggy brown bunch of bananas I spied a lovely scarlet-chested sunbird, and thought that it was indeed the bird so named. Typically, Kath pulled me up on my hasty identification and proclaimed it to be its very similar, dry country cousin the **Hunter's Sunbird**. I should have known it really, because weren't we in a 'Hunter's' camp at the moment? I was rather pleased for it was another 'lifer' in the bag.

Lunch over we set off towards the Zange Gate, where we came across the burnt patch of grassland again and stopped to see if there was any of the gorgeous Golden-breasted Starlings still around. Unfortunately there was none to be seen, but there was a pair of **Senegal Plovers** foraging about in the blackened earth to give us a fillip. On finally reaching the gate across the road, we predictably found it to be unmanned once more. Not to worry, for as we had learnt on our arrival, this was a good little place to while away the time birding until someone hopefully arrived to open the gate. So we did just that. We observed quite a few of the same species that we had seen on our entry here, but in addition we had a **Bare-eyed Thrush**, an **Amethyst Sunbird** and a **Smaller Black-bellied Sunbird**, before the ranger chap showed up. This latter species being yet another lovely 'lifer' bringing my total number of new birds for the weekend up to 17, and our species list for the Mkomazi Game Reserve to a respectable 108 all up.

The first thing the grinning ranger asked us was if we had seen any *simba* on our travels. "*Simba!*" I repeated after him, "They've been prowling around us the whole time!" I growled, "We've seen twice as many ruddy *simba* as people!" I truthfully retorted. He laughed his head off. I turned to Kath and muttered to her, "Just wait until I get my hands on Monica, I'll throttle her! For she never once mentioned the lions here!"

Driving down the main highway on our way back to Tanga, I reflected that we'd really had a truly unique African experience. What with the majestic scenery, all the wonderful (and not so wonderful) birds that we'd managed to spot, and our unforgettable encounters with the 'man-eaters of Mkomazi'. An experience that I wouldn't have missed for the world, but one that I didn't wish to repeat again too quickly!

7

Where Sparrows Fly Backwards . . .

Batley, West Riding of Yorkshire, England

I LEFT BATLEY, the place where I was born and bred, as a young man in 1973 and emigrated to Australia on an assisted passage scheme. My contribution towards my passage out there was £10. This is the reason we are affectionately termed '10 pound poms' in Australia! At that time, I had no intention of staying more than 2 years, the minimum length of stay required under the scheme. I only wanted to see a bit of the world, Australia being the furthest place I could go for £10, a sum incidentally that took me months to save up. But once over there, time just lapsed and I stayed. I liked the place. I found that this particular working class lad could earn in a week more money than I could possibly spend, three times as much in fact than I'd been earning in Batley. Consequently I lived the 'life of Riley', Australia being in effect one big ruddy playground, abounding in sun, surf and sin. Over the next 23 years or so I visited home no more than 2 or 3 times. That isn't to say that Batley was pushed into the nether regions of my mind and forgotten for all those years. How could I do that? I was a Batley lad through and through. Batley ran in my veins. Batley had forged my character and laconic sense of humour. Batley had endowed me with a strong 'Heavy Woollen District' Yorkshire accent which I'm very proud of to this day. In short I love Batley and its people, a place where most of my family still reside. If home is where the heart is, then Batley I still regard as home.

It came to pass that on a lovely clear, sunny morning in May 1996, I stood at the bottom of my mum's garden in Soothill, high on the hillside looking down fondly at my hometown in the valley below. I thought to myself as I surveyed this once familiar scene, "*Ee,* it's fair grand to be home! There is certainly no place quite like it." My mind wandered back to my happy childhood days, as I looked over the town to the opposite hillside of Mount Pleasant. Mount Pleasant is where I had been born in a 'one up and one down' back to back terrace house, on a cobbled street just a stone's throw away from the famous sloping ground of my beloved Batley Rugby League club. This row of terrace houses was deemed to be a slum and condemned, for our house only possessed one cold water tap and we shared an outside *closit*, which we had to walk 50 yards in all weathers to use, with our rear neighbours, a chamber-pot being essential for convenience during the night. I didn't realize at the time that this experience would later stand me in good stead for living in Africa! We were moved in the early 1950s to a brand new council house estate just up the road in Staincliffe. This house had hot and cold running water, an inside toilet and a bathroom – sheer luxury! We no longer had our Friday night, bath night ritual, where we would drag the tin bath out onto the peg rug in front of the coal fire, whereupon all of us would bathe in t' same *watter*. The muckiest, my dad, a builder's labourer at that time, going in last, the bath being kept topped up with hot water bubbling away in a kettle on the hob over the fire. It was on this council estate I spent my formative years. There being no televisions or motor vehicles at that time we *laiked* in the street under the street lamp. Many a time we got carried away playing 'touch and pass', turning it into a full-blown game of rugby league on the tarmac. I rarely had any skin on my hands and knees as I recall.

Batley in those days was a thriving woollen textile manufacturing town, specializing in 'shoddy and mungo' cloth. This cloth is made from old woollens and rags, shredded up and mixed with virgin wool before being re-woven. A Batley clothier Benjamin Law discovered this process in 1813, in doing so he brought prosperity to Batley and the neighbouring towns of Dewsbury, Ossett, Morley, Birstall and Heckmondwike, (termed the Heavy Woollen District) and left us with the word 'shoddy' which has now evolved to mean something sub-standard. I remember well whilst looking over the valley as a kid counting around 50 mill chimneys all belching out thick black smoke. Add to this smoke the smoke spewed out by each household's coal fires and you can well imagine the sulphurous smog that always hung over the valley, which over the years had left all the buildings in the town black, ingrained with soot. All this we took for granted, we were even proud in these parts of the saying, 'Where there's muck, there's money.' It was however a secure world that I grew up in, amidst the constant clatter of looms, the sound of mill hooters, the sight of mill lasses dressed in their *pinnies* and headscarves and blokes in greasy boiler suites, flat caps and clogs, wearily trudging home after a hard day's graft. Images straight out of a Lowry painting. All my great aunts and uncles worked in the mills and I had plenty of advice from them that when I left school, I should 'get a trade', preferably as a loom tuner, a highly skilled and respected trade in the mills. Who would have said that this great industry wouldn't last forever?

I now surveyed the valley, silent except for the roar of the traffic on the M62 motorway nearby. There was no smoke or mill chimneys to be seen, only the chimney-like minaret of a newly built mosque catering for the spiritual needs of the large Pakistani community now residing here. The woollen industry had folded in the space of one generation due to mainly three reasons: (1) The family-run businesses' failure to re-invest in modernizing the mills, and running off with their brass to invest it in more profitable ventures. (2) The advent of man-made fibres, and (3) cheap imported cloth flooding the market. It is so sad and to my mind nothing short of 'criminal' on the part of the government of the day in not only allowing it to happen, but actually assisting the decline. All that remains now to remind us of this industry are the many huge, empty, derelict, silent mills, or vacant sites where they once stood. A bank of white whirring things glinting in the sun caught my eye on the horizon, somewhere in the region of Hartshead Moor. I asked my mum what they were, she replied, "Oh them bloomin' things, they are a damned eye-sore. They are windmills generating electricity." I'd never seen *owt* like it before, there were perhaps a dozen of them in a row for all to see for miles around. I thought what an insult to all the local colliers who had fought so hard to keep their pits open, save their jobs and the coal industry, but they lost.

Putting these thoughts aside I reckoned it was time to get weaving and stop dreaming, for I was about to embark on a nostalgic walk to a few of my favourite old haunts. I had only visited Yorkshire once since I'd taken up bird watching as a pastime. That had been a couple of years ago when Kath and I spent 10 days here on our way from Australia to Tanzania. We had frantically gallivanted around the place visiting some great birding spots, such as Fairburn Ings, Bempton Cliffs, Bolton Abbey/Strid Woods and Nosterfield Gravel Pits. Our tally of British birds had added up to a grand total of 77 species. This trip I was to spend six whole weeks here, to look after my mum who was recovering from an operation, but I hoped to get time out to improve my British bird list. Maybe, with a bit of luck, I'd add to my list that day!

I hopped over my mum's back garden wall onto the top edge of a large hillside field planted with young trees. This area had been open-cast mined of 190,000 tons of coal by the National Coal Board in 1972. To their credit they had left the area neatly landscaped. This would be quite an attractive little woodland when the trees matured. I took the footpath along the top edge and descended down the hillside beside a new fence designating the boundary of this future woodland, being careful not to tread in dog muck which is plentiful here. I counted upward of 15 **Magpies**, quite attractive birds with their bright colouring and their long tails having a lovely green metallic sheen, but unfortunately they have a very anti-social habit of robbing other birds' nests. By all accounts their numbers are increasing each year to the detriment of other species. There was also a flock of **Starlings** and 4 or 5 **Carrion Crows** feeding on the ground of the newly mown adjacent field, together with, surprise, surprise, a pair of **Jackdaws**. I descended to a small copse by the long disused old Batley to Beeston railway line, where I startled a couple of **Wood Pigeons** into taking off with a clattering of wings, and investigated a chattering call coming from the bushes. It was an active little warbler, the lovely **Whitethroat**. I ventured up the old railway line into a dark, dank cutting until I reached the entrance of the old Morley tunnel. This tunnel which must be about a mile long, I had once, as a lad, walked through for a dare. Once in the middle of it you can't see the light at either end, and I had *flaid missen to deeath*. Now the entrance was bricked up so that no other silly beggar could repeat the same trick no doubt. I scrambled up the giant steps out of the cutting and skirted a field beside the Howley golf links, where I could spy on groups of gaudily clad players through a barrier of trees, the privileged élite of the town enjoying their game. I felt a bit like a lowly peasant sneaking a look at the local gentry, and was ready to doff my cap if I'd been caught. I came out onto an area of heathland, quilted with patches of heather and gorse bushes. I was intent on dropping down to Howley Ruins, when I flushed two plump birds out of the grass. They took off with a whirring and gliding flight, showing me a rusty-red short tail, before plopping back down into the grass a short distance away. I managed to locate and observe them. They were mainly grey and sandy coloured creatures with an orange-brown head. They were **Grey Partridges**. I hadn't expected to find any in Batley, in fact I understood that modern farming practices had resulted in this species becoming comparatively rare in many areas. Well, well, well, what a turn up for the books! I hadn't seen one before so it was a 'lifer' for me.

I happily ambled across to the ruins of Howley Hall. They were just in the same state as I remembered them as a kid. My parents used to bring my three sisters and me up here quite regularly for a Sunday afternoon walk, all dressed up in our Sunday best after going to the chapel. We would have our picnic by the ruins and then get *black-bright* playing in the dungeons looking for the legendary buried treasure. We were not alone enjoying our simple pleasures at this local beauty spot, for in the days before mass motor vehicle ownership hundreds of folk would be up here, all with their sandwiches, flask of tea and pac-o-macs carried in a shopping bag. These ruins were once a magnificent hall built in 1590 by Sir John Saville. In 1643 during the Civil War, the Earl of Newcastle 'besieged it with 10,000 men, brought his cannon to bear on the building and fiercely battered the walls. Sir John Saville resisted him but eventually the place was taken by storm.' It was demolished in 1730 when the then owner the Earl of Cardigan found the upkeep to be too expensive, and not as I had been lead to believe by Oliver Cromwell. I stood amongst the ruins and looked down the valley over my town. I could see in the distance Castle Hill in Huddersfield, it being such a fine clear day. Then I spotted swifts floating high in the sky. "Which one is it?" I muttered to myself, before realizing there is only one species in the U.K. – *the* **Swift**. I was admiring the sheer grace of their flight when three **Kestrels** caught my attention, hovering stationary with fast wing beats 20 feet above the heathland. They were great little falcons to watch as they searched for small creatures and insects in the grass. I went to investigate a twittering call emanating from a cluster of gorse bushes. I found a pair of **Linnets** to be responsible, the male having a lovely dash of red on his breast and forehead. I took the path down towards a farmhouse, where I spotted a yellow bird sitting in the open on top of a bush singing its little head off. It was the unmistakable song of the **Yellowhammer** saying, "A-little-bit-of-bread-and-NO-cheese," repeating its request monotonously. I strolled down the muck lane, hedgerows on either side of me, a little **Robin** popped out at the base of one directly into my path, then hopped it quick smart, deciding that I was much bigger than him. At the bottom of the lane I got onto a small flock of **Blue Tits** in the delightful garden of a newly renovated cottage, before taking the footpath that ran alongside Howley Beck towards Scotsman Lane. I hadn't gone very far when I saw a smashing little **Willow Warbler** scampering about in the foliage of a tree looking for insects. Maybe I'd seen this self-same bird in Africa a few weeks earlier. It will never cease to amaze me how these small creatures manage to travel so far in their migration! How do they do it? Then to my astonishment I spied a pair of finches with black caps, grey mantles, black wings and the male having lovely warm pinkish-red underparts. Both were sat quietly in a flowering hawthorn bush. They were **Bullfinches**, my second 'lifer' of the day. They were rather shy birds and took off, giving me a splendid view of their white rumps. I ambled on until I came to a stile. I was negotiating it when a bird, only feet away, exploded into loud song. It took me a while to spot it in the tangle of undergrowth. It was a titchy, brown-barred **Wren**, strutting about with its short up-cocked tail. I dropped down from the stile onto a newly surfaced narrow lane, which ran to a group of posh new houses built on the site of where Benjamin Law's Howley Low Mill once stood. I was *flummoxed* to see a new gate across this lane with a sign saying 'Private' tacked to it. "Funny, I'm pretty sure this was a public right of way!" I muttered, as I spotted a pair of **Pied Wagtails** bobbing up and down by the side of the beck, and a rather attractive **Chaffinch** in the well-kept orchard. I walked on through the tunnel under the main Leeds to Manchester railway line, where I spied in a field on the other side a large heavily spotted thrush with big sad looking eyes, the **Mistle Thrush**. "What's up wi' thee old lad?" I enquired, but it didn't take a *bit o' gaum on mi*. I was surprised to see the old level crossing keeper's house further up the railway line all done up and habitable. It had in all my youth been a derelict shell of a building. I well remember once spending a cold foggy winter's night huddled up inside it, *starved to deeath*. A few friends and I had hatched a hare-brained plan over a few pints of ale, that we were going to pack in being wage slaves, and head off into the hills to live off the land as nature intended. Such a romantic notion! We had only tramped as far as this derelict house which on such a night looked a quite cosy place to kip, and much more preferable than the heath. In the cold light of dawn, sober, stiff and miserable we had all silently trundled off home to a scolding from our parents. Now it was palatial, with a caravan and a horsebox parked outside. The old stone track, once the bridleway to Howley Hall, which ran past it, was now newly surfaced too. But where had the 'Public Footpath' sign gone? I had a feeling that these obviously well-to-do new inhabitants around here were responsible for their disappearance, so that they wouldn't have folk trailing past their abodes. If so, what a petty, mean spirited, contemptible trick.

I walked to the end of the narrow lane, crossing over the main Scotsman Lane, and carried on along another footpath through what used to be allotments. There were no *'en oils* or neat rows of vegetables to be seen. They were now securely fenced areas containing stables, to keep posh kids' ponies in, but surprisingly it didn't look all that different to how I remembered it. There was a **Blackbird** singing its majestic song on top of a bush, a row of **Swallows** huddled up together on an overhead wire, a strikingly coloured **Goldfinch** and a plump **Greenfinch** to be seen in this location. I ambled slowly up the path, a field of barley swaying gently in the breeze on my right. I was standing stock still observing a **Kestrel** perched on top of a fence post, when a movement caught my eye. It was a fox heading in my direction with a great big fat rabbit clenched in its jaws. It came within 10 yards of me before it saw me and turned tail. A grand sight indeed. I only wished that it had dropped the rabbit so that I could have put it in a stew for our tea. I was now in the vicinity of the old West End Colliery. This was a favourite haunt of mine, where I used to come with my pals in the long 6 weeks school summer holidays. We would catch tiddlers and newts in the old colliery dam and muck about in the old coke ovens, which at that time had been almost intact. Now I couldn't locate the dam or the coke ovens; they must have been filled in. The only sign now that there had ever been a colliery here was an outcrop of red shale, spoil from the pit. I was fossicking about in this waste, as happy as a sandboy, when I spotted a largish green bird on the ground. It took off and all I saw on it was a yellowish rump. I didn't have a clue what it was. I went off in the general direction that it had flown, to the edge of Birkby Brow Wood (known locally as Briar Woods). Where I picked it up again in my binoculars as it flew from tree to tree in undulating bounds. It had a green back, a bright red crown and black facial markings. Unmistakably it was the **Green Woodpecker**. Wow, I was as pleased as Punch, because I'd only ever seen them on cider bottle labels before! That made it my third 'lifer' of the day!

Green Woodpecker

I was now off the main track and down near the beck where I could hear a bird calling, "Chiff-chaff-chaff-chiff-chiff". You've guessed it! It was a **Chiffchaff,** an almost identical bird to the Willow Warbler, but its song unmistakable. I scrambled back up to the main track and was happy to find the two 'bomb holes' still there. These were two big round depressions in the ground where we would race around doing the 'wall of death', going as fast as our legs would carry us, with our *coit* tales held up behind us ready to take off in flight. I ventured into this mixed deciduous wood proper. To my delight it was carpeted with bluebells. They were drooping a little, obviously getting a bit 'back endish'; nevertheless, it was a breath taking sight. As grand a sight as I've encountered anywhere in the world on my travels. It were proper champion! These woods I loved, I'd seen them in all their glory, in all four seasons. I'd lived here as a kid in the school holidays, run through them every week on our cross country runs as a fourth and fifth grader at Batley High School, and in later years I'd taken various girl friends into them to do a bit of courting. So it's not surprising that I regarded these woods as 'mine'.

Just before I set sail for Australia, I had been working as a draughtsman for a small family firm engaged in making cutting machinery for the textile industry; the firm was housed in the old goods sheds at Batley Railway Station. I was made redundant when the firm suddenly announced that it had received incentives from the government to move lock, stock and barrel to Northern Ireland. They were to receive all re-location expenses and free rent for a year in a brand new factory over there, in return for them employing Northern Ireland labour. I was given one week's notice. This tale proves that the Tory Government of the day actually assisted the decline of industry in Batley. That is why I said earlier that it had been 'criminal'. I did however manage to get an unskilled job as a storeman/driver in a warehouse in Gildersome, rather than be unemployed. One dark winter's night at *loising time* I discovered that it was snowing like billy-o, 3 or 4 inches of it already lay on the ground, just a bit too deep to ride my bicycle home safely. I decided to walk the 4 miles home instead, and take a short cut through Briar Woods. I remember as if it was only yesterday pausing under the street lamp on Bruntcliffe Lane and marvelling at the snow flakes lighting up like twinkling stars in the glow, before leaving the road and entering the woods. To my delight I found that no other living soul had been through them, it was all virgin snow, now almost 6 inches deep. I could see even in the dark where the path ran in the strange yellowish light given off by the blanket of snow. The tree boughs were bowing under the weight of it and there was an eerie silence, the sound of my boots squeaking in the snow and my panting breath being accentuated. I was a young man in my prime, as fit as a *lop* and well rugged up against the elements in my donkey jacket. I remember pausing in the middle of the wood to drink in the sheer beauty of my surroundings. I had stepped into a world of my own, I felt like Alice in Wonderland. It was sheer magic, a moment of such beauty to savour all my life, a moment I've never quite experienced since. I gave a whoop of pure joy. I was the happiest man in the whole world. Yes, these are indeed 'my woods' and I've let it be known that if *owt* happens to me, here is where I want my ashes scattered. That's all I ask.

I traversed the main track, discovering that **Robins** and **Blackbirds** were quite numerous, then I got onto a small warbler clambering about in a tangle of brambles. I didn't get a very satisfactory view of it, but concluded that it was a **Whitethroat**, but was it the **Lesser Whitethroat**? It certainly was in different habitat than the other one I'd seen that morning, but did it have a dark grey smudge through its eye? Was it any greyer? It disappeared so I will never know for sure what it was. I slowly ambled along this well trodden path. I say well trodden because it was in this wood that Batley Luddites held their secret drill practices, before they marched off with other bands of local Luddites from Dewsbury, Birstall, Gomersal and Heckmondwike, armed with sledge hammers to smash the newly installed machinery at a Horbury mill in 1812, new machinery that was threatening their livelihood in their cottage weaving industry. A few weeks after their victory at Horbury, they went on to attack Rawfold's Mill near Cleckheaton. Unfortunately the millowner was waiting for them with a detachment of soldiers at the ready. Fifteen Luddites were captured, tried and sentenced to death. I like to think of myself as a bit of a Luddite, for I've never felt comfortable around modern gadgets, and would gladly help to smash up with a sledge hammer all the motor vehicles and computers in the world so that we could all revert to living life in a quiet, genteel slower paced world. Computers of course having deprived me of my livelihood as a draughtsman too, with the advent of Auto-Cad.

My thoughts were distracted when I caught sight of a bird with a white underside, flitter to the base of a tree trunk, creep its way up and around it, searching for insects in the bark with its long curved beak. It was of course a **Treecreeper**, a wonderful little bird to watch, and I noticed that it was being kept company in its foraging by three or four **Great Tits**. Further along the track I got onto a pair of **Blackcaps**, alerted to them by their loud blackbird-like call. These are grey looking warblers, the male having a black cap and the female a reddish-brown one. Then I noticed a largish bird with a white rump fly up off the ground into the mid-storey. What was it? I had no idea. So I took off up the hillside looking for it. I eventually, to my surprise, found three of them, hopping around on the ground. They were **Jays**, a lovely soft brown coloured bird with black, white and blue colouring in the wing. I was ecstatic, not only because they were such beautiful birds and I'd had excellent views of them, but because they were my fourth 'lifer' of the day.

I dropped back down to the main trail through a sea of wilting bluebells. I was now almost at the other end of the wood near Bruntcliffe Lane. I stopped, admiring an early blooming foxglove, when I heard a squeaking twittering sound; it seemed to be coming from an old dead tree by the side of the track. To my astonishment a magnificent **Great Spotted Wood-pecker**, a black and white plumaged bird having a nice red undertail, alighted on a hole on this dead tree and clung on underneath the entrance, whereupon a young woodpecker's head popped out to take the white substance proffered by the adult. They seemed completely oblivious of my presence only a few yards away. I retreated to a more reasonable distance so as not to disturb them and observed this feeding procedure 3 or 4 times at intervals of perhaps 4 or 5 minutes. It was wonderful to watch and in the intervals I busied myself watching more **Great Tits, Robins, Blackbirds, Wrens** and **Greenfinches** that showed up. But alas, I had to push on, for I had arranged to call in at our June's, my sister, for my dinner, and I was already late so I legged it up the main road towards Birstall, only stopping to identify a **Black-headed Gull** gliding overhead towards the nearby rubbish tip. I nipped through Howden Clough housing estate and passed the old windmill which used to stand alone amongst fields full of buttercups and 'mother-die', but is now hemmed in by new schools, and a sports centre, to our June's house in Upper Batley Lane.

"I *thowt* that *tha* 'ad gotten *thissen* lost," she said, to gently scold me for being late. "Nay lass, I've come *over* Howley, and through Briar Woods and I've *reight* enjoyed *missen*. Does *tha* know, they *'even't* changed a bit *sin'* we were *bairns*," I said to change the subject. Our June, poor lass, is in poor health and has been virtually house bound for years. Her husband Alan, a hard working soul, worked his way up in a local carpet making mill to be a manager, before it closed and he was made redundant. A Saudi Arabian chap came seeking him, for he had been told that my brother-in-law was the best carpet backer in the U.K., and made him an offer he couldn't refuse to start up and run a new plant in Saudi Arabia. He has been over there quite a few years now, whilst our June spends her days scrubbing and cleaning her house and molly-coddling two grown up kids. She fussed about and sat me down at the table, whereupon she plonked a whopping great Yorkshire pudding in front of me. It was filled with onion gravy, and she had even remembered that I liked mint sauce with mine. *By gow*, they were absolutely out of this world. I've often said that if I was a condemned man, and they asked what I'd like for my last meal on this earth, I would have no hesitation in requesting Yorkshire puddings with rabbit gravy! But if this wasn't enough I had more gastronomic delights in store, for she had made me a jam roly-poly with custard for 'afters'. Wow! I complimented her by saying that if the Prodigal Son's mother had fed him grub like this, he would have never left home.

I was sat contentedly staring out of the window watching the *Spadgers* and *Sheps* feeding on the bread crumbs put out for them on the lawn, amongst them was a *Spadger* with a grey head; it was a **Dunnock**. I drew my sister's attention to it, "Does *tha* know that *tha* 'as a Dunnock on *thi* lawn lass?" She looked puzzled for a moment, before she spotted it, and retorted. "That's *nooan* a Dunnock, that's an Hedge Sparrow." She was correct of course, but she didn't recognize its new fancy name that's all. They all took off when her lad came barging and crashing through the door, as youths do. I was shocked. The last time I'd seen him he had been an angelic teenager singing in the school choir. Before me stood a shaven headed, earring-wearing yobbo, carrying a couple of new shirts under his arm. "Do you like my new designer shirts, Uncle David?" he enquired. "Did you get 'em cheap?" I asked. "They look like 'seconds' to me, 'cos they've got t' labels sewn on t' outside, instead of t' inside." He grinned, he knew I was taking the micky! He took me out into the driveway to show me his new flashy car, which his dad had bought him. "*By gum* lad, it's a real 'bobby dazzler', its got 'pump up' tyres and everything!" I exclaimed. I recalled the new bicycle I had got at his age, just after I'd started my apprenticeship as a fitter at a large Gomersal engineering works.

I had got it on hire purchase for 6/- a week. I paid 2/- towards it from my 5/- a week spending brass. (My unopened wage packet being thrown on the table each Friday night, as was the custom.) My Grandma Nellie gave me 2/- a week towards it and my mum the remaining 2/-. How times have changed I reflected, but I'm sure I had been as equally proud of my new bike, as he was with his fancy new car. I had joined the Dewsbury and Batley section of the Cyclist Touring Club, and gone off with them religiously each Sunday on their club runs, whilst these kids seemed at a loss of where to go in their vehicles! I found though that despite my nephew's yobbo appearance he was still the same gentle sweet natured lad, underneath it all, and unfortunately unable to find employment. I sat and 'telled t' tale' with our June whilst she plied me with drinks, but after a while I thought I'd best be off whilst I was still able to walk straight!

I took off up the lane and toured around a new well-to-do private housing estate looking for the top gate of Batley Park, which I eventually found. By this gate overlooking the park stands the Bagshaw Museum. This fine, imposing Victorian mansion was once the home of one of Batley's mill owning families. It is just one of many such mansions standing upon this pleasant hillside. The term 'where there's muck, there's money' must have been coined by these mill owners, for the mill workers were never considered to be anything other than a cheap source of labour. My own favourite Great Auntie Minnie from the age of 12 worked in a mill all her life as a weaver. She lived in a rented back to back terrace house, never married, never went on holiday (except for the annual mill trip to the seaside), never drank, and never lived extravagantly. Her idea of extravagance was to open a tin of salmon for Sunday high tea, when she had visitors. Her only vices being in that she enjoyed smoking 5 Woodbines a day, and tended to swear a bit, often calling me 'a little *soiler*'. In other words she lived a very frugal existence. When the dear old soul passed away, I had to tidy up her 'affairs'. A second hand dealer gave me £6 for all her worldly possessions! Imagine, a lifetime's toil in the mill amounted to such a piddling sum! She lived in the muck in a 'one up and one down' in the valley, whilst the mill owners lived in the money in these mansions on this hillside. No wonder I'm a bit to the left of Arthur Scargill in my politics! The irony was that she wasn't interested in politics at all and was happy with her lot in life!

I stepped into the museum, walked purposefully past the three lady curators and up the creaking staircase, past the scale model of Howley Hall on the first landing and up the next flight of steps onto the interior balcony. I knew exactly where I was heading for. I was heading for a glass showcase with a rugby ball inside, which if my memory serves me right is over there. I looked towards an empty space, it wasn't there – my heart sank. I dashed inside all the rooms leading off this balcony in frantic search of it. It was nowhere to be found. This rugby ball I remember my dad proudly showing to me when I was a little lad. It was the ball used in the first ever Rugby League Challenge Cup Final in 1897, when Batley beat St. Helens by 10 points to 3. It conjured up names of legendary players like Wattie Davies, Jim Gath and George Main who all still resided in Batley in my schooldays. This team gave rise to the Batley club being nicknamed the 'Gallant Youths' for their battling performances. I was rather disappointed that this ball was no longer on display, then reflected that the once proud game of Rugby League had recently sold out to big business interests, all the teams now being given tacky, Yankee style names such as 'the broncos' etc. Batley were now 'the bulldogs'. How a team that's motto is 'Pride and Heritage' can go and call itself that, I shall never understand, but I wish them well.

I wandered back into one room where stood a floor to ceiling mock up of Bempton Cliffs. This exhibit had always fascinated me as a kid. Now it reminded me of the splendid time I'd spent at the actual cliff itself a couple of years ago with Kath, my sister Carol and her husband David. We'd marvelled at the thousands of sea birds wheeling around and nesting on the precarious rock ledges. The birds we'd watched were all represented here, the comical Puffins, the Razorbills, Guillemots, Kittiwakes, Northern Gannets and Herring Gulls. A fine display indeed, it only needed a tape recording of the cacophony of bird-calls to bring it to life. I then ventured into a room billed as a 'rainforest walk', or some such thing. I found myself magically transposed into a South American rainforest, the forest lighting up showing me its wonders as I walked slowly through it along a pathway. There were all kind of weird and wonderful animals, reptiles and birds. Amongst the brightly coloured macaws, tanagers and humming birds, I spied a Resplendent Quetzal. Wow, when I'd first heard this particular bird mentioned, I'd vowed that one-day I would seek it out. It has such an exciting name; I simply must see it for myself to see if it actually lives up to it!

Descending the stairs, I noticed that the 'official portraits' of former Mayors of the town that used to decorate the stairwell had been removed.

Why? These portraits of august, austere, mostly heavily whiskered, local dignitaries, attired in their regalia and chains of office used to fascinate me for some peculiar reason. Maybe because some of them had been great fighters for social justice in their time. Where had they gone? Now Batley had no longer got its own Borough Council, but was now merged into a large Metropolitan District christened Kirklees, with its headquarters in far away Huddersfield. I wondered if this new authority had spirited these portraits away, in order to obliterate the fact that Batley had once been independent? Maybe they had purged Batley of all such evidence, in order to ward off any rebellious thoughts by its people to regain their freedom! As I shuffled past the three lady curators, I dearly wished to ask them the whereabouts of the rugby ball, but thought better of it. I felt that they wouldn't understand why a middle-aged man wanted to look at a silly old piece of leather. I don't want to appear sexist here, but I believe a male curator would have understood! So I sneaked out of the door and headed down the hillside through the pleasant woodland.

I took a surreptitious route along overgrown pathways strewn with litter, pathways that had once been well maintained. I found that **Blackbirds, Robins** and **Great Tits** were quite numerous, and that the bandstand had been demolished, only the concrete base reminding me that it once proudly stood there. I walked through a tunnel under the disused Batley to Birstall railway line and came out at the ornamental lake. The once imposing Park Café where our June had held her wedding reception and I had danced the night away at Batley Cycling Club prize presentation dinners, was now all boarded up and looking all forlorn and neglected. There were no longer any rowing boats for hire on the lake, but I was pleased to see quite a few water birds about. Before I sorted them out though, I had to dash across to the public lavatories by the main gate, a consequence of our June's hospitality. To my dismay, I found that they were shut with a sign on the door apologizing for this fact and adding that it was due to vandalism. "Bloody Nora" I had no alternative but to seek a suitable bush. Now much more relaxed I went off to sort out the array of ducks and geese. I must point out that it is always difficult for a bird watcher to determine which species are wild and which species are domesticated on a lake such as this, so I started off by listing the obvious wild ones. There was a pair of **Moorhens** fossicking about in the trickling waterfall, a few **Tufted Ducks, Shelducks** and **Mallards** and a large gaggle of **Canadian Geese**. Along with these were a variety of ducks that beggared description, being hybrids of some sort, and a small pretty Oriental diving duck that wasn't to be found in my British field guide, together with obviously domesticated adaptations of Snow Geese and White-fronted Geese. I contentedly sat on a park bench watching this peaceful aquatic display when a chap with two small children showed up with a bag of breadcrumbs. All the geese and ducks immediately spotted them and came racing over at a great turn of knots from all corners of the lake, quacking and cackling with obvious delight. The kids, with dad's assistance, were frantically throwing the crumbs out onto the lake for these insatiable birds, but the birds were not content to stay in the water. They jumped out en masse and swarmed on the hapless kids, snatching the bag out of the hands of one of them. Dad had to usher his now bawling charges to safety, and leave the bag and its contents to the marauding hungry mob. I enjoyed this little scenario immensely from a safe distance; it did explain why the lake was choked with empty bags! I surveyed the surrounding gardens; they were not as immaculate as they used to be. People used to come from miles around to spend a leisurely day here, but it looked as though it was all being let to sadly run down. My mother had obviously been correct when she had told me that under Kirklees the rates had soared, but many services to the town had been cut or drastically reduced. Here for instance I hadn't seen any gardeners or park keepers at all. I recalled fondly that a Welshman called Mr. Tavener was the dreaded park keeper here when I was a lad. He used to always appear with his familiar shout of "Hoi" if we were up to any mischief. He carried a sharp pointed stick, which he not only picked up litter with but shooed us out at closing time with too. Two of my clubmates in the Batley Cycling Club had also been employed in this park in a large gang of gardeners. One of them, a ruddy faced, barrel chested, unassuming chap by the name of Peter Doolan was the local 'fast man'. In fact he was one of the fastest men in the country over 25 miles. He could regularly trot out a 57 minute ride in a time trial over that distance, on his favourite 90″ fixed wheel bike. He had been our mentor, all the lads in the club slavishly followed his punishing training regime, hoping to emulate him one day. I wondered what he would think about the sorry state of the park now?

I wandered up a pathway through rhododendron bushes in flower and recalled a silly little joke that my great uncle Harvey never tired of telling me – King Henry rode a horse, whilst King William rode-a-dendron! I warned you it was silly! I climbed up onto the disused Batley to Birstall railway line. The train that ran on this track, usually carried coal, which we called the 'Coddy Bob'. Now the line had been put to good use and turned into a pleasant tree lined bridle-way, where you could stroll in peace and solitude looking down onto the backs of old mills lining the busy Bradford Road. I enjoyed observing more **Blackbirds, Great Tits** and a **Willow Warbler**, before being very surprised to get onto 3 or 4 **Long-tailed Tits**. These are smashing little pinkish birds, with a white head, a black eye-stripe and a wonderfully long tail, far less common than the Blue or Great Tits. I sauntered on to where this bridle-way finished near Batley Hospital, to find that it is now a private nursing home. I strolled down Carlinghow Hill to the Wilton Arms and Bridge Hotel where I celebrated my 21ˢᵗ birthday – what a rum do that was! A sign in the window told me that they had a pianist playing every Sunday night. I made a mental note to be there. I like *nowt* better than a good sing song over a few pints of ale! I walked along Bradford Road past the Victoria Inn, which at one time had a reputation for serving up a good pint of Tetley's Bitter, but also for having a rather unsophisticated clientele. I remembered someone once telling me the reason that they didn't have curtains up on the windows was simply because some customers used to wipe their noses on them! I passed the old Burrows mill with its lovely arched gateway leading into the mill yard still intact, and paused outside my old local the Fleece Inn, now officially called by its nickname the Church Steps. This pub had been my second home at one stage in my development. I crossed the road and nipped through the grounds of the Parish Church, where I found myself walking on a pathway of grave headstones, laid side by side. I didn't like it. It was rather disrespectful. This path had been laid when the cemetery had been cleaned up to make a park-like area. I couldn't see why the dearly departed couldn't have been left to rest in peace. To my mind it was nothing short of vandalism, however well intentioned. For some peculiar reason I've always enjoyed strolling around neglected cemeteries, like this once was, and reading the headstones, some of which can be quite touching, others amusing, besides revealing a lot about the local history of a place – plagues, famines, mining disasters and so on. Not forgetting that they are good habitats for birds too.

I ambled up Branch Road towards the Market Place, the town centre. I was relieved to find that it hadn't changed a bit. It was Friday, a market day, and all the stalls were set up on the magnificent, sloping cobbled square. This square is bordered on the east by the Town Hall and Police Station, to the south by the Memorial Gardens, to the west by the lovely Library, with the Town Hall clock tower on it and the Post Office and to the north the Zion Methodist Chapel. I never appreciated the unique West Riding Yorkshireness this collection of stone Victorian buildings oozed, until I'd lived abroad. This setting is to be found nowhere else in the world except in West Riding mill towns. I take my hat off to the folk responsible for preserving these buildings and for preventing the cobbled market place from being sealed over with tarmac, which was proposed a few years ago. Instead these fine buildings bordering the market square had all been stone cleaned of years of soot and stood gleaming yellow in the sun, whilst the cobbles, or stone sets as they are properly called, had been lifted up and re-laid level. The only blot on this scene was the disappearance of the majestic Batley Co-operative Society building. In its place stood a new shopping complex built of red brick, would you believe, which didn't even pretend to blend in with the character of its surrounds at all. The Philistines responsible for this atrocity should be taken out and shot! I dashed into the library to see if I could get my hands on a leaflet telling me 'what's on' in Kirklees, during my holidays here. Yes, they had such a leaflet, and I discovered there was all manner of leisure activities, such as art exhibitions, guided walks, brass band concerts, plays, etc. But not surprisingly most were centred on Huddersfield, which may as well be on the other side of Timbuctoo as far as Batley folk without transport are concerned. I ambled contentedly around the market, it had shrunk in size over the years with no specialist cheese or tripe stalls anymore, and only two fish mongers to be found, but cheap clothes and shoe stalls, mainly run by Asians were well represented. I eavesdropped on many a conversation. The thrill and pure joy of hearing people talk in the same Yorkshire dialect as my own hadn't worn off yet. It was a novelty and comforting to be able to talk in my native tongue and be perfectly understood, without having to constantly repeat myself or without people commenting or trying to mimic it, as they often do. I was home, amongst my own tribe, I was happy. I spotted a sign reading 'Fresh dressed rabbit' and couldn't resist buying one because I hadn't tasted rabbit in years. (The one firmly grasped in the fox's mouth that morning had reminded me of this fact.) I also bought some vegetables too so that I could make a stew with it for our tea.

I ambled off, happily clutching my bag of victuals under my arm. I had noticed that most of the roads had been altered to create a confusing 'one-way' system, obviously dreamt up by someone who was a bit short of the full quid. Along Commercial Street I went, *gawping* in all the shop windows, and trying to buy my favourite Chorley cakes or Manchester tarts, which no one seemed to bake anymore, although I could have bought American doughnuts or muffins at a number of establishments! Commercial Street hadn't changed much over the years except they had demolished a long row of old shops on one side of the street. Nothing stood there now, only a head high hoarding, very imaginative I must say, which gave this main shopping thoroughfare a peculiar lop sided, unbalanced feeling, a feeling of incompleteness. I came to the end of the street by the Wilton Arms, and remembered that I'd arranged to meet my younger sister Janice there that night. She had warned me that we were going to 'tie one on' when David her husband joined us after his game of golf up at Howley! Whence we would nip over to the Batley Working Men's Club to watch the 'turn' – Mel, the Wildebeest, as he liked to be called, was on singing. She had cracked up laughing, when I'd mentioned that the Kiswahili word for wildebeest was 'gnu', made famous by the Flanders and Swan comic song, and couldn't wait to tell him. So I hurried down Hick Lane on my way back to my mum's, as time was getting on, to the Bradford Road intersection.

It was reassuring to find Batley Barless Fireplace Co. still in its odd triangular shaped building on the corner, with its little doorway on the apex of the triangle. This firm had been there for as long as I could remember and I had never witnessed anyone entering or leaving the showroom, the window display hadn't ever seemed to change either. I imagined there to be a little wizened old man in pince-nez spectacles and a stiff winged collar sat at a high desk pouring over ledgers somewhere in the back of the dusty shop. I ran across the road and passed the Victoria Hotel displaying gaudy fluorescent signs in every window, advertising the price of drinks and topless barmaids, it certainly must have got sleazier since I used to frequent it. Then my eyes caught a new structure, rather like a miniature version of the Marble Arch in London but of local stone, standing where the old taxi rank used to be. What on earth was it? It was a tall rectangular shaped stone structure, engraved with what looked to be a curious assortment of bats. I remembered my mother telling me that they had recently erected a monument, supposedly to be representative of Batley, to welcome people to the town, and that it had cost a small fortune. Whoever was responsible for it, must have been under the impression that bats had something to do with the town's name, or under the influence of drink. What an embarrassing blunder! What a dreadful monument! It is more likely to frighten people off than to welcome them. A statue of Benjamin Law would have been more appropriate and pleasing I would have thought. I looked around me and was saddened by the fact that Charlie's Pie and Pea business was no longer there, it was a Tandoori take-away or some such thing. A sign of the times we live in, but give me pork pies and mushy peas any day.

I set off at a gallop up Soothill Lane, *by gum* it seems to have got a lot steeper over the years. I paused by the Soothill cricket field to catch my breath, and noticed some **House Martins**, distinguished from Swallows by their short forked tail and white rump. They were to-ing and fro-ing from a huddle of mud nests built under the gutter of a terrace house nearby. How lovely. I turned my attention to a pigeon sat on the roof, it was a pinky/sandy colour, obviously not a feral pigeon or a Wood Pigeon. On closer inspection I could see that it had a black collar, that made it the **Collard Dove**. I was quite pleased because I hadn't seen this particular species that now resides in the U.K., it was another 'lifer' for me. That meant I had seen about 35 species of birds that day, including 5 'lifers'. To say that Batley lies in a very densely populated, once industrial region, surrounded by the cities/towns of Leeds, Bradford, Halifax, Huddersfield, Dewsbury and Wakefield, it is quite a decent number. I had been really surprised to find here the Jackdaw, Grey Partridge, Bullfinch, Green Wood-pecker, Treecreeper, Jay and Long-tailed Tits. I'd had a really pleasant day out in my home town, watching birds, visiting childhood haunts, reveling in old memories. Yes it had been quite a nostalgic, sentimental day. I don't know about you, but I need these sorts of days occasionally to put my life into some sort of perspective, and it helps to keep one's feet firmly on the ground. Yorkshire folk, especially family, certainly help you to do just that!

I took one last glance over my silent, smoke free town in the valley below, it suddenly struck me that I hadn't seen more than a handful of men working in the town! The curators in the museum had all been women, the librarians likewise, there had been all women working in the banks, travel agents, bakeries, shops, etc. that I'd *gawped* in. I'd even seen women driving buses and ambulances, and not one solitary policeman. The whole town I concluded was run by women! Where were all the men? I'd seen a lot of old retired men out shopping with their spouses, a fair sprinkling of unemployable yobbos with shaven heads, tattoos and earrings, but hardly any working men. Were they all unemployed and at home looking after the kids? After all it was a fact that all the traditionally male dominated industries, like mining, engineering, boilermaking, foundrying, tin smithying, etc. had all long since gone. Had the skilled men of the town been forced to migrate to new countries like myself? Were they working away from home on the North Sea oil-rigs or in Saudi Arabia, or some such place, like my brother-in-law? Whatever the reason it was an interesting phenomenon, a town run by women. It was, so I'm told, just like during the last war! To be fair the government had funded a project recently to try and promote new industry to Batley, and they have had partial success in attracting a few service industries, employing mainly unskilled labour, to occupy space in the empty old mills. I found this rather ironic, considering they encouraged industries to leave the area in the first place! It was a case of too little, too late. Twenty years too late to be more precise.

I took off 'home' and remembered that when I was a pupil at Batley High School I often met one of 'Batley's characters' on my way home on winter evenings. I've long since forgotten his name, but he was a snowy haired old chap, always clad in a blue boilersuit, over which he wore an old greasy, out of shape, sports jacket. He was employed by Batley Corporation and carried a short triangular ladder around with him, his job being to climb up and light the street gas lamps. He would stop all and sundry for a chat, and everyone knew him. In fact most people tried to avoid him, including me, knowing that once he'd collared you and started blathering on, you couldn't get away from him without being rude. As we say around here, "He's was all *reight*, but he went on too long." He managed to waylay me a few times and he always took great delight in telling me about the time he was a guest on the Wilfred Pickles T.V. game show, called ' Have A Go!' When Wilfred Pickles asked him where he came from, he replied, "BATLEY, WHERE T' SPARROWS FLY BACK'ARDS TO KEEP T' MUCK OUT OF THEIR EYES."

Well I'm afraid that doesn't hold true now, because now there is no industry, hence no muck, or indeed much money, and there is no need for sparrows to fly backwards anymore!

8

On the Trail of Carruthers ...
in Darkest Africa

Uganda, East Africa

After residing on the coast of Tanzania for over 2 years, I began to feel rather guilty that I had not attempted to sort out, or take much interest in the dreaded CISTICOLAS. A genus comprising 32 species in East Africa alone, all L.B.J.s, with a reputation for defying field identification. I had, up to now relied on Kath to I.D. them for me, a state of affairs I felt I must address. Whilst thumbing through the cisticolas in the field guide one evening, my eyes were drawn to a species named CARRUTHERS' CISTICOLA. I thought, what a very British name! I said it aloud, in a British public school accent. It rolled off the tongue beautifully. Kath thought I was talking to her, so I carried on in the same vein. "I say old thing, have you ever had a CARRUTHERS' CISTICOLA?" She replied in the affirmative. I continued, "Well by jove, I simply must see one at all costs, and I shall not leave this jolly continent until I do so!" Kath, who by now is used to my idiosyncrasies, replied that in that case I would have to do some birding in Uganda. And added that I would be able to pick up quite a few more 'lifers' there too, including a few West African species that just creep into that country.

A few months after this exchange, in late September 1996, I found myself on the shores of Lake Victoria at Entebbe airport, Uganda where Kath and I were met by our Australian birding companion Greg Roberts with a small 4wd hire vehicle. I explained to Greg, who is no stranger to the African continent, that on this sojourn I was merely along for the ride, for I hadn't even had the time to make a 'wish list', so I would be happy to go anywhere that he and Kath desired to chase their target species. That is on one proviso only – I must see a CARRUTHERS' CISTICOLA ...

The birding started straight away in the airport car park. "What's that?" I inquired excitedly. "A **Red-chested Sunbird**," came back the reply in stereo. "There's a tree full of black weavers over yonder," I said in astonishment. "Yes, they are **Viellot's Weavers**," replied Greg. "*By gum* isn't it grand to travel, and be surrounded by unfamiliar birds?" I thought to myself. Greg had been hanging around Entebbe for a couple of days awaiting our arrival, and had put his time to good use checking out the area. We stopped off at one of his spots on the shores of the lake, on our way to lunch at the Entebbe Club. In no time at all we had **Slender-billed** and **Northern Brown-throated Weavers** in the fringing reeds. **White Pelican, Long-tailed** and **Greater Cormorants, Squacco** and **Black-headed Herons, Spur-winged Plover, Pied Kingfisher, African Marsh Harrier** and **African Fish-Eagle** being on hand too. Over lunch Kath and Greg poured over maps and bird lists, and agreed on a rough itinerary for the forthcoming two weeks, before we took off for a stroll around the Entebbe Botanical Gardens. They were surprisingly quite well kept by African standards, and thronged with Sunday afternoon picnickers. I picked up the locally common **Black and White Casqued Hornbill**, but no CARRUTHERS' CISTICOLA. Too much disturbance I suspect. We moved on to the nearby Nabinoonya Camp Site in the grounds of a convent, the place was again jam-packed with family and church groups having a good time singing and picnicking by the lakeside. We made camp as far away as possible from the bedlam and went for a short bird walk before nightfall. I added to my life list an **Eastern Grey Plantain-eater** (Plantain being the staple crop in Uganda) and the largest of the turacos, the **Great Blue Turaco**.

What a magnificent sight greeted me when I struggled from our small tent at dawn. A fine mist hung over the calm waters of Lake Victoria, the sun emerging ghost-like through the haze. **Hadada Ibises** and **Hamerkops** were picking contentedly over the rubbish left behind by the revellers yesterday. Greg bobbed up from a vast expanse of papyrus, wearing a dorkish Foreign Legion style camouflaged hat, muttering something about being unable to get a clear view of the crake he was pursuing. We all clambered upon a huge rock with a statue of the Virgin Mary on top, a good vantage point to check out the papyrus for CARRUTHERS' CISTICOLA. I spotted what I thought was one as it climbed up a stalk to sing in the now fully emerged sun. The adrenaline flowed through my veins, until Kath assured me that it was definitely a **Winding Cisticola**, a very similar species, its call being reminiscent of an old fashioned railway time piece being wound up, hence its name. Oh dash! We checked out a rather good

Great Blue Turaco

piece of adjacent forest, and saw **Red-bellied Paradise Flycatcher, Speckled Tinkerbird, Green Crombec, Green-throated Sunbird, Orange** and **Weyn's Weaver, Banded Wattle-eye**, and a surprising **Blue-breasted Kingfisher**, which was a lifer for us all. We broke camp and drove into Kampala, threading our way through the bustling capital and eventually finding the Fort Portal road without the aid of any road signs whatsoever! The 320 km drive only took us 4½ hours, the road being bitumened for half the way. We arrived in this pleasant little town, at the north-eastern end of the Rwenzori Mountains, just before dusk, Kath remarking that she was relieved to have arrived there before dark because the road we had just travelled on was notorious for highway robberies ... We relaxed that night over a few Nile beers in the somewhat run down, old colonial, Mountains Of The Moon Hotel.

We were away in the dark at 5.30 a.m. the following morning to travel the 35 km to Kibale National Park. We arrived with an hour to spare before anyone showed up with a key, but we spent the time admiring the splendid view of the snow capped Rwenzori Mountains in the distance; and saw a **Green Sunbird** and a **Yellow-billed Barbet** as well. Greg desperately wanted to see chimpanzees, the only primate he hadn't as yet seen in Africa, so we all went on a guided chimpanzee walk into the mid-altitude tropical forest. Of course we all wanted to see Prigogene's Ground Thrush too, it being an endemic to this park. I picked up **Chestnut Wattle-eye** and **White-throated Greenbul** before we all got onto a forest floor skulker, flitting about. Kath said that it was definitely a **Common Akalat**; I said that it couldn't have been because it had two white wing bars, which akalats don't happen to have! Greg confirmed my observations, thus it could only have been the **Prigogene's Ground Thrush**. Kath was adamant, so we agreed on the two-bird theory, she dipping out of the endemic! We did not get to see any chimpanzees, thus Greg was rather disappointed as we drove to the nearby village of Bigodi. Here we booked into the Mucusu Lodging House and decided that we would have a quick lunch before exploring the swamp adjacent to the village, so ordered vegetable soup from the menu. That was a mistake. It arrived on the table two and a half hours later, but we did see **Yellow-backed Weaver** and **Grey-headed Negro Finch** in the garden whilst waiting, and the soup was fresh. So fresh in fact that unbeknown to us it had been still growing in the garden when we had ordered it. We eventually set off and hired a guide and gum boots from the village before being led off into the swamp. It was great birding, we all had new birds: **Dusky Blue Flycatcher, Grey-green Bush-shrike, Toro Greenbul, Hairy-breasted, Grey-throated** and **Double-toothed Barbet, African Black Duck, Purple-headed** and **Narrow-tailed Glossy Starlings** and **Western Nicator**, but I dipped out on a White-tailed Ant-thrush much to Greg's amusement. He told me that it had been out in the open, perched on a log directly in front of me ... I failed to say that it was almost pitch black by then. If we thought the soup was good for lunch, we were highly delighted with the local food dished up for our tea. The table groaned under the weight of it, it was my first taste of matoki, the local staple made from plantains. It was grand, and we all made a valiant attempt at clearing the table. Phew, talk about being *pogged* ...

The following day Greg decided to go after the chimpanzees again. Kath and I birded the road instead, seeing as the forest interior had been rather quiet the previous day. We saw **Stuhlman's Starling**, the shy **Brown Illadopsis, Honeyguide Greenbul, Black-billed Turaco** and a superb **Superb Sunbird**. Greg had a big grin from ear to ear when we picked him up at lunchtime to travel back into Fort Portal. The jammy beggar had seen 6 chimpanzees. Back in town we drove around and around trying to find a grocery shop that actually sold food. Some shops sporting 'grocers' signs we found only sold clothes, or shoes, etc. but luckily we eventually found a hardware shop that actually was a hardware shop but for some reason also sold tins of bully beef and beans, so we stocked up for 3 or 4 days camping in the Semliki National Park, our next port of call. We were even lucky enough to buy bottles of tonic water and coke for our duty-free gin and rum, without having any empty bottles to exchange. But we had to promise faithfully to return the empty bottles when we passed through Fort Portal again. We had fun and games too in the 'money exchangers', for they wouldn't exchange our U.S.$ notes unless they were dated later than a certain date, no matter if our 'old' notes were in a pristine condition or not. Kath and I by pure chance had enough 'new' notes between us to buy a mountain of Ugandan currency, but none of Greg's notes passed their scrutiny. He was absolutely livid and went on about why no one ever tells you these things before you arrive in the country! Kath and I fell about in fits of laughter over his outburst, assuring him that we would see him right.

Fully stocked up we set off on the 3-hour drive through a gap in the

Rwenzori Mountains on an abysmal road, encountering a heavy hailstorm en route. We stopped at a high vantage point where we could view the magnificent surrounding mountains and the Semliki River (the border with Zaire) below. The air was clear and fresh after the storm, and steam rising from the Sempaya hot springs was clearly visible. It certainly was a breath taking, picture postcard view, and enhanced only by a **Whistling Cisticola** and a **Lead-coloured Flycatcher** showing up for us to peruse. On our arrival we had no trouble in finding the delightful camp-site run by the Bundibugyo Natural Resources and Tourism Development Agency on the boundary of the Semliki National Park. There was only one other camper, a backpacker type; he clutched the Lonely Planet Guide Book in one hand, a joint in the other ... We relaxed and enjoyed our bully beef and beans that evening, sitting around the camp fire yarning.

In the morning we birded the road and saw quite a number of interesting species, such as **Fraser's Ant Thrush, Common Bristlebill, Blue-headed Coucal, Pale-fronted Negro Finch, Brown-backed Scrub Robin, Copper Sunbird** and **Fawn-breasted Waxbill**, returning to camp for lunch quite pleased with our morning's sightings. The backpacker was relaxed smoking a joint in the sun reading his Lonely Planet Guide Book. He innocently asked Greg if he could change some of his US$ for local currency! Greg, still smarting from his experience at the money changer's the day before, fumed, "You must be #*!@# joking?" After this exchange, I heard Greg mutter passionately to himself, "I hate #*!@# backpackers." We set off into the rainforest in the afternoon looking for Pittas and such like, but did not see a thing. It was very quiet, but I did get **Piping Hornbill** when we were almost back at our campsite at dusk. After our bully beef and beans dinner, we went out spotlighting in the vehicle with our backpacker 'friend'. The only thing we managed to spot was a **Fiery-necked Nightjar**, our friend who was quite 'high' by now had some sort of religious experience observing it! On our return to camp we heard a very loud, strange, sinister owl like noise, a sound none of us could identify. It called only once. What on earth was it?

The following morning we picked up a national park guide and drove down to the nearby village of Bundibugyo. I had to haggle with a local chap regarding payment for him to guard our vehicle, whilst we went into the forest. He outrageously wanted the equivalent of 2 weeks local wages for a few hours 'work'. I overheard our guide negotiating with him for a cut of the fee. He had no idea that Kath and I could speak a little Kiswahili, and hence knew what he was up to. I was not amused. We eventually took off into the forest onto a track that went down to the Semliki River. It was very quiet. I mean very, very, quiet. I only saw one **Eastern Bearded Greenbul** and one **Black-winged Oriole** for a 5 hour effort. My enthusiasm for birding, I had to admit, had waned somewhat. All I could think of was my rumbling stomach. What made our morning more interesting however is when we came across three little people on the track carrying bundles of what looked like plant stalks on their heads. Greg whispered to me, "Are they pygmies?" After a moments hesitation, I replied, "Bloody hell, yes they must be! Fancy meeting pygmies in the forest." I'd actually had no idea that they were around these parts. It had come as a complete surprise.

When we arrived back at our vehicle in the village, it was completely surrounded by a large mob of little people. I gave the vehicle guard the price we had agreed, but he was not happy. He wanted more! Whilst I was arguing with this fat greedy fellow, Greg and Kath were meanwhile being hassled by aggressive pygmies to buy artifacts. They were all obviously as drunk as skunks. When I'd sorted the guard out, we were in the midst of a yelling, frenzied mob of wee people, who were by now jostling us and shoving silly trinkets right into our faces. I could see Greg getting quite agitated and I didn't hesitate in jumping into the vehicle when he screamed, "Come on, let's get out of here." We made our escape from the mêlée, scattering people asunder, as he gunned the vehicle out of the village. Phew, that could have turned really nasty.

The highlight of my day was bathing by the scenic Mingilo waterfall near our campsite, and seeing a **Brown-chested Alethe** on the way back in the evening twilight. We heard the sinister owl call again whilst having our bully beef dinner. Kath was quick enough to get it on tape, but what on earth was it? Kath and Greg spent most of the night walking up and down the road trying to call it in, but to no avail.

The following morning we decided we had had enough of Semliki National Park, the birding was slow and we did not really care to have another pygmy experience, so we decided to have a last walk down to the Hot Springs and head off in the afternoon back to Fort Portal. Greg was distraught that he had lost his dork hat somewhere during the night. Off we went down to the boardwalk to the springs, placating him. I was amazed to see waterbirds in the sulphurous boiling water: **Purple Heron, Sacred**

Ibis, Egyptian Goose, Three-banded Plover, Common Sandpiper, and **Wood Sandpiper.** Kath reckoned that they have no nerves in their legs, so do not feel the heat! We also had a **Cameroon Sombre Greenbul,** and I at last saw the **Black-casqued Wattled Hornbill.** A bird that Kath and Greg had been seeing everyday and unsuccessfully trying to get me onto it. It was such a huge pterodactyl thing, I wondered why I'd had so much difficulty ... We packed up our camp at lunchtime, Greg misplacing one of his empty coke bottles. I mentioned while driving back to Fort Portal that a pygmy chap would probably find it and come chasing after us, just like in the film *The Gods Must Be Crazy,* and that he would be wearing Greg's dork hat! Heaven forbid! We finished up that evening at Kasese (50 km south of Fort Portal). We booked into the Margherita Hotel where we saw a **Piapiac** (a crow-like bird with a long tail) on the back of a sheep in the driveway. Ah! sheer luxury, an hot bath and some real food at last. Well at least they didn't serve us up bully beef and beans!

The hotel boasted a full English breakfast as part of the room tariff, so after having had only a couple of biscuits for breaky the previous four mornings, I ordered the works – bacon, eggs, sausages, and toast. My taste buds were salivating in anticipation, just as the electricity supply went off. One and half hours later I was served up one measly fried egg. Was I cranky ... I could not comprehend why if they had managed to fry me an egg on an alternative fuel supply, why they could not have managed the full works? Such is Africa ... You stop querying these things after a while. We had actually whiled away our pre-egg waiting time by watching raptors over the mountains. How on earth Kath can put a name to black dots in the sky miles away will forever remain a mystery to me.

We travelled south from Kasese, the bitumen road skirting Lake George to the east, and crossing over the equator where we turned westward into Queen Elizabeth II National Park, a huge expanse of savannah, a habitat we had not come across so far on this trip. Greg was keen to see a Short-tailed Pipit; he said they liked short grass, so we kept stopping and checking out the grasslands for these pipits. On one such stop Greg exclaimed, "Can you see what I can see over there?" I looked in the direction he was pointing, fully expecting to see a pipit, but there, sat a LION in the grass! We agreed in future not to stray too far away from the vehicle. We reached the shores of Lake Edward and had **Cardinal Queleas** and a lovely **Swamp Flycatcher** on our way to Mweya. Greg booked into the posh safari lodge and Kath and I, the destitute Institute of Ecology hostel nearby, which had warthogs running around in the grounds like domestic dogs. We relaxed over lunch on the verandah of the safari lodge; birds were flying around us everywhere. I had a lifer, **Black-headed Bush-shrike** whilst relaxing with a beer. "This is my style of birding; it beats bush bashing any day," I thought to myself. Meanwhile an interesting conversation was going on between Kath and Greg. Kath mentioned that the strange, sinister owl call we had heard in Semliki National Park may have been a Pel's Fishing Owl, and she said she would check its call out when we got home. I must add that the PFO is one of the most sought-after birds in Africa by visiting twitchers. When Greg regained his power of speech, he said that if he had known that, he would have liked to have stayed in Semliki longer to try and see it, pygmies or not! It was then that it finally dawned on me that Greg was completely loony. He was prepared to wade through sulphurous boiling swamps in the dark and brave hostile pygmy tribes just to see a bird!

We went off for a drive around the park in pouring rain and checked out the fringing reeds of the lake. We found **Goliath Heron, Jacana, Water Thicknee, Black Crake, African Crake** and **African Reed Warbler**. I was getting fearful that I would never see CARRUTHERS' CISTICOLA. To Greg's delight, we saw a **Short-tailed Pipit**, but Kath still remains sceptical about this record. We thought we had better get back to the lodge, after Kath got the vehicle stuck in the muddy track whilst trying to avoid a huge bull elephant. We were lulled to sleep that night by the sound of hippopotamuses bellowing and grunting directly under our window. Ah! The sounds of Africa …

We headed off out of Mweya, seeing quite an array of game, which was quite encouraging considering that most of it was almost wiped out by the retreating troops of Idi Amin and the unpaid, starving Tanzanian army who occupied the area after Amin's demise. We also saw quite an array of birds too, including **Didric** and **Red-chested Cuckoo; Malachite, Pied, Chestnut-bellied** and **Woodland Kingfishers; Sooty Anteater-Chat, Flappet Lark; Siffling, Singing, Chubb's, Red-faced, Winding, Zitting** and **Stout Cisticolas**, but no CARRUTHERS', even though we checked out all the stands of papyrus, their favourite habitat. We headed down the bitumen main road for a short while and then turned off down the Ishasha Road. This dirt road was being used by convoys of huge UN food trucks, taking food supplies into Zaire for the unfortunate Rwandan refugees, and was therefore badly churned up after the recent rains. We had quite a few heart stopping moments trying to get around UN trucks that were stuck in the mud, or had slipped off the road, but we arrived in the southern part of the park at the Ishasha gate, our original destination for the night, with the sun still high in the sky. So we decided to go on to Buhoma in the northern sector of the Bwindi-Impenetrable Forest National Park. We arrived in Buhoma absolutely shattered after miles of grinding along in low gear over rough roads, and booked into a banda run by the Buhoma Community Campground Development Association. This park, being famous for its gorilla population, wealthy eco-tourists, mostly Americans, are catered for in a luxury tented camp here, and are charged US$200 by the Uganda National Parks for the privilege of going on a 2 to 3 hour walk to see these gorillas. But we were there to see the birds that the park boasts, a species list of 350, 27 of which are found nowhere else in East Africa, and CARRUTHERS' CISTICOLA ... which had eluded me for over a week now. I read a notice in the banda, saying that meals were available in a canteen across the road, which was run by a villagers' co-operative, but three to four hours notice was required. Not wanting to miss out of a feed that evening I immediately dashed across the road to order three meals. I was shown a menu consisting of about 15 choices. Well now, with residing in Africa for over 2 years, I knew that there would be a few items on the menu which were not available. So in order to save time I began by asking if everything on the menu was available. I was told there was no chicken, so I ordered 3 goat stew dishes. To this request I was bluntly told there was no meat either, so I ordered 3 matoki dishes. I was further told there was no matoki either! "No matoki in Uganda, they surely must be joking!" I thought to myself. Undaunted, I perused the menu once more and came to the realisation that if there was no chicken, no meat and no matoki, then there was only a spaghetti dish left on the menu. I gingerly ventured to order 3 spaghetti dishes. The villager's eyes lit up, and she said with a big beam on her face, "Yes, we have that." I wasn't half relieved. No bully beef and beans tonight! It turned out to be rather delicious too, and they did have plenty of warm Nile beer!

I was perplexed to read in the park's literature that evening, that tourists are advised to bring raincoats, walking boots and *gloves!* The next morning, still half asleep, enjoying my early morning cup of coffee, I heard Kath beckoning me. She had got onto a lovely little bird perched in a bush, singing, near our banda. We both watched it for over 10 minutes before it flew off. I was confident of finding out what it was in our field guide, but I was unable to do so. Neither could Kath! To this day that little bird that we both had excellent views of, remains a mystery … We set off, gloveless, to bird the track that runs northwards through the mid-altitude forest (1,550 m). It was fantastic birding; there were birds everywhere! So different from our experience of the slow birding in Semliki. We spent all day on this track and ended up seeing six of the regional endemics: **Yellow-eyed Black Flycatcher, Handsome Francolin, Masked Apalis, Red-faced Woodland Warbler, Rwenzori Batis** and **White-bellied Crested Flycatcher**. I personally had 29 lifers in all for the day, my memorable ones being **Black-faced Rufous Warbler, Petit's Cuckoo-shrike, Banded Prinia, Red-fronted Antpecker, Elliot's Woodpecker, African Broadbill** at long last, after dipping out on it on numerous occasions in the past, and the stunning **Black Bee-eater**. The latter we observed perched on a dead tree in a small clearing in the sun, its light blue rump and scarlet throat clearly visible as it hawked insects from its perch.

We had no hesitation in birding the same track the following morning. We saw a further two regional endemics: **Red-throated Alethe** and **Ladgen's Bush-shrike** and I had a further nine lifers: **White-tailed Ant-thrush**, (a grip back) **Pink-footed Puffback, Dusky Tit, Montane Oriole, Buff-throated Apalis, Blue-throated Roller, Tit Hylia, Yellow-throated Tinkerbird** and the largest woodpecker I had ever seen, the **Yellow-crested Woodpecker**. After lunch we decided to drive to Ruhiza in the southern sector of the park. We went via Kitahurira and birded the forest edge in heavy rain, managing to see a lovely **Luehder's Bush-shrike** before we came across a fallen tree across the road. A motley collection of locals appeared from nowhere and offered to move it for USh 10,000 (US $10). It took them no time at all to chop it up and lever it out of the way. We carried on, but it was getting dark and the road turned into a deeply rutted, muddy mountain track, with a steep drop into the valley below. We could not have been very far from our destination but realised that our little 4wd vehicle would not make it; so turned around and drove back the way we had come, passing the cleared log, and finished up in the Travellers Inn at Butogota. A small town only a few kilometres away from Buhoma where we had started out from at lunchtime. It poured down with rain all night. I was happy to have a bed, having earlier in the evening, visualised the three of us sleeping in the bogged vehicle!

On the Trail of Carruthers ...

We provided entertainment for the local children while we breakfasted on the verandah of the inn on the main street of Butogota, and received a lecture on Uganda's 'Dark Ages' during the rule of Idi Amin from the inn-keeper. We decided to have another go at driving to Ruhiza, this time going via the main road around the park and approaching it from the opposite direction. The drive was mostly through cultivated areas where we saw a **Honey Buzzard** (sitting in the middle of the road) and a pair of **Crowned Cranes**, arguably the most striking cranes in the world. In a degraded forest section, we also saw **Stripe-breasted Tit,** another regional endemic, together with a lovely **Regal Sunbird, Doherty's Bush-shrike,** and a **Strange Weaver.** When I first saw the latter species, I told Greg that I was onto a strange-looking weaver. He replied, "How did you know its name?" I had no idea what he was talking about until he explained. We had to call into the town of Kabale to buy petrol before heading north, back into the park. We saw **Tullberg's Woodpecker, Northern Puffback, Thick-billed Serin** and **Collared Apalis** when we climbed up a mountain track into the bamboo zone (2,500 m), but we did not hang around there, for there were fresh signs of elephants everywhere we looked. Greg remarked that he could even smell them! We finally arrived in Ruhiza at dusk, one and a half days of travelling to cover about 20 km as the crow flies. We stayed at the hostel run by the Institute of Tropical Forest Conservation. We had the place to ourselves. It was quite cosy sitting before the log fire, warming up our bully beef and beans!

We set off in the morning with a guide to do the 4 km walk to Mubwindi Swamp. I was excited, this swamp being a known spot for CARRUTHERS' CISTICOLA. The guide warned us before we set off, that if we came across a troupe of gorillas to stay still, and if we came across any elephants to stay quiet! Our guide soon adjusted to our birding pace, which took us 4 hours to reach the swamp through the montane forest, the track finally descending steeply to the swamp edge. Greg had remarked on this descent that we would have fun returning up it! I'd consolidated ticks along the way there, but had failed to see any new birds, whilst Kath and Greg had been looking out specifically for the African Green Broadbill that is only known in East Africa from this swamp, but without success. Over our stale bread and sardine lunch, I was scanning the reeds in the swamp. I saw a small brown bird momentarily fly up and drop down again, not managing to see much on it. The adrenaline was pumping through my veins as I concentrated on the spot where it had disappeared. It magically flew up again, this time I saw its chestnut head, streaky back and black tail. I instinctively knew this was it, a CARRUTHERS' CISTICOLA at last! I put on my British public school voice, "I say, I believe I'm onto a Carruthers', what a topping bird. Hey what!" Kath confirmed it. I was ecstatic at seeing my one and only target species for this trip.

We started the long slow haul back up the steep track. We kept seeing birds with a black head, rufous back and grey belly and initially thought they must be juvenile Paradise Flycatchers, until Kath had a hunch they could be **Mountain Illadopsis**, but they have grey heads! She had a tape of this species and played it. Yes, that's what they sounded like and they even came in to the tape. We concluded that in this location they must be a black-headed form. We arrived back at the hostel having seen quite a few of the same birds we had seen at Buhoma, but dipping out of the African Green Broadbill. It still only being mid-afternoon we birded the roadway until heavy rain and cold set in, so scurried back wet through to dry out in front of the fire. I celebrated my CARRUTHERS' CISTICOLA by draining the dregs of our duty-free gin, but retired to bed shivering with a chill, or so I thought. The rain bounced down on the tin roof all night.

The rain had ceased by dawn. I had a dull headache as we set off in the vehicle back down the mountain track towards Kabale. We had a lovely **White-headed Wood Hoopoe** and a **Cassin's Hawk-Eagle** on the way. We did not hang about too long in Kabale as we had to get back as far as we could towards Kampala that night, for Kath and I had to catch a plane home on the morrow. We were surprised and delighted to discover the main road to Kampala was bitumened. We stopped along the way and birded some open savannah woodland habitat by the side of the road, looking for Bronze-tailed Glossy Starlings. We failed to find any but I picked up two more lifers: **Black-faced Waxbill** and **Yellow-bellied Eremomela**. We made it to the town of Masaka that evening and booked into the clean and comfortable Laston Hotel. I worked out over dinner that I needed another two lifers to bring my East African list up to a respectable 800 species. Would I do it tomorrow morning? Our last day in the 'Pearl of Africa' as Winston Churchill referred to Uganda.

I still felt a bit off-colour as we left Masaka, but perked up a bit when we stopped to check out a papyrus swamp with an adjacent tiny patch of forest. I had **Compact Weaver** and great views of a wonderful **Papyrus**

Carruther's Cisticola

Mad Twitching

Gonolek to bring up my tally to 800. I also had a **Pied Hornbill** as a bonus in the forest. We arrived back at Entebbe Airport with time to spare for a farewell lunch with Greg. He had a further week in Uganda before heading off back to Australia, and planned to go up to Murchinson Falls National Park. He seemed reasonably happy with his tally of lifers, but like Kath was disappointed in dipping out of the probable Pel's Fishing Owl and African Green Broadbill. I was more than happy with my tally of 128 lifers and over 300 for the trip, and ecstatic at actually seeing my target CARRUTHERS CISTICOLA.

I do not know who Carruthers was, but I have this image in my mind of a colonial public servant type. An amateur natural historian no less, who spent his free time busily collecting specimens, decked out in khaki safari clothes complete with pith helmet. Whoever he was, I wish I could tell him how much fun I had chasing after his cisticola!

P.S. On our return to Tanga, I was hospitalised for a week with malaria. It wasn't just a chill I'd caught after all!

9

A Man Before his Time

Washington D.C., United States of America

IN JULY 1997 Kath completed her three-year project in Tanga, Tanzania and secured a new position with W.W.F. (The World Wildlife Fund) based in Jakarta, Indonesia. Prior to taking up this new position, Kath was summoned to the W.W.F. head office in Washington so that she could be introduced to the W.W.F. system, and be shown how to fill in a time sheet correctly. I think the term they used for this was 'indoctrination'. Consequently Kath inquired if I wished to accompany her to Washington. Oh boy did I!

I must tell you that the one and only time I had visited the States was in 1988, (before I became a birder) when I'd ridden my bicycle from Los Angeles, up the west coast and into Canada. I'd had a wonderful trip, met some rather nice, friendly hospitable people, (quite a number of them commenting that I was a dead ringer for Sean Connery!) and I'd enjoyed the smashing hearty American cooked breakfasts that are often served up 'all day' in their diners.

You can probably imagine then what was going through my mind, considering that here was a lad who had lived a fairly Spartan existence in the wilds of Africa for the last three years, being offered the chance of 'pigging out' in the land of plenty for a few weeks? Yes, it would be rather relaxing to lounge around in some hotel room watching *movies* on T.V., not ever having watched a T.V. set in Africa. Yes, it would be champion to have a full American breakfast each morning, starting with *oatmeal*, followed by eggs – cooked to your choice of 101 different ways, bacon, sausages, tomatoes, *hash browns*, etc. and bottomless cups of 'proper' coffee. Yes, it would make a pleasant change to be able to try some American pipe tobacco. Yes, it would be grand to be amongst people who spoke more or less the same language as I for a week or two, after finding it rather tedious and exhausting trying to communicate in a foreign tongue to accomplish the most trivial tasks over the past three years. Yes, it would be rather a novelty to be able to browse around a department store, for Tanga didn't even have anything remotely similar to even a mini-supermarket. "Yes, yes, yes, yes, YES, I'd like to accompany you to Washington!" I pleaded, having to restrain myself from falling at her feet.

We left Africa in the midst of a riot in Nairobi. It was rather sad in a way to be leaving, not only because we were leaving our friends behind, our faithless staff whom I'd become rather fond of, and indeed the unique colonial life-style we had enjoyed, but because I only needed a further 7 species of birds to bring my African Continent tally up to a 1,000 species! Still, I had another 1,500 or so new species to go after in Indonesia over the next four years hadn't I ? We arrived in Washington tired and jet-lagged. My luggage didn't, and we took a taxi to a hotel in *downtown* Washington that W.W.F. had booked us into. It was disorientating to be driven on the 'wrong side' of the road, but nevertheless I was most impressed by the orderly way in which everyone drove, after the utter chaos of Dar-es-Salaam and Nairobi. Everyone here obeyed the road rules, what a novel idea! They even stuck to their lanes, drove very sedately, and didn't seem remotely interested in reaching their destination in the shortest possible time. I found this to be a very endearing quality, much to my style of doing things. We got dropped off outside the Tabard Inn, it looked to be a delightful old fashioned, if not a trifle trendy, hotel situated on a pleasant tree-lined street only a walk away from the capital's major tourist attractions. Our room was crammed with elegant old furniture, a cast iron bed, kitsch ornaments and lamp standards, a profusion of mirrors and the bathroom contained a large old-fashioned claw footed bath. "Yes, I'll be most comfortable here," I thought to myself, as I opened up all the old cupboards looking for the T.V. set. There wasn't one to be found! "Flippin' *heck*," I moaned to Kath. "This trendy bloomin' hotel doesn't even have a T.V. set. It may be a novelty for yuppie Yanks to stay here, who have a T.V. set in every other room in their home, but for me who hasn't seen one for three years it's a #*@# disaster!" I flung myself onto the flock mattress and sobbed. "There goes my dream of spending two weeks doing *nowt* but watching T.V. down the drain." Kath laughed at me and retorted, "Maybe you'll have to go out and do some bird watching?" "What?" I replied incredulously, for I'd never thought of that!

The following morning, still wearing my travelling attire because my luggage hadn't as yet caught up with me, we wandered down to the dining room for breakfast. Oh boy, was I looking forward to this. A waiter wearing a 'bum freezer' showed us to a table, where I snatched up the menu card, only to find that my dream of having a hearty American cooked breakfast every morning was shattered. I could have cereal or fruit and then a choice of a bagel (whatever that is), a croissant or a 'delicious oven fresh muffin'. I could have cried! I stoically pulled myself together and decided that a nice toasted muffin would have to suffice. So I asked the waiter, "Could I have a *delicious oven fresh* muffin please?" stressing the adjectives used on the menu. He gave me an old-fashioned look, as if he suspected I was taking the Mickey. He had the last laugh when he dumped a 'bun' down in front of me. It wasn't an English muffin at all as I'd presumed. Well you live and learn, I'd have never believed that folk could actually prefer to eat a sweet bun for breakfast! There was only one thing to do, find a diner and have a decent 'breakfast' for my lunch, for I had it in mind to spend the day roaming around, reconnoitring the place, whilst Kath went off to be indoctrinated.

I walked Kath to the W.W.F. office only a few blocks away, as they say here, and set off with a free tourist map in my pocket in the general direction of the White House. (As they call the Presidential Palace.) Washington, I found had a nice feel to it, lovely old red-bricked buildings, clean tree-lined streets, but there was something oddly missing. I couldn't put my finger on it, until it suddenly struck me that there were no menacing skyscrapers that disfigure the landscape in other major cities around the world. This gave the city a lovely small town feel about it. I still couldn't get over how orderly the traffic behaved. They even stopped their vehicles at intersections to let pedestrians cross the road, how terribly civilized. The *sidewalks* (pavements) were a different matter. They were full of cyclists, dressed in full Tour de France racing clobber, hurtling at break neck speed every which way you turned – on the sidewalk! These cyclists, unlike their motorized compatriots were definitely trying to get to their destination in the shortest possible time. If you somehow were lucky enough not to get mown down by one of these maniacal cyclists you would certainly be sent flying by one of the countless number of joggers and get trampled underfoot. The sidewalks were definitely a dangerous place to actually walk! I gingerly ambled on, browsing in all the exclusive, expensive shops like a country bumpkin hitting the big city for the first time, until I came across a large bookshop, where I became totally engrossed for an hour. I came out with a Peterson's *Field Guide to Eastern Birds*, surprisingly quite inexpensive too. I had asked the lady on the till if she could direct me to the nearest tobacconist shop (because I wanted to buy some American pipe tobacco). She had given me an incredulously puzzled, vague look as if she didn't know what a tobacconist's was, and I was forced to add, "You know, where they sell cigarettes and tobacco." She gave a gasp, as if I'd asked her to do something indecent, and screamed, "Cigarettes, you want cigarettes!" in a shrill voice so everyone in the shop could hear. I half expected her to give me a lecture on the evils of smoking, until I gave her my 'I've heard it a million times before' look. She only added, with a curled-up mouth, "Try a drug store." I'd obviously asked the wrong person! Now it was my turn to be puzzled. A 'chemist' shop would sell tobacco? I found a large 'Drug Store' and to my amazement, found it to be much more than a chemist shop. It sold just about everything, more of a mini-supermarket than anything else. I wandered around, wide-eyed like a kid in a toy shop – all these brightly packaged commodities for sale. The American citizens are certainly spoiled for choice. That's for sure! A packet caught my eye in the pharmaceuticals section of the shop. I read – 'Stop Gas – Eat beans and broccoli with confidence.' "What the bloomin' *hummer* is this?" I muttered. I hadn't known that medical science had made such a monumental break-through. This must surely rate with the discovery of penicillin! There was a whole shelf full of different brands, all advertising this miracle cure to stop you 'breaking wind'. Simply amazing! I realized then that I could be nowhere else on this planet but in America. What other nation would worry about farting? Or indeed could *thoil* to actually buy it, to stop what is after all a normal bodily function? They did sell cigarettes but no pipe tobacco, neither did all the other likely looking shops I went into. I never envisaged that I would have difficulty buying pipe tobacco in Washington, after all, the place once was a bustling tobacco port. Virginia, just over the other side of the Potamac River, is famed for its fine tobacco, so why couldn't I buy any? Neither did I spot any American 'diners', which I'd been looking out for. There were numerous fancy restaurants specializing in food from all over the world – Indian, Thai, Chinese, Japanese, Lebanese, etc., but do you think I could find a fair dinkum American diner – not on your Nellie! Fancy – no pipe tobacco or American diners in America's capital city! Well, not in this neighbourhood at any rate.

I was reduced to entering a sandwich shop that had a few little tables by the window. I perused the blackboard menu and the array of grated rabbit type food displayed in a glass cabinet, before deciding that it must be one of those health food places, I had inadvertently entered. I was just about to walk out when I spotted 'B.L.T.' on the blackboard. I knew what this meant, as my wife who hails from these parts often uses the term for Bacon, Lettuce and Tomato. So I politely asked for two B.L.T. sandwiches, but without the lettuce and tomato, and could I have my bacon *crozzled.* The young lady assistant laughed, and I realised that I had used a Yorkshire expression that she would probably not understand. I qualified it by saying, "You know, burnt to buggery ... well done ... crispy ..." She smiled in acknowledgement and asked me what type of bread I would like, rolling off her tongue a string of names in rapid succession, so fast that I didn't catch a word of anything that she had said. I wasn't used to having so much choice and not wanting her to repeat her litany replied, "Ordinary white bread will be fine." She smiled again, this lass was alright. I was about to sit down, when she enquired, "Anything to drink, Sir?" I didn't think she was talking to me, because I wasn't used to being addressed as 'Sir', but on realising that she was, replied, "Oh, a coffee please, black ... with milk and sugar." I ventured a little joke. She proceeded to spout a long spiel about what coffee she could offer me. It was all terribly confusing, I didn't recognise anything she said, and I began to wish that I'd never asked for one. I stammered, "Just ordinary coffee will do fine." She countered with, "*Regular* Sir." Then it twigged, that they use the word 'regular' here to mean 'ordinary'. This piece of essential terminology was to stand me in good stead for the rest of my stay here! I replied knowingly, "Yes, regular." I thought foolishly that I had finished my order, but I was wrong. She then inquired if I'd like cream or 'half and half'. I hadn't the faintest idea of what she was talking about, this was all getting to be too much for me. I was exhausted with all this tedious palaver, over a simple bacon *banjo* and a cup of coffee. So much for thinking that it would be grand to be amongst people who spoke the same language as I for a change! On twigging that she must be talking about milk, I ventured "*Regular* cow's milk please." See, I'm a fast learner! And it did make her laugh. I sat down and mused over the fact that in Tanga, we had bought our milk directly from a farmer who lived nearby. It was pure cow's milk, completely unadulterated by man, it hadn't been homogenized, sterilized or any other sort of ... ized, it was straight from the cow, and it tasted bloomin' marvellous. I would boil it and then leave it to stand overnight, before skimming the cream off to save to put on our desserts ... yummeeee! I remembered the time when the farm lad failed to deliver our milk one evening. I later found out that there was a simple explanation. There wasn't any because the cow had kicked over the bucket! Here I was on a different planet. I pulled out my new field guide and flicked through it. Wow, there were all kinds of interesting sounding birds in it, the likes of which I'd never heard of before, such as – Goatsuckers, Sapsuckers, Killdeers, Flickers, Titmice, Chickadees, Gnatcatchers, Mockingbirds, Vireos, Grackles and Towhees, etc. Such unusual names to whet my appetite, my mind boggled.

I left the sandwich bar suitably satiated, assuring the young lady that I was indeed a 'Limey'. (It made a welcome change from being called a Pommie in Australia.) And yes, I suppose I did sound a little like the Beatles. If I hadn't been old enough to be her father, I'd have thought that she was chatting me up. I must admit she was rather an attractive young thing, with all the bumps in the right places, but I guessed she was just being friendly, like most folk around here are. I walked down to the White House. Yes it was very nice, and very white. I carried on down 17th Street to the Washington Monument, a 555 feet tall marble obelisk. Yes it was very nice and very tall. I could see Lincoln's Memorial on my right in the distance, where Martin Luther King Jr. delivered his famous "I have a dream" speech, or so my map said. Both men incidentally meeting untimely deaths, both being assassinated – so much for being a civilised society don't you think? On my left were a number of National Museums and Art Galleries, and beyond was the Capitol, as they call their House of Parliament. They all looked very fine buildings, but I ignored them all. I had no desire to look around any one of them, maybe I would visit the Natural History Museum another day. I think I was a little travel weary, or a little peeved at our hotel not having a T.V., not being able to get an American cooked breakfast, nor tobacco. It was all the fault of these miserable, health-kick obsessed, trendy, cosmopolitan bloomin' Washingtonians. Wasn't it? I crossed over Independence Avenue and sat down under a tree beside the Tidal Basin on the Potomac River, directly opposite Jefferson's Memorial. A very nice marble adaptation of the Roman Pantheon, or so my map said. The only birds I'd seen so far had been **House Sparrows, Feral Pigeons** and **European Starlings**, but a grey bird with a longish tail was flitting about in an adjacent tree. I didn't have my binoculars with me, but I could clearly see that it had a large white patch in each wing and white outer tail feathers. I found it in my new field guide. It was the **Northern Mockingbird**. Wow, my first mockingbird, my first 'lifer' in Washington, my first 'lifer' in Eastern North America to be more precise. My spirits were lifted. But being weary and jet lagged decided to put my best foot forward and go back to the hotel for a snooze, taking a different route back, being still on the lookout for tobacconists and diners. I didn't find either, but I did spot a 'Spy Shop' specializing in audio and optical devices to enable Americans to spy on each other. I'd never come across one of these shops anywhere else in the world. It speaks volumes about the American psyche doesn't it? I began to wonder whether W.W.F. would violate the Human Rights Charter in indoctrinating Kath!

I needn't have worried, for when she arrived back at the hotel later she looked pretty well unscathed. I told her that I'd read the hotel literature, and I'd discovered that this hotel was used by congressmen in times of yore for illicit liaisons, and wondered if that is why they called them congressmen? It did explain the profusion of mirrors! I went on to say that we had better be careful as some of them might be two-way, and that the hotel management may present us with a video taped record of our stay here on checking out! We went out that evening for dinner with a large contingent of Kath's new work chums, to a Thai Restaurant. "Who on earth chose a Thai Restaurant?" I'd moaned to Kath beforehand, knowing full well that Kath adores Thai cuisine. "I fancied some American spare ribs, or a thick juicy steak to be followed by 'moms home-baked apple pie' and cream," I said in my best American accent. "We are going to have no choice but to eat Asian muckment for the next four years in Indonesia, for goodness sake," I added. Kath gave me one of her despairing looks, and I knew then that I'd gone too far! I kept my mouth firmly shut over dinner, which I surprisingly enjoyed, but I'd never admit that to Kath, would I? I had washed my nosh down with a couple of different American beers, and I now could understand why a lot of Americans drink bottled water – because there is not much difference in taste between either! I asked myself why it was that the most powerful country in the world hadn't yet mastered the art of making good beer? Even many a third world country could teach them this simple art. Tusker beer in Kenya, Nile beer in Uganda, Three Horses beer in Madagascar just to name a few examples, were far superior to this insipid stuff. Was it because the country had been founded by the puritanical Pilgrim Fathers and not by a bunch of regulars from the Ye olde Batley Working Yeomen's Club? Nevertheless we had quite a jolly evening, even though it didn't degenerate into a monumental booze-up that a similar gathering in Yorkshire or Australia would have without doubt turned into.

The following morning I'd risen early, bright eyed and bushy tailed, and was enjoying my first smoke of the day with my head hanging out of the bathroom window, (I'd failed to find an ashtray too), when a small brown dove landed on the chimney pot of the adjacent building. It had a long pointed tail with a fair bit of white in it, and lovely black spots on its back. I discovered in the field guide that it was the **Mourning Dove**, another 'lifer' for me. Then I spotted 2 or 3 smoky black tailless swifts flying around the roof tops, their bodies rather cigar shaped. I was surprised to find that that is how the field guide described the **Chimney Swifts** too, yet another 'lifer'. By now I'd finished my 2nd fag and had wafted all the smoke out of the window, so that it was safe to summon Kath to have a look. I didn't want to be accused of suppressing my 'lifers'. We breakfasted on 'delicious oven fresh muffins' before I dropped Kath off at her office. That day I was going to check out Theodore Roosevelt Island in the Potomac River, as the novelty of being able to go shopping had already waned. The previous evening I had been tipped off by one of Kath's colleagues that it was a good little wooded island containing a few birds. To get there I carried on walking west along M Street, and I had to pass through Georgetown, Washington's oldest neighbourhood. I found Georgetown to be quite a pleasant place, like a lot of old inner city suburbs of many big cities, it had after years of decline been tarted up to become a trendy place to live. It was full of expensive shops, little fancy eating places, art galleries and the like, interspersed with handsome Federal style houses and architecturally pleasing old banks and churches. I was nevertheless relieved to find that the further west I walked the less trendy and tarted up it became. There were even 'ordinary' or should I say 'regular' shops – a bicycle shop, an army and navy / scout shop – the types of shops I love browsing around most. I made a mental note that I must call in there on the way back to buy a shirt, so that I could change out of the one I had been wearing for the last 5 days, my bags still not yet having shown up! I came upon the Frances Scott Key bridge, where I read a plaque informing me that this bridge over the Potomac River was named after the chap who wrote the 'Star Spangled Banner'. I strode out along this bridge, wishing that I'd bought some of those 'Stop-Gas' pills. For I was suffering from the spicy Thai food I'd eaten the previous evening! I definitely wasn't playing the Star Spangled Banner though, it sounded more like God Save the Queen! I paused in the middle to take in the vista from this high vantage-point. Downstream in the middle of the river was Roosevelt Island, my destination. It indeed looked a splendid well-wooded little island. Over the island could be seen the infamous Watergate complex and the skyscraper free city. Upstream was equally pleasing, the river having well-wooded banks on either side and scullers in tiny streamlined craft were training on the river, which gave it all a rather tranquil air. There weren't too many pedestrians on this bridge, a bag lady pushing a shopping trolley, one or two business suited gents and a few ladies elegantly clad in office attire, but oddly wearing gym shoes! Not forgetting of course the ubiquitous cyclists and joggers in various stages of distress. Before I moved off I spotted a lone seagull flying up the river, it flew under the bridge beneath me where I could clearly see its grey mantle and black wing tips. It looked like a **Herring Gull** to me, but I wasn't sure if they were to be found in North America. I had to check in the field guide. On discovering that they were indeed here, and on checking the other species of gulls that occur here too, deduced that in all probability it was indeed the **Herring Gull**. That sorted out to my satisfaction, I strode off the bridge, out of the District of Columbia and entered the state of Virginia, famed for its tobacco and hams, both of which to my chagrin I was still not acquainted with. I took a cycle path that looked as though it was heading in the direction that I wanted to go. It was rather pleasant and relatively cyclist free. I came across a small party of **American Crows** picking over a tramp's cardboard lined lair in a copse, and spied a brown finch perched in a bush, having a pinky-red breast, eyebrow and rump, and heavily streaked flanks. It was the introduced **House Finch**. From a tangle of vegetation, just before the cycle path crossed over the George Washington Memorial *Parkway* (motorway), I heard a cat-like mewing, and managed to get onto an active slaty-grey bird sporting a black crown. I had no idea what it was, or for that matter, even which family it belonged to. I found that it was the **Grey Catbird** belonging to the Mimidae family or mimic thrushes. Anyway whatever its pedigree, it was a smashing little bird which I enjoyed watching immensely, as it darted around cockily flicking up its tail. I crossed over the parkway, and the cycle path descended onto the bank of the river to a large empty car parking area, where I could see a footbridge across to the island. I stopped to observe the antics of a **Northern Mockingbird** in a riverside tree before alighting onto the footbridge, where quite a lot of **Barn Swallows** were gracefully diving under catching insects.

On the island proper there was a National Park Service notice board welcoming visitors and a large pile of leaflets in a box, which I availed myself of. I sat down on a shady bench to peruse it. I'd had no idea that this island was managed by the National Park Service, and I found the leaflet to be most useful and very well compiled. Not only did it have a short history of the island together with a short precis of Theodore Roosevelt's life and achievements, of which I knew absolutely nothing, but it had a well-drawn map showing all the trails too. I read that this 91-acre wooded island used to be called 'My Lords Island' when King Charles 1st granted it to Lord Baltimore. Later, it had been owned by the Mason family, who built a mansion here in the early 1800s, where during the civil war Union troops had been stationed. In more recent times it was purchased by the Theodore Roosevelt Memorial Association in 1932 and that the monument had been built and finally dedicated in 1967. So this little island had quite a chequered history.

I set off northwards, for no particular reason, on a pleasant woodland trail. I hadn't gone very far when I got onto a **Carolina Wren** flitting about in the undergrowth. It was much bigger and prettier, with its conspicuous white eyebrow, than its British cousin. I slowly wended my way up the trail and found that these lovely creatures were quite numerous. On reaching the north-west corner of the island my attention was drawn to the canopy, where I could hear a bird whistling. To my amazement I got onto a bright red plumaged bird, with a long crest and endowed with a red bill and black bib. It was the stunningly beautiful male **Northern Cardinal**. It wasn't a bit shy either, as it came down to my eye level to take a closer look at me. I couldn't wait to tell Kath about this beauty. I spotted a couple of ducks in a small sheltered bay, so stalked over to take a closer look, and found that they were **Mallards**. At the same time on glancing over the river towards Georgetown there was a flotilla of **Canadian Geese** to be seen cruising the waters too. I slowly walked eastwards until I came across a trail sign posted to the monument. I decided that now was as good a time as any to take a 'butchers' at it. On moving off down this trail I immediately

Northern Cardinal

spotted 4 or 5 tit-like birds acrobatically gleaning insects from the underside of foliage. They were **Carolina Chickadees**.

I eventually arrived at the Theodore Roosevelt memorial. It was so well hidden amongst the trees that I didn't see it until I was on top of it. I was gob-smacked! I hadn't expected anything quite so magnificent or quite so awe inspiring. There was not a soul about. In fact I hadn't clapped eyes on anyone at all so far on the island. It was a chilling cathedral-like experience to stroll reverently around alone. I felt so insignificant. There were four segments of a circular reflecting pool, inside of which was a paved area with shrubbery leading to a statue of the 26th President of the U.S. of A., wearing a frock coat and with one arm raised in the air. Around this area are erected stone tablets with some of his poignant quotes inscribed upon them. I read on one:

MANHOOD
A MAN'S USEFULNESS
DEPENDS UPON HIS LIVING UP TO
HIS IDEALS
IN SO FAR AS HE CAN
IT IS HARD TO FAIL. BUT IT IS WORSE
NEVER TO HAVE TRIED TO SUCCEED
ALL DARING AND COURAGE
ALL IRON ENDURANCE OF MISFORTUNE
MAKE FOR A FINER AND NOBLER TYPE OF
MANHOOD
ONLY THOSE ARE FIT TO LIVE
WHO DO NOT FEAR TO DIE
AND NONE ARE FIT TO DIE
WHO HAVE SHRUNK FROM THE
ICY OF LIFE
AND THE
DUTY OF LIFE

I tip-toed around the back and to my surprise, I surprised 5 or 6 large blackbird-type birds that were hopping around on the ground. Some of them had a lovely red breast, others, obviously juveniles, having a speckled breast. I discovered that they were the **American Robins**, but they weren't robins at all. They belonged to the thrush family, so must have been named by the early settlers – the red breast reminding them of the robin 'back home'! My attention was drawn to movement in the trees along the trail I had come down, so back I went to see what it was. This time I did get onto two big iridescent blackbirds with long wedge shaped tails – the **Common Grackle** I figured. I retraced my steps to the northern shore and took a track going eastwards towards the Swamp Trail. Here I saw a small flock of noisy birds that reminded me of mousebirds in Africa. They were a lot smaller, having grey backs and lovely tufted crests – **Tufted Titmice**, of course. I dropped down a small hill to lower ground, where the trail was a little muddy in places. I found a fallen tree by a patch of tangles and decided that this was a good spot to have a sit down and a sandwich, and just see what came along. I was happy and content, being in this quiet, wooded retreat far from the madding crowd, watching birds. It was far better than rushing about shopping and viewing the city's attractions, which had made me all bitter and twisted the day before! I didn't have long to wait before a little black and white woodpecker showed up. My field guide showed that with its white back it could be either the Downy or the Hairy, the only difference being in general size (6½ inches against 9½ inches) and size of bill. It was still around, so I double checked. Yes, it was the smaller of the two with the short bill. That made it the **Downy Woodpecker**. Then I caught sight of a brown-backed bird with a white underside flitter onto a tree trunk, where it clambered around hunting for insects with its long de-curved bill. "It's got to be the same Treecreeper I've seen in Briar Woods in Batley," I muttered to myself. Yes it certainly was, except here its common name was the **Brown Treecreeper**.

Suitably rested, I set off south on the muddy trail, until coming upon a "Trail Closed" sign across the track. What should I do? There was not a soul about, the track looked OK ahead, just a little muddy, and the habitat was changing into an interesting looking tall grassland type. Hadn't I just read a plaque by Roosevelt extolling the virtues of 'Daring and Courage'? I courageously walked around the sign and daringly carried along the trail. I'm sure Roosevelt would have approved! If I came across a park ranger, I would just have to act dumb, which is not too difficult for me!

I ventured on until hearing loud whistled 'wheep' calls. It was a pair of large bulbul like birds, with grey throats, yellow bellies, chestnut tails, and slight crests – the **Great Crested Flycatcher**. A good tick! I was stood stock still, watching these flycatchers when a titchy warbler alighted in a small bush only a few feet away. It was a typical 'L.B.J.' having a plain brown back, pale underparts and a faint eyebrow. I had to flick through the field guide numerous times until deciding that it was probably a **Warbling Vireo**. I wanted to have another look at it, but it was a pity that it had taken off and I was unable to locate it again. On I went, my brogues now well and truly caked in mud. I was getting close to the concrete Theodore Roosevelt Bridge carrying the interstate highway high across the river, using the southernmost tip of the island as a base for mid-span piers. I spied another woodpecker, this one was much larger than the Downy, it sported a lovely red cap and had a black and white striped back, the **Red-bellied Wood-pecker**. I've no idea why it was thus called, because its belly was a sandy colour! I contentedly watched its antics, until a strange noise like a 'creaking hinge' drew my attention to a blackbird, proudly displaying red epaulets like some banana republic general. I remembered this bird well from my bicycle trip up the West Coast years ago, it was the **Red-winged Blackbird**. I walked further on until I was almost under the dark, sinister arches of the highway bridge where the track turned west and I found myself on a little wooden bridge over a tidal creek. I hadn't seen this creek whilst coming down the trail, for it had been hidden by the long grass. I stood on the little bridge looking up the creek and spotted what I thought was a Grey Heron fishing. Perusing the field guide I was rather pleased to find that Grey Herons don't occur in these parts, so it turned out to be the very similar **Great Blue Heron**, a 'lifer' for me. I scanned the mud under the highway bridge looking for other waders, I was disappointed in not seeing any, but my eye caught two or three large dark swallow-like birds swooping about. They were definitely not Barn Swallows, I knew that much. They were in fact **Purple Martins**. I was contentedly watching the heron once more, when I spotted two large birds in the very top of a tall tree. They had the same 'jizz' as the Great Crested Flycatcher, but on inspection through my binoculars I found that they were black-backed birds having a conspicuous white band in the tail tip, the **Eastern Kingbird**. Tick! I climbed up a little hill beside the highway bridge and came upon the back of another 'Trail Closed' sign. I hadn't the foggiest idea why the trail had been closed, but I was glad that I'd ignored the signs, for I hadn't been 'sprung' and my 'courage and daring' had got me 6 'lifers' I otherwise wouldn't have seen.

I had a quick look at the map of the island. I was intrigued to find that a 'Comfort Station' was nearby around the next corner. I had no idea what on earth a 'Comfort Station' was. Was it a lounge where one could change into slippers and be handed a cup of tea, a newspaper and a Stop-Gas pill by some silver-haired kindly matron? I rounded the bend but could find no such place. All I found was a lavatory block! Here I spied people, well not real people, but actually a party of pesky joggers. I felt like shouting to them, "Hoi, this is a lovely memorial park, not a flippin' athletics track." I didn't say anything of course, my courage had deserted me. I only acknowledged their grunts of friendly greetings as they sweatily passed by. I decided to explore a trail in the centre of the island that climbed onto a low wooded ridge overlooking the swamp. I hadn't got very far when I came across a small multi-species feeding flock of birds. I was kept busy observing one bird then the next. There were **Tufted Titmice, Carolina Chickadees**, a larger white-backed woodpecker with a long bill, that made it the **Hairy Woodpecker**, and to my delight there were a couple of lovely nuthatches, the **White-breasted Nuthatch**. Wow, what a smashing bunch of birds, you never know what you will come across next, do you? I did a loop trail that brought me back to the lavatory block, where I took a trail heading north, back towards the footbridge on the west side of the island. I didn't encounter any more new birds, but I did observe a lot of the wonderful creatures that I'd already seen, deciding that the **Northern Cardinal** was my favourite of the day, and quite numerous. Upon arriving at the footbridge, I found myself reluctant to leave this lovely island. Having half an hour spare before I would definitely have to be making tracks, I decided to take another look at Theodore's monument, and you never know, maybe I'd come across another new bird. I'd already seen some 30 species that day, 21 of them being 'lifers' for me, so I was rather pleased with my day's birding as it stood. I realize of course that most of the birds I'd seen were probably quite common species to any local birder but to a visitor like myself they were all rather exciting and delightful, and I had been more than happy to observe them on this wonderful, pretty, quiet, wooded island retreat. I say 'quiet', meaning relatively so, if you are capable of ignoring the noise made by frequent low flying aircraft, landing and taking off from the nearby international aerodrome.

I approached the monument from a path directly opposite the one I'd entered on that morning. I got the full impact of his imposing statue as he stood facing directly towards me. His outstretched arm seemed to be hailing me, it sent a shiver down my spine. I reverently tip-toed around this hallowed space and sat down on a low stone wall to read another stone tablet, inscribed with his thought provoking sayings. I read:

NATURE

THERE IS DELIGHT IN THE
HARDY LIFE OF THE OPEN
THERE ARE NO WORDS THAT CAN
TELL THE HIDDEN SPIRIT OF THE
WILDERNESS THAT CAN REVEAL
ITS MYSTERY ITS MELANCHOLY
AND ITS CHARM
THE NATION BEHAVES WELL IF IT TREATS THE
NATURAL RESOURCES
AS ASSETS WHICH IT MUST TURN OVER TO
THE NEXT GENERATION
INCREASED AND NOT IMPAIRED IN VALUE
CONSERVATION
MEANS DEVELOPMENT
AS MUCH AS IT DOES
PROTECTION

Well, I suppose that is more or less in line with modern thinking! I took out the leaflet from my pocket and read that he came to be President in 1901, at a time when America's natural resources were threatened. Four-fifths of prime forests had already been cut, and species like the bison and beaver were fast disappearing. As he was well known for being a naturalist and outdoorsman he was able to bring this to the attention of the American people, who thought at that time that America's natural resources were inexhaustible. He even threw down a prepared speech once and roared, "I hate a man who would skin the land!" I wryly thought to myself that now America had used up most of its own natural resources, it now plunders other countries, to support its consumeristic lavish lifestyle!

The leaflet went on to tell a tale about him on a hunting trip, when his aides tied up an old bear for him to shoot. His unwillingness to kill the defenceless animal was depicted in a newspaper cartoon, which in turn prompted a toy maker to manufacture 'Teddy Bears'. "Goodness me," I mused, "How would we have coped with the traumas of childhood without one?" I perish the thought. I went on to read that he was also responsible for protecting unique wilderness areas, such as the Grand Canyon and Mount Olympus, which later became National Parks. In fact he set aside over 234 million acres of public lands as National Parks, forests and wildlife refuges. He most certainly was a man of vision. A man who once showed up late for a cabinet meeting because he was out bird watching. Yes, there is no doubt about it, 'A MAN BEFORE HIS TIME'.

10

What a Load of Rubbish!

Bogor Botanic Gardens, West Java, Indonesia

K ATH AND I ARRIVED in the Indonesian capital Jakarta in August 1997, for Kath to take up her new job with the W.W.F. It was over 10 years since I had passed through this sprawling metropolis of 10 million inhabitants, whilst on a lone cycling trip. I didn't recognize the place, and couldn't believe how things had changed so much in just over a decade. The capital now has a network of modern freeways, that are still inadequate to cope with the ever increasing volume of motor vehicles. Towering new office blocks, posh international hotels and luxury apartment buildings now dominate the skyline in Central Jakarta, and sprawling multi-storey shopping centres are now dotted around the place to cater for the expensive tastes of Indonesia's burgeoning middle class. It was difficult to find the Jakarta that I remembered, a lot of the slums having been bulldozed away and *becaks* and street pedlars having been banished from certain districts. But despite these showy signs of the rapid economic growth that has taken place, it is still essentially a hot, chaotic, overcrowded, noisy, smelly, colourful Asian city, with the majority of its citizens not having two 'ha'pennies' to rub together, eking out a living as best they can.

It took us a few months to settle into our new home in a relatively quiet street in the central suburb of Menteng, amidst the foreign embassies. We explored our surrounding areas by foot, marvelling at the new sights, sounds and smells, but much to our chagrin discovered that the place was far from pedestrian friendly. We found it almost impossible to walk on the footpaths, for they were generally in a bad state of repair, with a lot of inexplicable deep holes and manholes minus their covers, into which you could quite easily fall and never see the light of day again. When we came across a footpath that was navigable they were invariably blocked by parked vehicles, motor bikes, street vendors' stalls, groups of security guards *ligging* and lolling about playing cards, unkempt bushy hedges and piles of rotting rubbish. I must explain that the householders here place their rubbish, not in a dustbin, but in an open concrete enclosure about 1m square and 75cm high near the footpath. Some have a hinged iron lid and a hatch at the bottom that opens up onto the footpath to enable the rubbish collectors to rake it out and throw it into the rubbish carts. The problem arises when scavengers rake the rubbish out onto the footpath to sift through it looking for re-cycleable items, and leave it there. You don't have to be a genius to realize that having piles of rotting rubbish on the footpath isn't too good for public health, indeed rats flourish in this environment. There are some quite large healthy looking specimens, which the folk here are so used to seeing, that they don't even rate them a second glance. We also discovered on our walkabouts that Indonesians love wild birds. Sadly not in the same way that many other nationalities do, by feeding them in their gardens, providing bird baths and nesting boxes, etc. Instead they prefer to keep them in small bamboo cages hung up under their verandahs. These birds can be bought at large 'bird markets' in any major town, or from street pedlars, each carrying *umpteen* cages swinging from the ends of a bamboo pole, the birds usually being in an agitated and distressed state. On a walk down any suburban street one can hear the tranquil call of doves and the loud whistles of songsters. For our first couple of months here, Kath and I would peer through hedges and railings to identify these caged wild birds. We even spied a White-bellied Sea-Eagle on one occasion, so it was not surprising that our caged bird list was longer than our legitimate Indonesian one.

Naturally with being preoccupied with settling into our new home and Kath into her new job, we hadn't had time to do any serious bird watching. That is until Kath had to attend a 'workshop' in Bogor. Bogor was in Dutch colonial days an important hill station. It is only 60km south of Jakarta, but at 290m above sea level it is appreciably cooler than the hot sticky plains of Jakarta. It was here that a Dutch Governor General built a large country residence, which was later used by Sir Stamford Raffles in 1811 to 1816 during the short British occupation. He described Bogor as a 'romantic little village', but now it has grown somewhat and is more or less an outer suburb of Jakarta. The main attraction in Bogor is the 86 hectare Bogor Botanic Gardens, which were built in the 'backyard' of this country residence, and opened in 1817. We had heard that these gardens were an ideal place to get acquainted with typical Javan town and lowland birds, and they are on the itinerary of every overseas birding group visiting Java so we were eager to visit them and kick-off our legitimate Indonesian bird list.

Mad Twitching

We approached the gardens, located in the centre of Bogor, from a northerly direction at the opening time of 8a.m. on the Sunday prior to Kath's workshop. What a magnificent sight we beheld as we pushed our noses through the iron railings to view the Presidential Palace, gleaming whiter than white in the morning sun, set in a lovely green lawn, manicured by a large herd of deer. This palace incidentally is not the original residence of the Dutch Governor General, that was destroyed by an earthquake, but one built in 1856 to replace it on the same site. We walked around the western perimeter of the gardens to the 'Sunday Gate' and fought our way through the horde of souvenir sellers and food vendors to gain admission. It was a relief to emerge from the rugby scrum and into the gardens proper, where we were confronted by a tall bamboo grove from which we could hear birds calling. We ventured into the midst of the dark interior of the grove on a delightful cobbled path towards the perpetrator of a loud melodious warbling song. There on a low skew-whiff bamboo pole sat a flycatcher singing its little head off. In the dimness we could discern that it had a blue back, orange breast and white belly. It was the male **Hill Blue Flycatcher**. We were contentedly watching it, when another little bird flew into our view and busied itself clambering about frantically in the clumps of bamboo stalks. It was a L.B.J., which we eventually decided was a **Horsefield's Babbler**. Then two predominantly green and yellow birds flew speedily by chasing each other. We stealthily moved in the direction that they had disappeared in. After a few minutes Kath said quietly, "I've got them, they're spiderhunters." I got quite excited, I'd never seen any spiderhunters before; it was a completely new genus for me. I focused my binoculars on the ginger plants I could see that were moving in the undergrowth and held my breath! Up popped a bird with a fantastically long de-curved bill, longer than any sunbird's. It was the **Little Spider-hunter**. I was ecstatic, 3 lovely lifers and we had only been in the gardens for 15 minutes. Kath and I can be 'dead jammy' at times!

A large group of geriatric Dutch tourists noisily squeezed past us on the narrow footpath with their guide, each inquiring what we were looking at, or rather had been looking at, as all the birds had by now taken fright with all the commotion they were creating. They instantly lost interest when we told them birds. We gathered that they were only interested in seeing monkeys. They were wandering over to view the small cemetery in the midst of the bamboo grove, complaining bitterly about the mosquitoes,

Little Spiderhunter

which we had been too absorbed in our endeavours to notice. The cemetery contains the tombs of past (or should I say passed-away?) Dutch colonial dignitaries and the grave of Heinrich Kuhl, a 19th century ornithologist who died of the fever in 1821, after only 3 years in Java. He discovered a sunbird, which used to bear his name, but unfortunately for him, is now usually referred to as the White-flanked Sunbird. We wandered out of the bamboo grove into the hot sunshine, and found ourselves at the back of the Presidential Palace, our eyes adjusting to the brilliant whiteness of it, rather like emerging from a dingy pub at lunchtime. We crossed an avenue of tall trees to an ornamental lake having a small island in the middle. We sat on a bench in the shade of the tall trees and whilst watching the antics of the numerous **White-bellied Swiftlets** over the water, discovered a colony of **Black-crowned Night Herons**, roosting on the island. We could hear a pigeon cooing above us, but we couldn't locate it. Nevertheless we saw **Olive-backed Tailorbird, Olive-backed Sunbird** and **Common Iora** whilst searching for it. A flash of blue caught my attention as Kath called out, "Kingfisher." It had flown out of the tall trees we were sitting under and darted across to the island. We both spied it as it sat quietly on a low branch in the midst of the herons. It was a smallish one, with a royal-blue back and orange under-parts – the **Blue-eared Kingfisher**. How lovely it was! I was admiring it, when a fruit dove climbed into my view. It had a whitish head with a black nape, green back, yellow belly and a red undertail. This was the colourful **Black-naped Fruit-Dove**, right out in the open for us to relish.

The kingfisher took off, and so did we to the southern end of the lake, where stands a memorial to Lady Raffles, who died here in Bogor in 1814. We were now near the main gates of the gardens, where I was astonished to see armies of folk streaming in. I'd heard that these gardens were a popular place for people of Jakarta and Bogor to visit on a weekend, but I hadn't realized that they were *so* popular. Arriving in droves were large family groups carrying their picnics in plastic bags and their mandatory sealed containers of steamed rice; young courting couples (being careful not to hold hands in public, which is a taboo here) and large noisy gangs of youths intent on having a good time, each of them carrying plastic bags chock-a-block with drinks and snacks. A lot of these youths saw Kath and me as a good source of fun and would shout things out to us, which drew merriment from their pals. I've no idea exactly what they were shouting, but I can well imagine from my days of being an uncouth youth. In response to this unsolicited attention we decided to leave the footpath, to avoid them where possible, and headed down to the river via the Mexican section of the gardens, where we saw **Scarlet-headed Flowerpecker, Plain-throated Sunbird** and **Sooty-headed Bulbul** in relative peace, these birds being common garden species for us in Jakarta. We crossed over the boulder-strewn river by means of a suspension footbridge and strolled towards the south-east corner of the gardens. This is the 'wild corner' of native trees, having a dense ground cover of ferns makes it ideal habitat for the Orange-headed Thrush and White-rumped Shama, both renowned songsters. We found it to be a relatively quiet corner, it only being popular with young courting couples who were naturally more interested in each other than in us. We sat down in the shade on a secluded bench in this splendid location. We could hear orioles calling. It wasn't long before we saw a flash of yellow in amongst the foliage, and eventually got excellent views of the **Black-naped Oriole**. We could also hear the damn pigeon cooing away again, but this time we both got onto it high up in the canopy. It was a long way away, but we saw enough of it to guess that it was in all probabilities the **Grey-cheeked Green Pigeon**.

We sat contentedly on our secluded bench for quite a while, enjoying the peace and quiet. I recounted to Kath the tale of being caught with a lass in Batley Park, by a local bobby, when I was a teenager. The bobby shone his torch on us and demanded, "What are you two up to?" I stammered back, "We're just 'necking' officer." He retorted back gruffly, "Well put *thi* neck away lad and get *thissens* off home." '*Ee by gum*, happy days! We didn't hear any thrushes calling, just our bellies rumbling, so reluctantly moved off in search of sustenance. We followed an overgrown path by the side of a smelly stream and saw a pair of **Collared Kingfishers** along its course. The path emerged out of the wood into a vast, sloped lawn where numerous soccer matches were in progress. An ornamental lily covered pond lay at the lower end and Café Botanicus, our destination, overlooked all this on the hillside. We ate a splendid lunch, being kept amused by the antics of the geriatric Dutch patrons, and a pair of noisy **Bar-winged Prinias** foraging about in the bushes immediately in front of the café, keeping one step ahead of the café cat stalking them. We lingered here a while enjoying the ambience and chatting about an article I had recently read entitled, 'Bird survival in an isolated Javan woodland: island or mirror?' by J. M. Diamond, K. D. Bishop and S. Van Balen. This paper is about a study conducted in these gardens, and states that they became isolated when surrounding woodland was destroyed in the 1930s, and is now one of west Java's few forested islands in a sea of cultivated land! It goes on to say that 60 years ago these gardens supported 62 breeding bird species and 77 non-breeders, but has now lost 20 of its breeding species. Of the surviving breeding species, 40 occur in the surrounding countryside, the other 2 species are absent from the surrounding countryside and being completely dependent on the gardens, are unlikely to survive here for long. Thus the gardens are mirroring the erosion of surrounding bird populations, these gardens being simply too small a wooded island to support by itself a secure population of many woodland birds. It concludes that the most important causes of extinction were 'the risks inevitable to small populations in a fluctuating environment, combined with the disappearance of sources for potential recolonization from the surroundings.' How sad.

On this cheery note, we ventured out of the safe haven of the café to brave the milling mass of day-trippers. We ducked and weaved our way through various ball games on the lawn and nearly got decapitated by kite strings as we crossed over the river by a metalled road bridge, and made our way up the wooded hill back towards the lake. Quite a few locals were determined to catch our attention by calling out to us, " Hello misterrrr." Then asking us the usual standard questions: Where you from? – Where you work? – How old are you? – How many children you got? etc. etc. This sort of friendly inquisitiveness can be a lot of fun or get rather tiresome, depending on what sort of mood you are in, or whether you are trying to watch birds or not! Kath and I realized that it was pretty hopeless trying to watch birds with so many folk about, so we relaxed and enjoyed it. For reasons known only to themselves, they like having their photograph taken with foreigners, so we posed for quite a few. I have no idea why pretty young girls wanted their picture taken with a grizzled old bugger like myself, but I was happy to oblige. Kath doubled up with mirth when I mentioned that it could be because they'd mistaken me for Sean Connery! By now every square inch of shade was taken up by happy picnickers. I noticed that they all sat on spread-out newspaper sheets to protect their Sunday best clothes. Cor blimey, I hadn't seen as many folk enjoying themselves in a local park since I was a kid, when my mum and dad used to take me and my sisters to Roundhay Park in Leeds every Whitsuntide, before the days of mass motor vehicle ownership. I envied these folk their simple pleasures and their delightful gardens in which to enjoy themselves. Indeed these botanic gardens I rate amongst the finest I have ever visited anywhere in the world.

We made our way slowly around the lake and back towards the bamboo grove, where we observed a **Pied Fantail** sitting on a nest, before we exited the gardens. We hadn't seen too many species of birds but we had enjoyed ourselves, and I had a whole day tomorrow to 'while away' here on my own, whilst Kath would be attending her workshop.

The following morning I had to enter the gardens from the main gate, it being the only one opened. I strolled down the main avenue towards the lake and couldn't believe what my eyes beheld. A sea of rubbish, rubbish every which way I turned. Flippin' rubbish everywhere! I mumbled to myself in disbelief, "Well I never … in all my born days I've never seen *owt* like this before."

I didn't know whether to laugh or cry. It was simply disgusting. Yesterday I was full of empathy with these day-trippers enjoying their unsophisticated pleasures. Today I was sadly disappointed in them. How could anyone leave a place in such a sorry state? They had got up from their picnics and just left their newspaper sheets spread out over the ground, together with their leftover food, plastic bags, empty wrappers, plastic bottles and cans. Slobs the lot of them! They don't deserve to have gardens such as these. There was simply no excuse for such behaviour, as there were concrete rubbish containers every 100 paces or so, with signs saying, " Place your rubbish here." These were all blinkin' empty!

I sauntered down the main avenue, kicking rubbish from underfoot, like fallen autumn leaves, when I spied a **Slender-billed Crow** having a feast on the rich pickings. I went to sit on a bench in the bamboo grove, having to swipe it clear of rubbish first, and I watched the **Hill Blue Flycatcher** and **Little Spiderhunters** again, but failed to see the **Horsefield's Babbler**. "Lucky that I saw it yesterday," I thought. I then walked over to an adjacent area and sat under a shady tree, re-arranging some cleanish newspaper sheets to sit on. " *Ee* it's grand when you've *nowt* to do and all day to do it in." I said to myself before observing two **Asian Magpie Robins** and a **Spotted Dove** on the ground, and got onto a **Plain Flowerpecker** in a small tree – species that had evaded us yesterday. After a while I strolled back to the lake, where an army of men were now busy raking up the rubbish and throwing it into the back of a truck. There was even one man on a make-shift bamboo raft in the middle of the lake who was fishing out plastic bottles and cans. They were doing a thorough job I'm pleased to say.

I wandered through the gardens towards the river through this sea of rubbish, and spied a small flock of **Javan Munias** rummaging through empty crisp packets, and saw **Oriental White-eyes** foraging about in a tree festooned with empty plastic bags and stranded kites. I crossed over the river by the suspension bridge and sat quietly down on a bench along a boulevard of almond trees. I got onto three or four **Sooty-headed Bulbuls** bathing themselves in a concrete splash tray under a garden tap. They flew off when a young man appeared carrying a couple of small sticks about 2 foot long. He was carrying them very gingerly by their ends, as though he had just painted them and didn't want to get any paint on his hands. "Now what on earth is this chap up to?" I thought, as I watched him carefully place the sticks across the concrete splash tray and set the tap to a fast drip. "What the *hummer*!" I exclaimed, when it dawned on me that he had put some sort of sticky resin on the sticks and was trying to trap the bulbuls in this manner. He straightened up to look around him, and saw me watching. He fled. He shot through like a Bondi tram, as they say in Australia. I went over to inspect his handiwork. The sticks were indeed smothered in some type of glue. I picked them up by their ends and tossed them into the river.

He didn't venture back, so I ambled up to the patron free café for another excellent lunch, which I'd been looking forward to all morning. Suitably satiated I decided a snooze was in order, and what better place to have one than on the secluded bench in the 'wild corner' where Kath and I had hid for an hour yesterday morning. On approaching this delightful spot from the top of the hill I spotted movement in the mid-canopy of a tree at my eye level. There, sat side by side on a dead branch were two grey drongos with long, deeply forked tails, the **Ashy Drongo**. Great, another 'lifer' for me. I found 'our' bench, re-arranged the newspaper sheets already spread out for me, laid myself down tramp like, and shut my eyes. Such bliss! That is until the ants found me and I opened my eyes to de-louse myself, when to my surprise just above my head sat a female **Black-naped Fruit-Dove**. It wasn't until a male appeared carrying nesting material that I realized she was sitting on a partially constructed nest. I watched the male to-ing and fro-ing for quite a while in my recumbent position until I fell into a deep sleep, ants or no ants.

I've no idea how long I'd been asleep before I was rudely awoken by a dreadful screeching noise. "What the Dickens is that?" I muttered, as I shot bolt upright. I couldn't believe my eyes when I saw a **Yellow-crested Cockatoo**. I thought I'd woken up in Australia for a moment. I said to myself, "I don't think they are supposed to be here in Java, we are on the wrong side of Wallace's line." It certainly was a real one, and I never heard it say, 'Pretty Polly', but I figured it must be an escapee.

I decided it was time to move on, not having heard any thrushes calling, and would make my way back towards the lake taking a surreptitious route. I found myself in the creeping plants collection, stealthily moving along the cobbled pathway when I got onto a **Hill Blue Flycatcher** and a **Little Spiderhunter** amongst the tangle of plants. I heard someone 'pishing'. "Oh there must be another bird watcher about," I thought. I looked around and was astonished to see a scruffy looking local chap, crouched down on his haunches in the undergrowth gently pishing at the flycatcher. He was so absorbed in calling it in that he hadn't seen me. When he eventually did, a look of sheer terror came over his face and he took to his heels. Goodness me, I never realized I looked that bad! He was obviously up to no good, my guess is that he had smeared sticky resin on a few branches and was trying to lure the flycatcher on to one of them. Another flippin' bird poacher! It did mention in the article that I had recently read that the authors didn't consider trapping to be a major factor in the decline of species in the gardens, and that they had never witnessed it. That may have been the case when the paper was written in 1987, but I suggest that it could be a factor now. I had witnessed two individuals trapping birds in one day.

I eventually reached the lake. I only had another hour to kill before Kath would pick me up outside the main gate, so I sat on the bench overlooking the small island. I added to my bird list a **Striated Heron** which I spotted fishing on the mud bank of the island, and a **Grey Heron** that flew overhead. I turned my attention to the numerous 'swift type birds' flying around, birds that I have great difficulty in sorting out without Kath's assistance. "Was that one with the red rump a **Striated Swallow** or a **Red-rumped Swallow**? Oh, and there goes a **Fork-tailed Swift**." I said aloud. Referring to my notes, I worked out that I had seen a total of 33 different species of birds in the gardens to kick off my Indonesian list. A pretty dismal total really, considering that these gardens boast a list of 150 species, including migrants and escapees that is.

I sat there trying to figure out the Indonesian psyche. It puzzled me firstly why they preferred to keep wild birds in cages, and secondly why they were so indifferent to rubbish everywhere? They obviously took great pride in their personal appearance, why not in their surroundings? Why do they dirty their own doorstep? I was pondering these questions when a night heron crapped all over me from a great height, covering me from head to toe in watery white muckment. Serves me right I suppose for having negative thoughts about these otherwise friendly people!

II

Christmas Crackers

Central Sulawesi, (Wallacea), Indonesia

CHRISTMAS 1997 – it was our first in Indonesia, the world's largest archipelago, consisting of over 17,000 islands. Kath had a few days holiday up her sleeve so seeing that we had already done a little bird watching on the island of Java, where we now resided along with 100 million other people, we decided we would take the opportunity to bird another island. Where should we go first? That was the difficult question, because Indonesia is divided up into a number of quite distinct biological regions, each having its own unique bird species. After considerable deliberation we plumped for the island of Sulawesi in the biological region termed Wallacea.

Wallacea is named after the Victorian naturalist/explorer Alfred Wallace, a contemporary of Charles Darwin. He noticed that on Lombok and the islands to the east, the flora and fauna was Australasian – where cockatoos, marsupials and thorny arid plants could be found while in complete contrast, on Bali and the islands to the west, the flora and fauna was Oriental – where tigers, rhinoceros and monkeys roamed the lush tropical vegetation. He thus drew a line on a map between Lombok and Bali and extended it in a north-east direction between Sulawesi and Borneo. This marks the dividing boundary between the two continental regions. Wallacea is made up of the islands of Sulawesi, Maluku and Nusa Tenggara and is the major *transitional zone* between the Australasian and Oriental faunal regions. Hence birds originating from both these distinct faunal regions are found here. Just imagine, woodpeckers and woodswallows can be seen in the same tree! For this reason, together with the oceanic isolation of these islands for thousands of years, there has evolved a very high degree of endemicism, Sulawesi with 88 Wallacean endemic species, was to be our first foray out of Java into the Indonesian archipelago.

I was more than happy to be leaving the crowded, traffic-polluted city of Jakarta behind as we flew towards Sulawesi. My main concern was how on earth was I to recreate a traditional Yorkshire Christmas in Indonesia of all places, something I've always striven to achieve in my years of living in the antipodes, with varying degrees of success in Christmases past. I'd come to the depressing conclusion though, that this Christmas there would be more chance of it snowing than of finding an eating establishment serving a traditional Christmas turkey dinner in this predominantly Muslim country. I'd combed the Christmas-carol-musak-playing shopping malls of Jakarta in search of Christmas goodies to stuff into my small travel pack, but with little success, although I did manage to purchase a Santa Claus hat which would have to suffice. I was less concerned about our prospects of seeing a fair number of endemic bird species, after all Kath was with me, and if anyone can locate and identify birds, Kath can. We were also luckily armed with the new, hot off the press field guide to the 'Birds of Wallacea', and we had procured a few trip reports by various authors. In fact I don't believe I've ever before embarked on a birding trip with so much information at my fingertips. It is debatable whether this is a good thing or not! Kath had contacted The Nature Conservancy office in Palu, the provincial capital of Central Sulawesi, where we were headed, and they had kindly arranged for us the hire of a 4wd vehicle with driver, and permits to visit Lore Lindu National Park. So there would be no messing about with the vagaries of local transport and wasting valuable birding time.

We landed in Palu at lunchtime on the 23rd December. Our guide book said it was possibly the driest place in Indonesia, but we had to scurry through a tropical downpour to load ourselves into the awaiting vehicle. I got a good feel about the place, as we headed in the direction of The Nature Conservancy office to say "Hello" and pick up our park permits. Unlike Jakarta, Palu was not teeming with humanity, but was a clean, pleasant little town, with tree-lined streets plied by jingling *dokars*. Very picturesque! Eventually we got going on the road to Kamarora, the headquarters of Lore Lindu National Park, a pleasant one and a half hour winding drive on a tarmac road. I laboriously gleaned from our driver along the way, (my scant Indonesian matching his scant English) that he was a Muslim. This eased my conscience no end, as it meant we weren't depriving this poor soul from his family during his festive season. It also meant, hopefully, that we wouldn't have problems getting him out of bed early to take us birding, because he would already be up before dawn saying his prayers.

We'd arranged to stay at a park guest house at Kadidia Hot Springs situated 2km west of Kamarora village on a dirt track skirting the forest. The park guard there was expecting us and had filled up the tiled pool, adjacent to the simple but adequate guest house, with water from the spring. Unfortunately it was scalding hot when we arrived, much too hot to jump in. Just as well really because we had more pressing things to do than bathe. There were still a couple of hours of daylight left and we were anxious to kick off our bird list. We also had to purchase food as the guard informed us that there wasn't a *rumah makan* in the village, but if we bought some he would cook it for us. So off we set on foot back along the track to the village, our expectations pretty high of seeing a few new species. We had only been going for a short while when we heard a loud honking noise and a flapping of wings.

We both got onto a huge black bird with a white tail, a gigantic yellow bill with a large red knob on top and vivid blue jowls. Wow! It was the endemic male **Knobbed Hornbill**. What a stunning creature to kick off our list. We were rather disappointed with the remainder of our trip to the village, as the forest was very quiet indeed. We only saw a pair of **Hair-crested Drongos** on our way back, a species we were familiar with on Java. Nevertheless we toasted our first Wallacean endemic with a Bintang beer by the poolside at dusk. The stillness of the evening was broken by loud plaintive whistles low overhead. On looking up I could discern 4 or 5 of the largest nightjars that I've ever clapped eyes on, leisurely gliding above us hawking insects. They did not have any white in the wing as one comes to expect from this family. They couldn't possibly be anything else but **Great-eared Nightjars**. Could they? They were a pleasant sight at the end of a long, tiring day travelling.

I was awoken at dawn by the sound of clinking glasses, and the aroma of fresh coffee. Where was I? What day was it? Where's Kath? I gratefully sipped my coffee on the verandah pondering these questions. I was at Kamarora, elevation 680m, situated on the northern boundary of Lore Lindu National Park, the largest park in Sulawesi. It was Christmas Eve and Kath appeared saying that she had just heard a babbler but couldn't get onto it, and that she had heard an owl calling during the night too. I'm fairly used to these sorts of morning greetings from my wife by now, and know that no response, other than a grunt, is necessary. Kath started shouting out names of birds whilst gazing through her binoculars, before I was even fully awake. "**Ornate Lorikeet, Slender-billed Crow, Grey-sided**

Knobbed Hornbill

Flowerpecker," she cried in quick succession. "Cor Blimey, I'd better get my act together quick smart or I'll dip out," I thought to myself. This I did, and we set off along the track towards the village and then beyond to the park H.Q., a distance of about 3km. We discovered that the forest was not quiet like the previous late afternoon, but alive with bird calls and movement. We saw a pair of **White-necked Mynas**, slender black birds with a white neck collar and extremely long tails, and a noisy flock of **Grosbeak Starlings** (Finch-billed Mynas), ashy-grey birds with thick yellow bills and red-tipped rump feathers. These starlings, being active sociable birds, made them quite entertaining to observe. We also saw the lovely **Yellow-sided Flowerpecker**, a **Crimson Sunbird** with its metallic blue front and moustachial stripe clearly visible, a large flock of **Grey-cheeked Green Pigeons** feeding high up in the canopy, a lone **Sulawesi Triller**, a fast flying **Yellow-and-green Lorikeet**, and in the long grass by the side of the track small parties of **Scaly-breasted** and **Black-faced Munias**. Almost at the park H.Q. in a dead tree sat two predominantly grey and white birds. "Are they Ashy Minivets?" I ventured to ask Kath. "Don't be daft," she replied. "They are **White-rumped Cuckoo–shrikes**." (Only one dead Ashy Minivet had ever been recorded on Sulawesi, and that was in the last century!) "Oh um, I wish I'd kept my mouth shut!"

We met the one and only park employee at the H.Q., just as he was about to jump on his motorbike to travel back to Palu for his Christmas break. We chatted to him as it began to rain heavily. He reeled off the names of eminent birders who had stayed here with him in the past. I felt that we were following in their footsteps, rather like the serf gathering winter fu-u-el in the footsteps of good king Wenceslas! The rain abated as we observed **Pacific Swallows**, **Grey-rumped Tree-swifts**, and **Blue-tailed Bee-eaters** hawking insects over the H.Q. clearing; and a noisy **Sulawesi Serpent-Eagle** working the forest edge. We set off into the forest to bird the waterfall trail that started behind the H.Q. ... I was amused to discover fancy, ornamental, fake log, concrete bridges over the numerous creek crossings. They would not have been out of place in Disneyland! It wasn't long before we came across a mixed feeding flock (a feature of Asian birding) containing **Black-naped Monarch**, **Yellow-vented Whistler**, **Black-fronted White-eye**, **Citrine Flycatcher** and **Hair-crested Drongo**. We also had good views of a pair of semi-nocturnal **Blue-backed Parrots** snuggling up to each other, the male having a red bill and the female a white one. As we climbed higher up the trail leaving the Disneyland bridges behind, and inevitably getting our feet wet as we boulder hopped up the creek, the forest got rather quiet. The waterfall was quite picturesque but the water much too cold to frolic in. We rested here a while munching on bananas, and I reflected on many past Christmas Eve afternoons spent revelling at office parties, supping copious amounts of ale and flirting with the office lasses. "Happy days, what am I doing here?" I mused. On our way back down the trail we saw a pair of wonderful **Sulawesi Crested Mynas**, such unusual looking birds, sporting a short purple crest on their forehead and crown. Almost back at the H.Q. clearing, whilst standing stock still checking out the undergrowth for rails, a small bird alighted on the ground beside me, too close for me to use my binoculars. It was a **Rufous-throated Flycatcher**. I'd a devil of a job trying to get Kath's attention without making any sudden movements or noise, but she cottoned on quickly as I nodded and rolled my eyes in its direction. I was quite pleased with myself for getting onto that one first. Kath with her superior birding skills usually has to get me onto the more cryptic species! On our way back to Kadidia Hot Springs I spotted what I initially thought was a 'chook' bathing in a puddle on the track, but I realized I'd never seen a chicken doing such a thing. On closer inspection it turned out to be an **Isabelline Bush Hen**. Great! That brought our species tally up to 40, not many you might say, but that was 25 lifers for me, including 16 Wallacean endemics! Not too bad for starters.

The water had cooled down somewhat in the pool that evening, so we luxuriated in it, sipping on a few beers and watching the antics of the nightjars once more. The trees around us were magically lit up by thousands of fireflies, making them resemble Christmas trees. Oh dear, I began to feel homesick and wondered what mischief my grown up kids in Australia were getting into, and whether my family in Yorkshire would be singing Christmas carols around the tree at my mum's house as usual? A loud **BANG!** like a gun going off, instantly brought me out of my musings. "A fire cracker," Kath assured me. They continued to be let off at regular intervals all evening, and all bleeding night. **BANG!** So this is how **BANG!** they celebrate Christmas **BANG!** in Indonesia, with bloody crackers! **BANG! BANG! BANG!**

"*Selamat hari Natal* misterrr," **BANG! BANG!** was the sounds that greeted me as I staggered out, half asleep, onto the verandah at first light. A group of bleary-eyed smiling kids were sat around the steaming pool dressed in their now crumpled Sunday best. They had obviously been up revelling all night, most probably down at the Sally Army citadel we had noticed yesterday (evidence that missionaries had been active hereabouts). I sauntered back into our room to rummage in my pack for the Santa Claus hat, and to the kids' delight returned with it on my head doing a bad impersonation of him, before breaking out into the strains of my favourite carol, 'Christians awake salute the happy morn ...' They joyously responded by singing for me a beautiful rendition of 'Hark the herald angels sing,' in Indonesian. Kath meanwhile emerged from the forest, tape recorder in hand. She had managed to tease the **Sulawesi Babbler** into showing itself, and was wondering what all the noise was about. The kids one by one came up onto the verandah to shake our hands, rather like at a prize giving ceremony, and wish us "*Selamat hari Natal.*" The last little lad was rather shy and he had to be cajoled onto the verandah to shake our hands, I plonked the hat on his head amidst shrieks of laughter.

Twenty minutes later we were bouncing down the track in the vehicle, leaving the sound of kids and Christmas firecrackers receding into the distance. That day we had decided to bird the main road near Dongi Dongi, the site of an old logging camp, elevation approximately 1000m, and then drive on over the pass to stay in the village of Wuasa, in the next valley that evening. The drive along the track by the forest edge to the bitumen road at Tongoa afforded us splendid views over the cultivated valley Kamarora lay in, to the mist shrouded forested mountains beyond. We flushed a **Barred Button-quail** and a **Lesser Coucal** from the roadside herbage along the way. Upon reaching the road bridge over the fast flowing shallow river at Dongi Dongi, we alighted and requested our driver to come looking for us at 3.00 p.m. 'somewhere along the road.' "*By gum*, this is a grand spot," I said, as we were drawn down towards the river bank by a weird piping whistle. It was the endemic **Piping Crow**. Then we got onto three more endemics in rapid succession, a magnificent pair of the large **Yellow-billed Malkohas**, with a pair of **Bay Coucals** in tow, and a **Sulawesi Blue** (Mangrove Blue) **Flycatcher** caught our eye in a bush beside us. Great! We slowly wended our way up the road, riverine lowland forest on both sides, when a mixed feeding flock came through. I was kept so busy looking at one species after another that it took me half an hour to get a chance to bend down and tie up my shoe lace, I was so intent on not dipping out on anything! The flock contained, in addition to a few species we had seen the day before, **Rusty-bellied Fantail, Caerulean Cuckoo-shrike, Little Pied Flycatcher, Grey-streaked Flycatcher, Sulawesi Drongo, Island Verditer Flycatcher** and **Black-billed Koel**. After seeing the latter species I couldn't resist making up a silly little ditty for Kath's benefit, to the tune of 'The first Noel'. It went something like this:

> "Our first koel, Dave Houghton did say,
> Was to certain poor Kath in Lore Lindu that day.
> In Lore Lindu where she was twitching like mad,
> On a warm Christmas day that wasn't half bad.
> Koel, koel, koel, ko-o-el,
> We have just seen our first Black-billed Koel."

"Don't give up your day job!" was Kath's response. Before our driver came to pick us up, we also added to our list **Sulawesi Pygmy Woodpecker, Purple-winged Roller, Gould's Bronze Cuckoo, Large Sulawesi Hanging Parrot, Maroon-chinned Fruit-Dove, Barred Honey Buzzard,** and **Sulawesi Hawk-Eagle**. In addition we were surprised to see two species I didn't think we would come across until we birded the montane forest, namely the weird looking **Fiery-browed Myna** and the rather splendid **Purple-bearded Bee-eater**. This latter species we observed with a back-drop of the mighty endemic *Eucalyptus deglupta* trees. Their wonderful rainbow-coloured trunks complementing the bird's plumage to a tee. As we were in the vehicle climbing up to the top of the pass, Kath and I were discussing the lowland species that we had not yet seen. The list was quite a long one, considering that we'd had two decent days of birding so far, but we decided we would go after the montane species on the morrow, targeting the lowland stuff again later on. We descended into the picturesque Napu Valley stopping to watch **Ivory-backed Woodswallows** on the way. Our driver pulled into a *losmen* he knew in the village of Wuasa. We took advantage of the remaining daylight by setting up the scope to scan the rice paddy fields. Astonishingly we added a further 15 species to our list in an hour, which included **Spotted Kestrel, Purple Heron, Pacific Black Duck, Wood Sandpiper, Javan Pond Heron, Little Black Cormorant, Golden-headed Cisticola, Chestnut Munia, Yellow-bellied White-eye** and were those **Cattle Egrets** congregated around the wallowing buffalo or Buffalo Egrets?

Now for Christmas dinner! Was I going to get anything remotely resembling one? Not on your Nellie! My heart sank as I surveyed the fly-blown interior of the *rumah makan* next door to the *losmen*. We could have anything we wanted as long as it was chicken and rice! Not quite what I had in mind, but I nevertheless tucked into the rather tough chicken which surely must have died of old age. We then retired to our dingy, mosquito infested little room before the village generator was turned off at 9pm, leaving us in the dark. "It was Christmas day in the workhouse …" I started to recite.

Boxing Day – at first light we were headed back up the road in the vehicle to the top of the pass, elevation 1620m, disturbing numerous lone **Grey Wagtails** sitting on the road. I was excited at the prospect of finding today most of the montane endemic species the park had to offer. Our driver dropped us off at the start of the 9km track leading to the old logging camp of Anaso, elevation 2600m. The first species we encountered was the noisy **Mountain Tailorbird**. These ones here we observed had only a slight wash of yellow on their flanks, whilst the ones we were familiar with in the mountains of Java had completely bright yellow bellies and vents, much prettier. After a while as we climbed higher up the track we came upon a mixed feeding flock at last, containing **Mountain White-eye**, the ubiquitous **Yellow-vented Whistler**, **Streaky-headed White-eye**, **Sulawesi Drongo**, **Island Verditer Flycatcher**, **Pygmy Cuckoo-shrike**, **Rusty-bellied Fantail**, **Sulawesi Leaf Warbler** and **Blue-fronted Flycatcher**. Wow! We continued up the track, it got quieter, steeper and hotter. I had expected that at such an altitude as this it would be a bit on the cool side, and had dressed accordingly. Now my uncustomary long trousers were stuck uncomfortably to my clammy legs and my shirt was wet through with sweat. A **Black Eagle** circled over our heads, vulture like, to check us out. We observed small flocks of **Golden-mantled Racquet-tailed Parrots** noisily hurrying by, and had fantastic views of **Fiery-browed Mynas** popping in and out off their holes in a dead tree trunk. I began to wilt with the heat and the steepness of the track, and cursed the birding guidebook for describing the track as 'overgrown and in places deeply eroded.' The author's idea of 'overgrown, etc.' was obviously different from mine. In fact I wouldn't have balked at driving up it in a conventional vehicle. I moaned to Kath that in hindsight we should have got our driver to drop us off at the top, so that we could have leisurely birded on the way down … Yes, you've guessed that I'd completely lost it by this stage, and whilst I was busy moaning, Kath had seen a **Greater Sulawesi Honeyeater** (Dark-eared Myza) and a **White-bellied Imperial Pigeon** which I dipped out on! We staggered further up the track and being 'somewhere near the top' and not having seen a bird for ages, turned around and dilly-dallied our way back down. I nostalgically mused that it was our family tradition on Boxing Day, for all the men of the family to go and watch the local Rugby League derby game, between Batley and Dewsbury.' *Ee by gum*, I've witnessed some right royal battles, fought out by these two homespun teams. Ah, I could vividly recall the smells from the terraces of stale beer, tobacco, liniment and leather. (And that was only the chairman's wallet!) Kath jolted me back to the present by pointing out a **Red-eared Fruit-Dove**, and then at last we actually got to see the **Flyeater** (Golden-bellied Gerygone) which we had been hearing call all morning. Its sweet cadence sounding identical to the Mangrove Gerygone in Australia. We topped off our montane birding for the day by stalking one of Sulawesi's specialties in the undergrowth, the enigmatic **Malia**. It doesn't resemble any other bird I've seen before, but it is babbler like in behaviour as it hops about in branches close to the ground. A joy to watch as it digs around in rotting timber looking for insects. By this time I was absolutely *jiggered*, the heat and terrain had taken their toll and we were late for our appointed rendezvous with our driver back at the main road. So I was much relieved to hear him driving up the 'overgrown and eroded track' to look for us. Even in my weary state I was still happy and content with all the great birds we had seen that day. We headed straight for the fly-blown *rumah makan* in Wuasa to sample once more the delights of deceased chicken and rice. Kath was getting rather peeved that her diet had been relatively vegetable free for quite a while. I personally was craving for the humble spud, I never thought that I'd ever miss them so much! After tea we had half an hour to scan the paddy fields with the scope before it got too dark. Lo and behold we spied a number of large swifts flying very fast amongst the ubiquitous **Glossy Swiflets** and **Pacific Swallows**. **Purple Needletails** we agreed after consultation with the field guide. Tick!

The following morning we were leaving Lore Lindu National Park behind, our destination – Lake Poso. There we hoped to see a few of the lowland species that had eluded us so far. However, firstly we were going to have another crack at the montane species on the way. The road we were travelling on was a new vehicular road that was being pushed over a mountain ridge, following the path of an ancient pack horse trail from Wuasa to Sanginora, elevation 2000m at its highest point. We drove through tea estates as we climbed up the mountainside. The road being still under construction, we passed numerous temporary road gang camps and crossed gingerly over frail looking temporary timber bridges adjacent to new ones as yet not completed. On reaching the forest at the summit we birded the roadside for a couple of hours, and managed to see most of the birds it took us all day to see the day before, including the **Malia,** but without exerting ourselves unduly. In addition we had **Rusty-breasted Cuckoo,** and two of the endemics we needed, namely the **Crimson-crowned Flower-pecker** and **Sulawesi Myzomela**. Grand! We also heard what we believed to be the **Blue-faced Parrot-Finch** giving its high pitched tsit-tsit call, that we're familiar with in Australia, but we never did get to see the flippin' thing. We then continued down the other side of the mountain, through splendid forest all the way until we reached the cultivations and bitumen road at Sanginora, and then onto the little pretty coastal town of Poso. Here we indulged ourselves in a substantial late lunch and a *cold* beer in a posh restaurant built on stilts over the sea's edge, affording us fine views over the harbour. Refreshed we headed on the road south to the town of Tentena on the northern edge of Lake Poso, Indonesia's third largest lake. We took the scenic lakeside road to Siuri Cottages, situated on a lovely lakeside beach, amidst lowland forest. This was a bit more 'upmarket' than we had become accustomed to. Our cottage was spotlessly clean and well appointed, but they had a slight problem, they had run out of fuel for the generator. This meant that there was no running water or electricity. Which posed no problem for us as our *mandi* was filled up from the lake and we enjoyed a candle lit dinner for two. So romantic …

At first light from our verandah, I was idly watching the **Pacific Swallows** and swiftlets overhead when I noticed that one of the 'Glossy Swiftlets' didn't have a white belly, so mentioned it to Kath. "They have a pale rump too," she added. That made them into the endemic **Mollucan Swiftlets**. A lifer before we even started birding in earnest. A good start to the day. We sallied off to bird the roadside and marvelled at all the doves in the tall fruiting trees, **Superb, Black-naped** and **Maroon-chinned Fruit Doves, Brown Cuckoo-Dove** and the endemic **Sulawesi Black Pigeon** (White-faced Cuckoo-Dove). How lovely! We enjoyed our morning's birding and I felt that I was getting familiar now with these Sulawesi lowland birds. In addition to seeing a lot of the birds we had already seen in Kamarora, we had **Black Sunbird** (besides **Brown-throated, Olive-backed** and **Crimson**), **Asian Palm Swift, Rufous-bellied Eagle** and had excellent views of a **Bat Hawk**. Kath mentioned that all the **Bat Hawks** we had seen in the past had always been beside a lake, as in this instance. However my best sighting of the morning was undoubtedly a rather attractive young lady I surprised whilst she was having her *mandi* in a creek. She quickly covered her ample charms in a sarong, and after regaining her composure, flashed me a wonderful smile. Wowee! Kath said that I should have been a gentleman and looked the other way. I protested that I did behave gentlemanly, 'cos I'd taken my cap off to her! Enough of this ... Back at the cottages for lunch we watched two **Brahminy Kites** perched in a tree overhanging the lake. Kath got rather excited over spotting a darting kingfisher. Was it an endemic one? No such luck it was a **Common Kingfisher**. That afternoon we 'birded' the road again, not one bird did we see. Not a dicky! By now we had come to expect it to be quiet in the afternoons, but where do they go?

That evening we had to travel into Tentena for our tea, as it was the cook's night off at the cottages. I had envisaged that Kath and I were probably the only tourists in Sulawesi over Christmas, so imagine my surprise on entering a restaurant to find the place throng with mature, 'well-to-do' looking tourists. I did not try the restaurant's specialities of eels or goldfish, but instead I was over the moon at being able to tuck into a large plate of potato *collops*. We failed to pick up any nightjars or owls in the vehicle's headlights on our return. Our driver who obviously thought we were 'crackers' was now actively assisting us in trying to find birds. He suggested that on the morrow he should take us a short way along the road to Bada where the road climbed up a mountainside through some good forest. This we readily agreed to.

He was dead right, the following morning we were birding the steep, narrow, winding road amongst a wonderful forest, marvelling once again at the array of pigeons in the tall canopy. We viewed in the scope **Grey-headed, Green**, and **White-bellied Imperial Pigeons** together with the **Large Sulawesi Hanging Parrots**, trying to turn some of these into the Small Sulawesi Hanging Parrot, but without success. Then I'll be blown, Kath got onto a pair of **Sulawesi Pygmy Hornbills**, the other hornbill that had alluded us so far. They were foraging in the midstorey, and I got the **Sulawesi Babbler** in the undergrowth at last. Great, I'd got four endemics in less than an hour, two of them being 'grip backs' on Kath. We called a halt to our birding here at 9.00a.m. because we had decided to return to Lore Lindu that day, a 7-hour journey, to mop up the species we still wanted, Lore Lindu being a known spot for all of them. So off we headed back over the new mountain road to Wuasa. This time rain was coming down in buckets, and the road churned into a mudbath in parts. The incredulous expression on the driver's face said it all when we asked him to stop at the top of the mountain again so that we could have a quick 'butchers' in the downpour. Yes, we were completely crackers! Predictably we didn't see much except for a troupe of Tonkin Macaque monkeys, and Kath reckoned she glimpsed the classic pose of a large woodpecker against a tree trunk, but it disappeared in the general murkiness. On our arrival back in Wuasa we did not patronize the grubby mosquito infested *losmen* again, but found the one that The Nature Conservancy office in Palu had recommended, a much better choice altogether, it being quite homely and clean. We had no choice but to celebrate Kath's birthday by chewing on chicken and rice, but we did wash it down with bottles of Guiness that I'd spied gathering dust on a shelf. (Evidence of missionaries of the Roman Catholic persuasion perhaps?)

By morning it was still *teeming* down with rain as we set forth up to the top of the pass, but we were not going to bird the Anaso track again. Instead we were going to try our luck on a footpath we had noticed that left the main road more or less opposite it, leading to Lake Tambing. We had quite a few birds still on our montane wish list but we were not too optimistic of seeing much in these weather conditions. On the outskirts of Wuasa however a **Barred Rail** scurried across the road in front of us, and on reaching the Lake Tambing path the weather brightened up somewhat, as did our spirits. For the first half hour or so the forest was fairly quiet, except for a frequent high-pitched trilling call emanating from the undergrowth, but we couldn't locate the bird responsible. Then activity at last when a mixed feeding flock came through. I got onto a bird with yellow legs and bill in the midstorey, I thought it was a starling of some sort. Kath announced, " I think it is a **Sulawesi Thrush.**" I exclaimed, "You must be joking." Sure enough after consulting the field guide she was proved correct as usual. Not long after we were thrilled to bits to see two of the endemic birds on our wish list, the **Maroon-backed Whistler** and the **Yellow-flanked** (Olive-flanked) **Whistler**. The latter species we observed at close quarters as it unconcernedly gorged itself on berries from a palm tree. During frequent heavy showers we contentedly sheltered under my outstretched poncho whilst seated on a makeshift bamboo bench by the lakeside. We whiled away the time observing the antics of a lovely **Red-throated Grebe**, and a couple of **White-breasted Waterhens** noisily chasing each other in the fringing reeds. In between the showers we birded the path and eventually got the **Lesser Sulawesi Honeyeater** (Dark-eared Myza) and Kath managed to tease the bird responsible for the trilling calls, from out of the undergrowth, by judicious use of her tape recorder. It was the endemic **Chestnut-backed Bush-warbler**. Another two birds were finally crossed off our wish list. *By gum*, doesn't time fly when you're having fun? We had spent 6 hours birding a 300m long footpath! Our driver was fast asleep in the vehicle. 'Fast' being the operative word because it was the first day of Ramadhan, the Muslims' holy month when they fast from dawn 'till dusk. In practice they seem to be up all night and cat nap most of the day. (Just like some blokes I've worked with in the past!) He certainly was having a good cat-nap, we had to almost rock the vehicle over to rouse him! Eventually we got underway and motored down the pass towards Kamarora. Kath not knowing when to call it a day, suggested that we stop and bird the road again at Dongi Dongi in the rain. I reluctantly agreed. I'm rather glad that I did for we saw a pair of the endemic **Ashy Woodpeckers**, the other woodpecker that Kath glimpsed the day before. We had our chicken and rice that evening in a *rumah makan* (which doubled as the family living/bedroom) in the village of Tongoa, then drove the final few miles to the park H.Q., where we were greeted by the same park employee we had introduced ourselves to on Christmas Eve. We relaxed on the verandah of the spacious guest cottage that evening listening to the sound of an owl calling. Which one was it?

In the middle of the night I was vaguely aware of Kath moving around and the door being opened. Glancing at my watch it said 4 a.m. A couple of hours later I was sitting on the verandah having my coffee and a fag when Kath returned. She had heard the owl calling and decided to go after it, knowing better by now than to disturb me at that ungodly hour. She had located the owl but did not get good views of it, just its general 'jizz'. She believed it could be the **Ochre-bellied Boobook**, and added that she had also heard a pitta calling too! We decided that we would bird the forest edge along the 4km track towards Tongoa and then take a trail sign-posted Gunung Nokilalika into the forest proper. So off we went, keeping an eye out especially for raptors and the elusive cicadabird. Alas, it was fairly quiet except for the usual noisy flocks of **Knobbed Hornbills**, **Grosbeak Starlings** and pairs of **White-necked Mynas**, which we had grown accustomed to seeing by this stage.

It was a relief to turn off onto the shady Gunung Nokilalaki trail and get out of the sun. We sauntered up this pleasant trail for a few hours, but it was rather quiet too, so we turned around and retraced our steps to the main track. Then we took the main road, negotiating cocoa beans spread out to dry on the bitumen in the hot sun, into Tongoa, to the *rumah makan* for an early tea. A large rat scampering about amongst the merchandise entertained us whilst we dined. Our bill for two soups, two chicken and rice meals, two soft drinks, two coffees and a packet of cigarettes came to the princely sum of the equivalent of US $2! Daylight robbery, don't you think? The floor-show came free! On the return to Kamarora, Kath and I were busy observing a lovely **Purple-winged Roller** when a brown snake wriggled out of the long grass, slithered between Kath's feet and disappeared in the grass on the other side of the track. She was completely oblivious of it, whilst I just stood there, speechless. At this point three giggling, glassy-eyed men, unsteady on their feet accosted us, and invited us to partake of a murky liquid they were each carrying in filthy plastic jerry cans. Obviously they had already started their New Years Eve celebrations. We declined gracefully, if somewhat reluctantly on my part. Back at the park H.Q. with an hour of daylight left, we went off to bird the Disneyland bridge section of the waterfall trail, to see if we could pick up any of the rails reputed to be in this area, such as Snoring, Bare-eyed and Barred. We did not see or hear any, but we did flush a **Sulawesi Ground Dove** from the undergrowth, it kindly alighted in a bush nearby so that we could take a good look at it. This was my only 'lifer' of the day. Relaxing on the verandah that evening I surprised Kath by pulling out of my pack a bottle of our favourite champagne. We toasted the New Year in style, at least a bit better than with the home brewed local stuff I suspect. I began to wonder who would be the tall dark handsome stranger who would 'first foot' it into my mum's house, and throw the lump of coal over the roof for good luck. I drifted off to sleep listening to the distant sound of fire crackers being let-off in the village, and in my minds eye could picture Andy Stewart belting out 'Roamin' in the gloamin'.'

White-necked nigna

Our driver greeted us with, "*Selamat tahun baru*" before taking us to the top of the pass, so that we could bird the strenuous Anaso track once more. This time however we had decided to restrict ourselves to the lower reaches, up to where we had seen the **Malia** on Boxing Day. We hoped to see, with a lot of luck, maybe a Geomalia, Sunda Serin, Great Shortwing, Sombre Pigeon or a Woodcock perhaps. Kath by the way subscribes to a 'bird chat' line on the e-mail network, thus at 7.00 a.m. she informed me that some keen birdo on 'bird chat' had suggested that everyone make a list of the birds they observe between 7.00 to 8.00 a.m. on New Year's Day. So this we did! Thanks to a few mixed feeding flocks coming through we saw a total of 19 species. Not a great tally, but that amazingly included 14 Wallacean endemics! We both enjoyed this added endeavour, but we didn't have any luck seeing any of the species we most wanted to see. So off we sallied back down the steep track to the main road, and from there we walked all the way back to Dongi Dongi. Our driver, as pre-arranged, picked us up in Dongi Dongi at 4.00 p.m. and he drove us post haste to the *rumah makan* in Tongoa. I said to the young waitress, when she came to take our order, rather tongue in cheek, "Fish 'n chips, mushy peas, a pickled onion and tea, bread 'n butter. Please love." No prizes for guessing what I got plonked in front of me! Kath and I reflected that we had seen quite an array of montane and lowland birds that day, but as yet, it had been our first 'lifer free' day of the trip. There was only one thing to do, go after the owl that night. It didn't call ... Such is life!

I was feeling rather sad at first light, as it was our last in Lore Lindu. We had to travel back to Palu in the afternoon to enable us to catch our return flight to Jakarta on the morrow. We decided to have one last attempt for the rails, pitta and the two endemic kingfishers, Green-backed and Scaly-breasted, on the waterfall trail. My spirits were lifted when I spied an **Oriental Hobby** flying fast over the clearing as we set off. We heard a strange haunting, mournful whistle by the Disneyland bridges. Was it the Green-backed Kingfisher? We spent the next hour trying to locate the source of this strange call (meanwhile hearing a pitta call too). We eventually spied a **Black-billed Koel**, which turned out to be the culprit. Further along the trail something moved on the forest floor. At last we got our first sighting of the **Red-billed Pitta** – what a top bird, one we have seen previously on Cape York, in Australia. Then whilst observing a mixed feeding flock, Kath drew my attention to a black bird that was foraging with two **Hair-crested Drongos**. It was smaller than the drongos. It had a dark eye unlike the drongo's white one, and had white barring on its under tail coverts. Kath informed me that it was a **Drongo Cuckoo**. "What!" I exclaimed! It just goes to show that I hadn't done my homework because I didn't know that such a bird existed.

It was all too soon that we had to give our birding away, not having seen any rails or kingfishers, and sadly leave Lore Lindu. Our driver put his foot down and showed off his cornering skills on the road back to Palu. Yours truly had to shut my eyes on a number of occasions when we narrowly avoided buffalo drawn carts meandering in the middle of the road. He could smell home! It rather reminded me of the time Kath and I were on a camel safari in East Africa, when the camels we were riding on, sped up and started trotting when we got close to 'home'. There was simply no way that we could hold them back. He dropped us off at a swank hotel in the centre of town. I gave him a generous tip to help him celebrate his religious festival 'Idul Fitri' which commences at the end of the Ramadhan fasting month. He had after all been a very helpful, cheerful and uncomplaining companion for the past 11 days. The hotel was sheer luxury, hot showers, western toilet, air conditioning and a T.V. Such decadence! After a luxurious s**t, shave and a shampoo we went for a stroll around the pleasant town. It felt strange not having binoculars dangling from around my neck, and I suffered a few panic attacks when on noticing they weren't there, I thought I'd lost them. We came across a large tree lined 'roundabout,' where upon we heard a **Flyeater** calling. It is funny that we only encountered this species in montane forest in Lore Lindu, whilst here it was in suburbia at sea level! Then we spied a small flock of munias with white heads. They were the Wallacean endemic **Pale-headed Munia**. What a bonus, I'd thought our birding was over for this trip. We were as pleased as punch and congratulated ourselves. That brought our species list up to 126, which included 53 Wallacean endemics. Not too bad at all.

We were both wide awake at first light next morning. We didn't have to be at the airport until 10.00 a.m., so decided we would go for a walk before breakfast to the 'roundabout'. This time taking our binoculars so we could have a good look at the **Pale-headed Munias**. We sat quietly on a bench in the middle of the 'roundabout'. "What are those doves up there Kath?" I asked, whilst watching a pair, one being a fairly uniformly drab brown colour while the other had a pale head and was a lovely warm reddy brown, both sporting a black hindneck collar. To our delight we discovered they were the male and female **Red Collared Dove**, a probably introduced species that had been recorded here since 1978. Thus a legitimate 'tick', another bonus bird. We actually saw nine different species on this 'round-about' right in the middle of town, quite astounding. We strolled back towards our hotel. The road was thronged with gangs of Muslim youths emptying out of the mosque after morning prayer. I was thinking to myself, "Well I've had a smashing Christmas holiday here in Sulawesi, and thoroughly enjoyed myself, even though it's been *nowt* like a traditional Yorkshire Christmas. *Nowt* like at all. We've been off chasing birds from dawn 'til dusk, for 11 days in all weathers! Our driver was spot on, we're BLOODY CRACKERS alright!" At this juncture a fizzing object rolled in our direction across the road, from a group of jeering youths, and exploded with a deafening **BANG!** at our feet. A firecracker! I roared with laughter, what a fitting end!

12

Javan Hawk-Eagle at Last

Gunung Halimun National Park, West Java, Indonesia

IT WAS EASTER 1999; Indonesia was going through a very interesting but rather traumatic stage in its development as a nation. When we had arrived to live in the capital Jakarta 20 months ago, the country, ruled by the despot Soeharto with the help of his huge army, had been stable for over 30 years. However the country's fortunes had changed dramatically since we'd arrived. Firstly the economy collapsed – the Indonesian Rupiah became virtually worthless, banks collapsed, companies went bust, and consequently a lot of folk became unemployed at the same time that the prices of basic commodities in the shops skyrocketed. (The International Monetary Fund were partly responsible for rocketing prices, as they insisted, in their wisdom, that subsidies that existed on various basic commodities be dropped before they would contemplate bailing Indonesia out of the economic mire.) This situation predictably led to a lot of unrest; the students took to the streets, staging daily demonstrations that were closely monitored by Soeharto's security forces. The inevitable happened in May 1998 when four students were shot dead during a demonstration, as the troops opened fire for no apparent reason. This angered ordinary folk, who had up till then been more concerned in struggling to put food on the table than in demonstrating. They began running amok in the capital – torching buildings, looting and pillaging which surprisingly (to me) led to Soeharto 'stepping aside'. The people were only appeased when promised free and fair democratic elections to be arranged as soon as possible by the caretaker government, who also promised 'reforms' to the system which had allowed Soeharto to abuse his power over the previous three decades. This new spirit of '*reformasi*' led to a freer press, people were no longer afraid to say what they really thought, the consequences of this being that people's aspirations, grievances and old grudges that had festered under the surface for donkeys' years, erupted.

So Easter 1999 there was a lot of bother all over the Indonesian Archipelago, where Indonesians were fighting Indonesians, the motto of which ironically is 'Unity in Diversity'. The troops sometimes tried to keep the warring factions apart, sometimes subtly helped one faction against the other, sometimes looked on disinterested, and sometimes went on shooting sprees themselves. Folk were fighting in East Timor, Irian Jaya and Aceh (Northern Sumatra) for their independence from Indonesia. The Muslims and Christians were at each other's throats in Maluku. The Dayaks in Kalimantan were ethnically cleansing their traditional land of migrant Madurese and the folk in Sulawesi were sporadically fighting each other for reasons that were unclear to me. People were losing their lives daily in these conflicts, with thousands being displaced. You could say that all in all the country was in a bit of a sorry mess. ("In a *wahr* state *ner* Russia!" my dearly departed Great Auntie Minnie would have said.) With most of the expatriate community and wealthy Chinese Indonesians wisely fleeing for fear of further riots in the run up to the forthcoming elections,why were we foolishly still here?

That was the question I kept asking Kath. For it was rather disquieting walking to the local shops having to pass water cannons parked up at the bottom of our street, and coming upon detachments of trigger-happy armed soldiers on every street corner. It was like living in a war zone. Was it because Kath valued her career and work here above our personal safety? Did Kath optimistically believe that there would be no further trouble in Jakarta? Had she put her faith in the American, Australian and British Embassies, that we were collectively registered with, to evacuate us safely out of the place if trouble flared again? Or was it the simple fact that we couldn't leave just yet because we hadn't been able to clap eyes on the elusive, rare **Javan Hawk-Eagle**? I rather suspect that we were still here for the latter reason!

To quote from the recently compiled Javan Hawk-Eagle Species Recovery Plan – "The Javan Hawk-Eagle is a rare crested eagle endemic to Java. It resembles the mythical *Burung* Garuda the national bird symbol of the Republic of Indonesia. Based on recent studies, its population in the wild is threatened by illegal poaching, habitat degradation, and the use of insecticides for agriculture. Hence, it is an endangered species by Presidential Decree No. 4 (1993)."

Recent population estimates of this secretive rainforest raptor, are only put at between 141 to 204 pairs. (It always makes me chuckle why scientists have to be so precise in their 'guesstimates'!) So no wonder that Kath and

I hadn't come across any during our bird watching forays around the birding 'hot spots' of Java during the past 20 months. I had personally given up all hope of ever seeing one but we were going to check out the northern slopes of *Gunung* Halimun (a known spot for them only a few hours drive from Jakarta) over the Easter break seeing that it was a bit too risky to travel to other islands in Indonesia looking for other endemics – what with all the bother going on everywhere. We hoped in the process to pick up a few more 'lifers', although new 'ticks' were becoming less frequent for us within driving distance from our home. I reckoned I'd be more than happy to get a couple, for we had already birded the eastern slopes of this mountain not so long ago.

We set off on Good Friday in a hired vehicle that took us up to Bogor, then on through to the town of Cigudeg where we branched off the main road onto a narrow secondary road that wound its way up into the hills, rice paddies on all sides. After getting lost on our way towards a village called Cisarua, where we knew that from there to our destination was only accessible by foot, we eventually found the right dirt road that wound its way higher into tea plantations, before the boggy track became impassable for the vehicle. We had to resort to 'Shanks's pony' much earlier than we anticipated. One and a half hours after waving goodbye to the driver we finally reached Cisarua on ascending tea plantation tracks, not encountering another soul along the way, a rare experience in itself in this overpopulated island. Here we were relieved to find a sign pointing the way to *Wisma Tamu* (Guest House) in the village of Leuwijamang, our destination. We were on a ridge, about 1000m above sea level, but could not see any mountains from where we were, although in theory we should have been able to surely. *Gunung* Halimun was obviously living up to its name of the "Mountain of Mist", but it was debatable whether mist or smog obliterated it! The footpath towards Leuwijamang was being upgraded, a path of uneven ankle twisting rocks had been freshly laid, making it hard going as it lead us off the ridge down to a fancy stone built archway about half a mile away, welcoming us to the National Park. Here the tea plantation abruptly gave way to pristine rainforest, where we could hear dicky birds singing the minute that we entered into it. A welcome change, for up until now we had only encountered a few of the common **Long-tailed Shrikes** and **Golden-headed Cisticolas** on our hike through the tea.

Within seconds I was surprisingly viewing my first 'lifer' of the trip, a

Rufous-chested Flycatcher. In the same location, only 200 paces from the entrance archway, we had in hardly any time at all, the **White-browed Shrike-Babbler**, **Sunda Minivet**, **Common Iora**, **Oriental White-eye** and a large, long-tailed member of the cuckoo family the **Chestnut-breasted Malkoha**. Wow, this was great; as good as it gets in West Java in fact. We slowly descended on the trail, and were observing a common inhabitant of these forests the **Black-winged Flycatcher-shrike** when a large woodpecker showed up in the same gigantic gnarled tree. It was a green one with red wings and a black tail, a red crown and malar stripe with a lovely bright yellow crest at the back of its nut. The male **Crimson-winged Woodpecker** we deduced, another 'lifer' for me. (Kath having seen it before in Malaysia.) I was congratulating myself when Kath heard what she thought was a Jay. Now if she was correct this was the **Crested Jay**, a bird that we'd had on our 'wishlists' forever, another bird that I'd given up on ever seeing. Sure enough there was the harsh shrill metallic *gnurrrrr* call again, and a black coloured bird with a splash of white on it somewhere or other darted across the trail and disappeared. Flippin' *heck*, we couldn't locate it again, and I never got the chance to see the bloomin' thing properly. With my impeccable high standards I ticked it, but requested that we spend time over the next few days looking for it, to enable me to see the thing properly. I'd already exceeded my expectations of getting only a couple of 'lifers' and we'd only just arrived. I was well pleased. We had great views of a small flock of noisy, fig parrot size **Yellow-throated Hanging Parrots** before the light faded and it started to rain so we put our best foot forward and slithered down the slippery steep trail until coming out of the forest, finding ourselves on the high banks of a steep sided cultivated valley, with a fast flowing river way down below us. The rocky path makers had been busy here too, the trouble was that the path divided, one path taking off up the valley and the other going down the valley. Which way would the *Wisma Tamu* be? We were deliberating when we spied an 'L.B.J.', the almost tailless **Pygmy Wren-Babbler** checking out the freshly hacked out mud banks of the newly laid rock path. It was strange seeing this usually shy secretive mouse-like creature out in the open, for we had only ever observed them before creeping about in the most dense forest undergrowth imaginable.

On seeing smoke coming from below us, then on further investigation glimpsing roof tops through the murky drizzle down in the valley below, we took the low road. Talk about steep, I had to go down sideways in the manner that you would descend a scree slope whilst out fell walking. Now I knew why this trail was unfit for vehicles of any description. It was only fit for mountain goats really. We arrived on dusk, wet through to the skin in the small village of Leuwijamang where we were given directions to the *Wisma Tamu*, which entailed us having to cross the raging river on a suspension footbridge, that looked to have been designed by Mssrs. Heath Robinson and Sons Ltd. "Lord love a duck!" I exclaimed upon examining it. For rotten timber boards were crudely suspended from two rusty ancient cables by an assortment of coat hanger wire and bamboo sticks. I had to hang on for dear life in the middle when the thing started to vibrate uncontrollably with my every movement. I prayed that there was some other means of crossing the river on our way back home! There was simply no way that I was going over on that contraption again. We found the *Wisma* in the dark. It was locked up and deserted. They obviously weren't expecting us, although we'd booked through an Eco-Tourism Agency that were responsible for setting up three such guest house ventures with the local villagers in and around *Gunung* Halimun. We sat under a coconut-thatched shelter in the pitch black, shivering in our wet clothes. Half an hour later the village bush telegraph worked and a group of people arrived with paraffin lamps, prepared a room for us and thrust a glass of boiling water into our hands for us to drink. I mentioned to Kath that a few tea leaves floating in it wouldn't have gone amiss! To their credit they took us up to the village headman's house for our evening meal, where we were unwittingly the focus of attention for all the village folk, who kept bobbing their heads around the door to peek at the *bule*. There being no vehicular access, no electricity, no telephones and no televisions in this region it was hardly surprising, for we must have been a strange rare sight to them. We heard a **Buffy Fish-Owl** calling near the Wisma later, a bird that apparently sits in the paddy fields to hunt, but seeing that it was still raining decided to go after it some other night.

The following day was clear and bright if not a little cooler than we'd grown accustomed to in Jakarta. During our breakfast, which consisted of a huge pile of greasy *nasi goreng*, a guide showed up and inquired if we needed his services. I don't as a rule enjoy going with a guide, for they generally get in the way, and either rush you around at break neck speed or like to take you bush bashing for some reason which I find to be as a rule fairly unproductive in seeing birds, birding from a roadway and clearings being far more rewarding not to mention much easier going. But this chap was all togged up ready to go so after perusing the little signed visitor's book, we deduced that he probably hadn't had a day's guiding work in yonks. Thus we felt sorry for him and hired him for the day, stressing upon him that we wanted to primarily watch birds. Thankfully we set off in the opposite direction to the suspension bridge on a path that took us up to an adjacent village called Soronge. From there he marched us between paddy fields on the muddy, slippery six inch wide bund walls, before taking us up a hillside as steep as a house side to the forest edge where great views over the valley could be had. We did get excited at one time when we spotted a raptor, but it wasn't the one we craved to see, it was the rather common but nevertheless nice to watch **Crested Serpent-Eagle** with its unmistakable loud shrill *kwee-kwee, kwee-kwee-kwee* call. So far so good, then the inevitable happened – he disappeared off the little track into a tangle of undergrowth wielding his machete. Looking round for us, making signs that we should follow him. "He must be bloody joking!" I muttered to Kath. I balked, saying that I would rather stay on the little pathway we were on, but he insisted that it was much further and more difficult to the 'waterfall' that way. "Waterfall! Who wants to see a flippin' waterfall?" I whinged to Kath, "I've seen plenty of them in Indonesia already." I relented and followed him grudgingly into the dark depths of the impenetrable forest.

The next two and a half hours were probably the hardest, most punishing, most miserable hours I've ever spent in my entire life. He bush bashed us up and down horrendously steep mountainsides in mud up to our knees, until thankfully we came out onto another path near the bloomin' waterfall. To make matters even worse we never clapped eyes on any birds whatsoever during that time. We heard a few alright, but we were too busy clinging on to the vegetation to stop ourselves from slithering to our certain deaths on the mountainside to pay them any attention! Worse was to follow I soon discovered, when he led us to the banks of the raging river and told us that we had to ford it. I completely lost my composure, and burst out, "This bloke's a blithering idiot! Does he think we are a couple of fit adventure seeking 18 year olds, instead of sedate middle aged bird watchers." I looked on in dismay as he took out of his knapsack a nylon climber's rope, took off his wellies and after securing one end of the rope to a tree, plunged into the raging torrent. Sinking up to his chest and clawing his way across grabbing onto mid stream boulders and pulling on the end of his rope to stop himself from being swept away. "This is #@!$# ridiculous!" I cried, thinking to myself that the time has finally arrived in my life when I should retire from this sort of wilderness experience bird watching. I longed to be in England, where all one had to do to spend a good day birding, was to park your vehicle up and walk no more than 40 paces on a well constructed path to a comfortable bird hide! He secured the end of the rope to another tree on the opposite bank and we both followed him across one by one clinging to the rope for dear life, emerging like drowned rats on the other side. I took out of my flat cap my dry ciggies and lit one up like the Marlboro Man. We arrived back at the *Wisma Tamu* in mid afternoon, completely knackered and wet through, with only a further one bird – the endemic **Javan Sunbird** added to our list. What a day! When the guide asked if we needed his services on the morrow – Kath had to restrain me from throttling the living daylights out of him!

We were up bright and early the next morning sat outside our traditionally built chalet watching birds in the vegetation surrounding the adjacent paddy field waiting for our pile of greasy *nasi goreng* being prepared. We had **Bar-winged Prinia**, **Javan Munia**, **Great Tit** and **Plain-throated Sunbird** in the shrubbery, with the ubiquitous **White-bellied Swiftlets** flying bat-like overhead. Kath and I decided that we would have an easy day, and slowly work our way up the main trail back towards the entrance gateway, where hopefully we might get onto the Jay again. We set forth, passing through the village where preparations were underway for some kind of festival that evening, and I managed to cross the manky suspension bridge over the river with rather more aplomb on this occasion, what with all the village folk coming out to watch us. We took a breather at the top of the steep climb out of the valley on the forest edge and observed 5 lovely **Blue-winged Leafbirds** foraging in a tree above our heads before a couple of smashing little **Orange-bellied Flowerpeckers** showed up to join them, and **Grey-rumped Tree-swifts** flew gracefully by overhead. I was beginning to enjoy myself again. We wended our way slowly up the path, greeting numerous bare footed porters struggling to carry heavy produce, contained in woven baskets swinging at each end of a bamboo pole that was slung over their shoulders, down the slippery steep trail to the village. I admired their fortitude. We got onto a pair of **Ashy Drongos** and a **Greater Racket-tailed Drongo** in the process, the latter as the name suggests having extremely long outer tail streamers with rackets at the tip. On nearing the self-same spot that we had glimpsed the **Crested Jay** the other day, we heard to my relief the familiar harsh *gnurrrrr* call once more, whereupon two of them flew across the trail and alighted in an adjacent tree for us to peruse. Wow, they were absolutely magnificent creatures, their long crests were erected not vertically, but held out horizontally in front of them, and the splash of white that I'd seen on an otherwise blackish body was an attractive neck patch. This was indeed a 'mega tick' for me.

Upon nearing the entrance archway Kath alerted me to the sound of a bird singing by cupping her ears. Eventually we tracked down the call to a bird sat on a dead branch way up on the very top of a tall tree in the distance. It was too far away to see much on it, therefore Kath suggested that she would try and call it in with her tape. It responded straight away, and landed close by where we had no problems in identifying it as the **Long-billed Spiderhunter** with its streaked yellowish breast, and I read to Kath from the field guide, "Sits on bare high branches to sing." Q.E.D. Another 'good lifer' under my belt. Five minutes later in the same spot we heard a Broadbill calling from close by. Now Broadbills are very special birds to me, for they are generally very elusive creatures. I had only ever seen two species of them before – the African Broadbill in Uganda, and the Green Broadbill in Sumatra, and was yet to actually see one in Java, although I'd heard them calling in two locations before. I held my breath and almost immediately spied a bird sat quietly in the mid-canopy with its back to me with its yellow rump and yellow flashes in its black wings attracting my attention. I whispered to Kath that I had got onto it, giving her directions. We watched it for ages as it occasionally moved its position in the tree, giving me excellent views of its purplish/ pinky underparts with darker breastband. It was the **Banded Broadbill**. I was overjoyed at getting another 'mega tick' in the space of under an hour.

We decided it was time for our banana lunch and a snooze in the shade of the Broadbill tree. I must have dozed off for a while when Kath rudely awakened me by jumping to her feet shouting, "Raptor!" I just had time to see the thing momentarily as it passed by a window in the foliage above my head. Kath took off trying to get another view of it, but came back to where I'd settle myself back down, shaking her head. She grilled me on what I'd seen of it, which was not much, except that I thought it was a buzzard of some sort for it had broad roundish darkish barred wings. She showed me the illustration of the Javan Hawk-Eagle in the field guide, which showed the underwing to be white with a bright rufous leading edge. I assured her that it was most definitely not that one, but she remained silent for a long while pondering over what it might have been whilst I went back off to sleep.

Kath being one of those annoying people who can't sit still for more than two minutes, soon had me back on my feet and ambling back down the trail towards the village, where we promptly got back onto the Jays once more. We were busy observing them when I spied a large Kingfisher with a bright red bill and blue back perched on a branch. It was the **Banded Kingfisher**, yet another 'lifer' for me. I couldn't believe my luck. We stayed in that same spot for ages, having to step aside numerous times to let family groups, dressed in their Sunday best, pass by on their way to the festival in Leuwijamang. All of them were very polite and asking *permissi* to pass us, besides being intrigued in what we were up to. We did actually observe a large troupe of agile Javan Gibbons pass through before we legged it back down the track. On nearing the village I spied a white rumped swallow-type bird with a square cut tail amongst the many swiftlets. Kath pronounced it an **Asian House Martin** without much ado, not knowing that it was another 'lifer' for me. Well I never, we'd had a smashing relaxing day and seen heaps of birds. A totally different day to the punishing assault course, birdless day we'd had with the guide. We had to push and shove our way through a throng of folk in the village to get back to the *Wisma Tamu*. They had gathered around a wooden platform where musicians were setting up their instruments, around which many make-shift food stalls had sprung up since that morning. After our evening meal we ventured back into the village in the dark to find out what was going on. There were hundreds of folk milling around, munching goodies and listening to a traditional gamelan orchestra, that was composed mainly of drums, gongs, flutes and xylophones. We stayed a while to be polite, but it wasn't really to our taste, so left them to it. The incessant music went on all night.

Easter Monday, we were up bright and early again. Kath was suffering with the 'runs' and my stomach turned over too when I was faced with the huge pile of greasy *nasi goreng* once more for breakfast. I muttered to Kath pushing away my plate, "I think I've suddenly lost my appetite." We packed our gear up and bade farewell to *Wisma Tamu*, sighing with relief after crossing the rickety suspension bridge over the raging river for the last time. We trundled slowly back up the trail towards Cisarua, stopping for a rest again at the top of the steep climb out of the valley on the forest edge. We were watching once more the **Blue-winged Leafbirds** and **Orange-bellied Flowerpeckers**, plus **Sunda Minivets** (on a Monda too) in this spot when Kath got onto a noisy babbler in the undergrowth beside the trail. It took her a while to get me onto it, for I wasn't *framing missen* too well, I was busy *faffing* about with my pipe, but eventually saw a largish chestnut bird, having a dark face and a white chest band. Lo and behold it was the Javan endemic **White-bibbed Babbler** – what a bonus 'lifer' to get on our way home. Further up the trail near our Jay spot we both got onto a largish long-tailed, rufous (streaked with white) backed black babbler foraging around in the mid-canopy. I knew that whatever it was I hadn't ever clapped eyes on it before. Kath announced it as the Javan endemic **Spotted Crocias**. I was utterly delighted and couldn't believe my good fortune. Moments later a raptor flew by low over the canopy. I recognised it as the one that we had glimpsed the day before in more or less the same spot. I shouted excitedly to Kath, "Raptor, flying right, the same one we saw yesterday." It flew out of my line of sight, so I ran up the track just in time to see it land in a tree not very far away. I got Kath onto it just as another one appeared from out of nowhere on the same branch in full view of us. My mouth drooled open in astonishment when I saw that it had two long crests sticking vertically in the air like a bunny rabbit's ears. I was speechless for a moment, before managing to blurt out, "It has a crest." Knowing full well that the only raptor around these parts having a long crest was the **Javan Hawk-Eagle**! Then to my further astonishment they mated and just as quickly, without having chance to ask, "Did the earth shake for you too dear?" they disappeared into the blue yonder. Kath and I both looked at each other gobsmacked, before I jumped into the air punching my fists like a footballer who has just scored the winning goal, shouting, "Yes, yes, yes, the **Javan Hawk-Eagle** at last!"

Without further ado we walked quickly up to the village of Cisarua, elated at not only seeing the Hawk-Eagle, a definite 'mind blowing tick' if ever there was one, but ten other 'lifers' too, including three Javan endemics. Our journey back to Jakarta was memorable for the different modes of transport that we used to get there, for we managed to hitch a ride on the back of a dilapidated lorry piled high with bales of freshly picked tea leaves and laughing 'coolies' down from Cisarua through the tea

Javan Hawk-eagle

plantation to the nearest bitumen road. From there we hopped in a mini van to take us down to Cigudeg where we squeezed into an *ankot* public transportation vehicle with seats for 12 people but carried 20, down to Bogor. From the bus station in Bogor we rode in a *becak* to the train station where we caught the train to Jakarta, finally arriving home in style in a taxi from the station. All in little more time that it had taken us in a hired vehicle to get there.

Sat supping a cuppa in our lounge room that evening, whilst bringing my bird lists up to date, I worked out that my Indonesian list now stood at 508 species. Then on mulling over life in Jakarta, I ventured to say to Kath, trying to imitate John Wayne's drawl. "Well pardner, after finally eyeballing that critter, the Javan Hawk-Eagle at last, there ain't nuthing left to keep us around this ol' town. So let's get the hell out a here!"

Epilogue

A FEW WEEKS PRIOR to the start of the new millenium, I only needed another 19 species to bring my life list up to the 2000 milestone. The big question was, would I get to see 2000 birds before the year 2000 was ushered in? My chance came when Kath and I, together with an American birder friend called Chris Frost, went off to Way Kambas National Park in Lampung, South Sumatra for a long weekend. Our first evening there I picked up two new ones, the splendid **Crested Fireback** and a **Brown Hawk-Owl**. Our first full day birding got me a further ten 'lifers' that included the smashing **Asian Fairy Bluebird** and the **Scarlet-rumped Trogon**. That left me seven new birds to find on our last full day in the park. The adrenaline flowed as I began to tick them off slowly one by one. **Banded Woodpecker – Blue-rumped Parrot – Short-tailed Babbler – Jambu Fruit-Dove – Thick-billed Green Pigeon – Fluffy-backed Tit-Babbler** until I was actually trembling, TWITCHING uncontrollably in fact, when I got onto a pair of **Black-thighed Falconets** to bring up my 2000 species. I was very happy indeed.

Since I first started watching birds on my 40th birthday it had taken me going on for 12 years to reach the 2000 milestone. Nearly 12 whole years spent searching for birds over 5 diverse continents. In that time I'd endured oven-hot dusty deserts, mosquito ridden stinking swamps, leech infested rain forests, rough seas, fields full of dog muck, and climbed many a giddy mountain track. I'd encountered crocodiles, lions, buffalo, elephants, tetse flies and hostile tribes, and succumbed to malaria, dengue fever and dysentery at one time or another, all in my quest to see more and more birds. I recall the legendary Yorkshire and England fast bowler Freddie Trueman's words, when after he'd broke the record for the number of wickets taken in 1st class cricket, and asked if he thought it would ever be broken again. He replied in words to the effect, 'If it is, whoever does it will be tired!' I could say the same thing about anyone who has a life list of over 2000 birds. They'll be tired! However Fred, whoever did eventually break your record, I bet that they got a great deal of satisfaction out of taking every single wicket, just like you did, and just like I have in observing every single bird. I also bet that some of your wickets were more memorable than others, just like some of my 'lifers' were more memorable than others.

Some people consider TWITCHING to be a silly pastime. Well I agree with them wholeheartedly, but aren't all pastimes, such as golf and train spotting for instance, equally as silly? So what! The thing one has to keep in mind is that it is only a pastime like all others, and as such you have to refrain from becoming too obsessive about it. Otherwise you'll be in deep trouble and in danger of losing your marbles completely.

I know one thing for sure, I've certainly had a great deal of fun searching for my 2000 birds, and enjoyed the good fellowship of my companions too. And, it's an exciting prospect to think that another 7000 + aesthetically pleasing, scientific wonders, called birds, are out there waiting to fascinate and frustrate me!

Mind how you go,
Dave Houghton